The cons r schools

STUDIES IN INCLUSIVE EDUCATION
Volume 1

Series Editor
Roger Slee, *McGill University, Canada*

Scope

This series addresses the many different forms of exclusion that occur in schooling across a range of international contexts and considers strategies for increasing the inclusion and success of all students. In many school jurisdictions the most reliable predictors of educational failure include poverty, Aboriginality and disability. Traditionally schools have not been pressed to deal with exclusion and failure. Failing students were blamed for their lack of attainment and were either placed in segregated educational settings or encouraged to leave and enter the unskilled labour market. The crisis in the labour market and the call by parents for the inclusion of their children in their neighbourhood school has made visible the failure of schools to include all children.

Drawing from a range of researchers and educators from around the world, Studies in Inclusive Education will demonstrate the ways in which schools contribute to the failure of different student identities on the basis of gender, race, language, sexuality, disability, socio-economic status and geographic isolation. This series differs from existing work in inclusive education by expanding the focus from a narrow consideration of what has been traditionally referred to as special educational needs to understand school failure and exclusion in all its forms. Moreover, the series will consider exclusion and inclusion across all sectors of education: early years, elementary and secondary schooling, and higher education.

The construction of disability in our schools

Teacher and Parent perspectives on the experience of labelled students

By:

Kathryn Underwood
Ryerson University, Canada

SENSE PUBLISHERS
ROTTERDAM / TAIPEI

A C.I.P. record for this book is available from the Library of Congress.

ISBN 978-90-8790-220-9 (paperback)
ISBN 978-90-8790-221-6 (hardback)
ISBN 978-90-8790-222-3 (e-book)

Published by: Sense Publishers
P.O. Box 21858, 3001 AW
Rotterdam, The Netherlands
http://www.sensepublishers.com

Printed on acid-free paper

For Jay, Henri and George

Contents

CONTENTS

List of Tables

List of Figures

Acknowledgements

The research conducted for this book was part of work carried out at the University of Toronto. Many people supported this research. I would like to thank especially Anne Jordan for her immense support in the first drafts of this work. I would also like to thank Paula Stanovich, Keith Stanovich and Brent Kilbourn as well as Roger Slee and Jane Underwood for their work on later drafts of this work. Thanks to Christine Davidson for her editing support. In addition I greatly appreciate all of the work done by fellow researchers who interviewed, analysed and reflected on the experience of students, teachers and parents in the schools where this research was conducted. Thanks go to Eileen Schwartz, Melissa Romain, Donna McGhie-Richmond, Esmé McKenzie, and Sandi McCrory. Thank you also to the many parents and teachers who were willing to share their stories. I was honoured by their openness and their deep commitment to the success of children in whatever form.

Financial support for this publication and research were provided by an Ontario Graduate Scholarship from the Government of Ontario, and a publication grant from the Faculty of Community Services, Ryerson University. Thank you to both organizations for their valuable support.

For personal support thank you also to my parents Jane and David Underwood and my sister Kristen Underwood and her family, and especially to my husband Jay Friedman and my son Henri Friedman.

CHAPTER 1

Introduction

This book is about the meaning of disability in schools. The experience of children with disabilities in schools has undergone substantial change over the last twenty years (and more) with many children who would have once been living in institutions now going to school alongside their peers. With this monumental shift and the continuing increased participation of people with disabilities, one might wonder what disability means. In the age of institutionalisation disability referred to those people who were not able to actively participate in society. As it turns out, many of the people who were deemed unable to participate were so only because the society in which they lived had kept them from active participation through institutionali-sation. In Ontario, Canada, where I live and work, many adults with disabilities continue to live in institutions and are also active in their communities. So it is not just the institutions that "disable" people. There are many reasons that people fall into the classification of "disabled" and for some this classification begins in an institution, often in the institution of school. This book explores the different beliefs that teachers and parents hold about disability and the types of barriers that cause disability, and how these beliefs translate into education practice.

I have spent the past eight years studying the way that students with disabilities are treated in schools, examining the relationships between disabled students and their peers, between disabled students and their teachers, and how teachers instruct students with disabilities. Throughout this research, the many issues associated with teaching and learning are complicated by the way in which the category of disability is used in schools. As with all researchers, my work is influenced and perceived through my personal experience. Many of my colleagues in this field began as special education teachers or as parents of children with disabilities. Indeed these are important experiences for understanding the complexity of disability and school. I have never worked as a special education teacher; most of my teaching experience has been as a teacher of English as a Second Language, another specialization to help students access the curriculum. I am not the parent of a child with a disability. But I became a parent while working in this field, which has dramatically altered my understanding of the experience of parents. I am the child of a person with a disability. This is common for people with older parents, but my father has a visible, physical disability and began using a wheelchair while I was in school. Prior to adulthood, I did not spend much time thinking about the meaning of disability, but my early experiences of disability, stigma, and perception of people identified as disabled has provided me with experience on which to reflect as I talk to other people about their experiences with disability and people identified as disabled.

Critical disability theory establishes disability as a socially constructed category, but this is not widely accepted or understood in the professional practice of teaching. The majority of students with disabilities are identified as such after they have enrolled in schools. Teachers are under immense pressure for their students to succeed in school. Likewise, there is a culture of blaming parents for children's failures. These pressures make it attractive for teachers and parents to identify internal characteristics of children, such as learning disabilities or behavioural disorders, as the cause of school failure, taking the focus off teachers and parents. This book explores how teachers and parents use the category of disability in their everyday activities. Sometimes the category of disability helps students and sometimes it hinders their potential. In almost all cases described in this book, teachers and parents were trying to do the right thing for students, but their beliefs and practices varied dramatically. That is, despite the intentions of the people with the most power in schools (not the students) there were both good and bad practices in place. In many respects the tensions that exist for students and their teachers and parents come down to systemic factors such as how success or failure in school is defined.

I begin this book with several assumptions. The first assumption is about students. As outlined in Article 26 of the International Declaration of Human Rights, and Article 13 of the International Covenant on Economic, Social and Cultural Rights, education is an inalienable human right. The right to education extends to all children in our society, including those with disabilities because, like other children, those with disabilities should have access to full citizenship and to a livelihood that affords them a dignified living, as well as active social participation in their communities. Thus students with disabilities attend school for the same reasons that students without disabilities attend school. Inclusive education is teaching students with disabilities, alongside their peers, in their neighbourhood schools, with appropriate supports. Inclusive education is the antithesis to special education, or programs of support for students with disabilities which take place outside of regular education classes, such as withdrawal programs in resource rooms, self-contained classes or specialized schools. Some of the most respected researchers in inclusive education have recently concluded that ethics, human rights and social justice arguments for inclusive education are so powerful that they supersede arguments for inclusive education that are based on pedagogy, or empirical studies of student achievement (defined in academic, social or participatory terms). For example, Slee (2006) says

> Stepping away from the discourse of special needs to establish inclusive education as a precondition for democratic schooling, as an ethical project helps to place the technical questions of placement, resources and the deployment of expertise into their second, nevertheless important, order place. (p. 118)

Similarly, Kenworthy and Whittaker (2000) present the argument for inclusive education as a matter of children's rights. They promote a message to advocates to "make the affirmation of children's rights their primary goal, before resorting to detailed educational debates" (p. 219). I agree with the arguments for inclusive education as a right, as a matter of ethical imperative or social justice. However, for the people who are living the experience of schooling, including the students, their parents and their teachers, it is not so easy to separate the theoretical underpinnings of being included from the technical aspects of being part of a system. In this book I begin by examining how teachers and parents think about disability, but the book is structured around the practical elements of schooling, such as identification of disabilities and reporting grades for students who are working on a modified curriculum. I hope that this discussion never strays far from the primary concerns about the rights of students, but the central purpose of the book is more technical. The book's focus is on how the practices of teachers and parents, informed by their beliefs about barriers to learning, either support or detract from the goal of including students and supporting students to maximize their potential.

The second assumption in this book is about parents. Parents and/or primary caregivers usually know their children better than anyone else, and therefore have information that is useful for teachers in connecting with students. When teachers ignore or devalue the expertise of parents they are harming students. On the other hand, parents, like teachers, have widely variable perspectives on the nature of disability and there is often dissent amongst teachers and parents about the "best" way to teach children.

The final assumption that I consciously begin with is that teachers' and parents' beliefs about barriers to learning are shaped by so many factors it is impossible to identify the source of these beliefs. However, I think it is safe to assume that personal experience and cultural norms have a significant part to play in shaping beliefs, and conversely when I describe the beliefs of individuals, the personal experiences and cultural norms are reflected. The perspectives of individual teachers and parents presented in this book are, therefore, used to examine the construction of the category of disability in schools rather than criticizing individuals for their beliefs.

A Note on Language

The use of language in describing disability and the people who have been labelled by this language is sensitive. The damage that language has caused for people labelled with disabilities is evident in the rate at which terms become expressions of offence and then are deemed inappropriate. Working in North America, the current trend is for "people first language". That is saying "person with a disability". In disability studies, this language is obsolete and it is considered most appropriate to use the term disability as an adjective, as in "disabled person" (Barnes, Mercer, & Shakespeare, 1999). I use the terms interchangeably in this book as a nod to both the tradition of the North American disability rights movement and the traditions of disability studies. I hope that they will be read with respect given to both the local and the global context.

The second point on language is about the use of the term disability in a school context. It is common for researchers and policy makers to talk about students with special needs or students with special educational needs. These terms are used as a catchall term for students who are traditionally identified with disabilities and for students who would otherwise not be considered to have a disability but who are having difficulty in schools. The latter could include, but is not limited to, students who are living in poverty, students who have experienced violence, or students who are attending school in a language other than their mother tongue. The terms special needs and special educational needs are thus used to differentiate between students who are seen to be unable to perform to meet school-based expectations and people in general society who are viewed as being unable to perform certain activities. If we understand disability to be a socially constructed identity, based on a lack of ability to perform a set of norm-referenced activities, then I don't think it is necessary to make a distinction between people who are disabled in general and students who are disabled specifically in the context of schools. The distinction between school-based disabilities and experiences of disability outside of school are simply a matter of who is constructing the category of disability and how. And so I refer to the students discussed in this book as students with disabilities, meaning students who are viewed as lacking the ability to perform the normative tasks expected in schools.

Finally, I refer to parents throughout the book. In most books which address similar issues reference is made to parents and guardians. In my research almost all of the guardians I spoke to were also parents of the children being discussed. These parents included adoptive parents, step-parents, and foster parents. Foster parents are in fact guardians, and in many cases the children still have contact with their own parents, which was the case for the foster parent I interviewed for this book. However, in this case the child referred to the foster parent as "mum" and the school referred to her as the "mother". I use the term "parent" with the intent that it will be widely interpreted.

THE POLICY CONTEXT

My research has been conducted in Canada in the province of Ontario, primarily in and around the city of Toronto. In Canada, education is funded and legislated at the provincial level, which means that each province has a different system of education. Context is important in understanding the experience of individuals. At the same time, I believe that the experiences of teachers and parents are informative for educators, researchers and parents from all over the world. In order that you, the reader, will be able to compare the experiences of teachers and parents I have interviewed to your own or others' experiences in your local environment, the policy context of Ontario is described in some detail here.

To begin, special education policy in Ontario has shifted from totally segregated placements, often in residential institutions, to special education classrooms in regular schools. Surprisingly, it was not until 1980 that legislation was passed making the education of children with disabilities a responsibility of the regular education system. Prior to 1980 this was a responsibility of social and health services, although many children with disabilities did go to regular schools. Currently the majority of students getting support in schools are placed in regular classrooms with their peers. However, Ontario has one of the highest rates in Canada of segregating students with disabilities into special education classes or specialized schools. Approximately 35% of students with cognitive disabilities in Ontario are in special education classes compared to only about 13% in the province of Prince Edward Island (Statistics Canada, 2004). Ontario also reports one of the highest levels of students identified with acute learning needs in North America (Bennett & Wynne, 2006).

There are two central components of Ontario special education policy: Identification, Placement, and Review Committees (IPRCs), and Individual Education Plans (IEPs). The IPRCs are used to formally identify students as "exceptional" and to decide on placement. Identification labels described for students in this book are often based on the Ontario Ministry of Education categories of exceptionality. The IPRC decision can be appealed under Ontario law by a parent who disagrees with the identification or placement of his or her child through the Special Education Appeal Board, and subsequently through a Special Education Tribunal (Education Act, 1998). The IPRC, however, is being used less often, particularly in school boards that have adopted more inclusive placements, because placement in a regular classroom can take place without an IPRC. One of the school boards where I interviewed teachers and parents had almost eliminated the use of IPRCs. The biggest implication of this practice is that without the IPRC there is no formal recourse for parents of children with disabilities to appeal the placement. Regardless of the school board's policy on inclusion, parents have the legal right to request an IPRC for their children. In general, the Special Education Appeal Boards and Tribunals are thought to favour decisions by school boards; however, that seems to be changing based on recent cases documented in the media (Kalinowski, 2003b, 2004). Over the last few years, two prominent cases have found in favour of parents' wishes at the tribunal stage (the next stage after the Appeal Board).

The second major education component governing special education in this province at the time of the study was the IEP Standards (Ministry of Education, 2000a). The IEP is a written document outlining programs and services to be provided to a student, and how these programs and services will be implemented and monitored. The IEP must be provided for students identified as exceptional through an IPRC or when mandated by a Special Education Appeal Board, or a Special Education Tribunal. However, the IEP may also be prepared for students who have not been formally identified as exceptional but are receiving special education services (Ministry of Education, 2000a). The IEP Standards require that parents be consulted in the development of IEPs . The nature of this consultation process is one of the components of policy implementation that I discussed with parents. This mandated consultative role on the part of parents is also an impetus for examining the role of parents in educational provision for students with IEPs .

The IEP and IPRC policy are affected by the funding structure of special education. At the time of interviewing teachers and parents for this book, there were three main types of funding for students with IEPs in Ontario. The first is the foundation grant given to boards based on the number of pupils in the board. The second is the Special Education Per Pupil Amount (SEPPA) based on the board's student enrolment, and the third funding category (which has 4 levels of support) is the Intensive Support Amount (ISA) (Ministry of Education, 2001). ISA funding is based on student need and requires that school staff and families of children with high levels of need supply proof that the child qualifies for the funding. It has been claimed in the media that school boards feel that the funding is inadequate to meet the needs of students and that long waiting lists for assessments and extensive paperwork involved in securing ISA money have led to a serious shortage of funding for these students (Kalinowski, 2003a). On the other hand, a policy review, funded by the Ministry of Education, also documented the need for greater funding but did not find the need to reform the overall funding scheme (Rozanski, 2002). The funding model has since been reformed, but many of the criticisms are unchanged.

The IPRC, IEP and Special Education funding thus provide the basic policy context for special education practice in Ontario. Although these three policies work in conjunction with each other, in my research the IEP is the primary focus of interviews with parents and teachers because it is the policy component which addresses program and is most familiar to the people closest to the classroom. Nevertheless, discussion about IEPs inevitably involves reference to IPRCs and funding policies. The students discussed in my interviews all had IEPs.

The students discussed in this book are in both segregated classes and regular classes. However, I would describe very few of the experiences of these students as being fully inclusive. Placement in a class is just one component of being included. Certainly placement is important for inclusive practice, but in both special education and general education there are components of what is needed to include students, such as respect for the student and a determination to support student achievement. Students from both segregated and regular education classes were included in my research. Interestingly, all of the placements encountered in my research were described by school administrators as inclusive.

Inclusion Policy

In 2001, in a Canadian Council on Social Development national key informant survey on special education, 82% of respondents reported that their special education system had changed significantly over the previous five years (Kierstead & Hanvey, 2001). The ongoing reforms that are taking place in the Ontario school system have in recent years included a major review of funding and programming policies and new guidelines for Individual Education Plans (IEPs) particularly in relation to Report Cards. Ontario education policy reforms are influenced by major social changes that have taken place over the last several decades on a global scale. Yet, the Ontario Human Rights Commission (OHRC) reports that many students still face barriers to learning. These barriers according to the OHRC include physical access to schools, access to accommodations, timeliness in accessing services and funding, and discrimination through the zero-tolerance disciplinary legislation known as the Safe Schools Act (OHRC, 2003). Our education system has also been influenced by international trends toward standardization and accountability (McGlaughlin & Jordan, 2005).

While education policy has been volatile, research on the best practices for teaching students with disabilities has also been subject to current trends. Many studies in special education now reflect inclusive education as an objective of teaching practice (for example, Danforth & Rhodes, 1997; Lipsky & Gartner, 1996; Skrtic, Sailor, & Gee, 1999). But, the trend toward inclusion is not without backlash. In particular, Kauffman (1999), Sasso (2001), and Barrow (2001) argue that the current trend in special education towards inclusive practice is based on inadequate scientific evidence, leading them to conclude that inclusion is therefore not justified. Kauffman (1999) asserts that:

> Data to date may support the claim that some students with disabilities can be taught appropriately in general education if support services are provided. However, data to date do not support the claim that *all* students can be taught appropriately in neighborhood schools or in general education. We need at least as much care to prepare special educators who will offer truly specialized instruction in special settings as we do to prepare special educators who will collaborate and work in general education settings. (p. 251)

This argument against universal inclusion is based on the lack of empirical evidence to support it, rather than on empirical evidence that it does not work. The inclusion versus special education debate is inevitably part of a discussion about how disability is constructed in schools, in part because it is the most dominant policy shift in the recent history of this field. Further, as will become evident, it is inseparable from the beliefs of teachers and parents about the nature of barriers for students with disabilities in schools.

Several researchers say that segregated or special education programs promote inequity for students with disabilities. Fulcher (1998) argues that theory used to inform policy and practice have a close relationship, and she outlines why she believes special education policy has supported harmful practices:

> ...the notion that some children have handicaps divides the school population [...] An alternative view comes from the discourse that children are firstly *pupils*: this provides a different theory and articulation: it unites the school population and identifies what children share, it provides an objective of including all children in regular schools and directs us to a particular means for achieving that, it invites us to focus on pedagogy. This is an inclusive ethos. (pp. 8-9)

Corbett (1996) says that the language of special education policy, including the word "special", have created distinct layers of education with elite programs, such as private education, having the most status and special education programs with the least status. This, she says, leads to prejudice amongst educators and the larger society. Slee (1997) describes how this prejudice is lived out in practice:

> Few writers in the tradition of special education problematise school failure beyond defective individual pathologies in need of special provision to support their own specific educational needs and delimit the disruption such children cause to their own academic and social progress and that of their "non-defective" peers (p. 408).

There are, therefore, values underlying the practices of special education and placement of students with disabilities. Similarly, values underlie instructional practices within classrooms regardless of placement. In my experience many educators understand inclusion to be a policy that directs students with disabilities to be placed in regular classrooms, and they do not understand inclusion to be an instructional practice that meets the needs of students with disabilities, and indeed of all students. The work presented in this book seeks to lay bare the values about disability that underlie school-based practices.

Why IEPs, Teachers and Parents?

The question of how disability is constructed in schools is answered in my research by interviewing teachers and parents about their experience of planning for children with Individual Education Plans (IEPs). The use of IEPs is premised on the notion that tailoring instruction to the individual needs of each student will allow each child to learn at their own pace and their own level. This theory comes from the work of Vygotsky who said that each child has a "zone of proximal development" and learning takes place within this zone defined by previous knowledge and a level of challenge (Vygotsky, 1978). The theory being IEPs are in fact good teaching for all students and this is apparent in the practice of teachers making anecdotal notes about students and tracking their progress in order to advance their learning. IEPs are a formalized version of this process used in many educational systems around the world specifically for students with disabilities.

The literature on effective teaching for all students, as well as the special education research which targets effective teaching for students with disabilities, indicates that all students need a combination of direct or transmissive teaching and holistic approaches which encourage constructive learning. The best teachers according to current research are flexible, adaptable and know their students well. This study examines teachers' reported practices in relation to their coded beliefs, but does not assume the relationship between belief and practice as in previous studies.

There has been much written on the topic of IEPs and I don't want to replicate that work here, but IEPs were used as the basis for discussing practice with teachers and parents in my research because they are a documentation of program adaptations, goals and needs of students with learning difficulties and disabilities in this province. Legislation directs both teachers and parents to participate in the development of IEPs. Teachers and parents, therefore, use IEPs to define students and student characteristics into categories of "able" and "disabled ". In my research the IEP serves two base functions: first, the IEP is the criterion for selection of participants in the study. That is, only parents and teachers of students with IEPs were interviewed. Second, as a record of decisions and strategies in place for students with learning difficulties and disabilities, the IEP is the point of reference for the interviews conducted.

There has been much debate about the factors that influence design and implementation of IEPs. Rodger (1995) claims there have been four general phases of IEP research: a "Normative" phase, focused on how to develop an IEP and on policy and paper work; an "Analytic" phase, focused on teacher and parent involvement in IEP development, and contributing factors in stakeholder participation, collaboration and decision making; a "Technological" phase, where the administration of IEPs using computer software was examined; and finally, a "Quality and implementation" phase which focused on the quality and implementation of IEPs. The general findings of this research were that there was minimal understanding of parent participation in IEP development and that IEPs did not reflect the practice that actually happened in classrooms. Further, IEPs did not appear to influence student achievement outcomes or improve teaching. There was some evidence that IEPs accurately captured student peer relationships. Outside of the IEP document, teachers vary in their ability to individualize instruction (Fuchs, Fuchs, Hamlett, Phillips, & Karns, 1995). It may be that the effectiveness of IEPs and teaching practice is dramatically influenced by school norms, as defined by school leadership and education policy. The goals of an IEP, although authored by classroom teachers, are now thought to be more closely linked to school norms than they are to the individual needs of a student (Pearson, 2000; Stanovich & Jordan, 1998). Thus, while the IEP serves as a point of reference, it is important to ask parents and teachers more specific questions about the program in place for each student and the reasons and purposes of that program.

Despite the lack of research directly linking IEPs to student achievement, since the 1980s student achievement gains have been linked to program in many studies. For example, Rea, McLaughlin, and Walther-Thomas (2002) used IEP goals and objectives to provide functional definitions of program. They found that students with learning disabilities in inclusive programs earned higher grades and did better on standardized tests than students with learning disabilities in pullout programs. They also found better behavioural records and better attendance for the group in inclusive placements.

While the IEP is primarily a program plan for students, it is also implicated in the relationship between teachers and students with disabilities. The IEP Standards in Ontario mandate parent consultation in the development of the IEP document. Family participation in individualized planning has long been a focus of advocacy for students with disabilities. The goals of parent participation, however, are far from clear. In their review of research on parent participation programs, Mattingly,

Prislin, McKenzie, Rodriguez, and Kayzar (2002) found that the relationship between parent involvement and student achievement was inconclusive, partly because there have been no large scale studies. However, Epstein (2001) says that empirical evidence of a correlation between parent involvement and student achievement is moot because family background is part of student character, and thus is a component of the school experience regardless of direct parent involvement. Furthermore, Epstein claims that teachers, parents, and students all report benefits from parent participation in the educational process. Corter and Pelletier (2004) argue that Epstein and others are prematurely concluding that parent and community involvement in education leads to improved attainment by students based on the current evidence. Corter and Pelletier also speculate that student achievement may be a result of family factors such as higher economic status and lower family stress, which in turn may lead to more family involvement in education. Their argument is that family characteristics are a better predictor of student achievement than family involvement in school. This leaves a lot of questions about the purpose of parent involvement in the education of children with disabilities.

Research on parent participation in school is inconclusive about the impact on outcomes for students. However, socio-economic status, a family characteristic, is predictive of educational outcomes. Socio-economic status also predicts parent participation and the level of collaboration between parents and teachers. Research on parent participation for students with disabilities indicates that parents who are able to advocate and have access to information are successful in keeping their children in inclusive placements, which is important to them. Much of the research on parents of children with disabilities focuses on their emotional state, coping and acceptance of the disability, and pathologizing the families. In this study, theories of belief that have been used to understand teachers' professional beliefs are applied to the analysis of parent beliefs. Using the same framework for understanding parent and teacher beliefs equalizes the treatment of these two participant groups where traditionally professional knowledge has been elevated.

Teachers

"Teachers hold disparate assumptions and beliefs about the nature of ability and consequently of disability" (Kagan, 1992a). Kagan (1992a) has commented that epistemological beliefs may be at the very heart of teaching. Several researchers have suggested that differences in beliefs are associated with different teaching practices and consequently affect the opportunities for a child to learn (Jordan & Stanovich, 2004; Kagan, 1992a; Stipek, Givvin, Salmon, & MacGyvers, 2001). This is, however, a challenging field of study because of the difficulty in reliably measuring beliefs, and showing the relationship of those beliefs to practice.

The literature on teacher beliefs has flourished in recent years as it is speculated that this is one of the central components of understanding teacher practice (Kagan, 1992a; Muijs & Reynolds, 2002). The definition of beliefs, however, has remained elusive with similar constructs being called attitudes, understandings, and knowledge in other research (Fenstermacher, 1994; Pajares, 1992). From an empirical standpoint, teaching beliefs are much harder to capture than teaching behaviours or practices which are easily observed. However, as Muijs and Reynolds (2002) say:

> While findings appear robust for basic instruction, (the) focus on teacher behaviors has been subject to criticism that has focused among other things on the lack of attention given to teachers' own beliefs about and attitudes to teaching and the subjects they teach, arguing that these deeper structures are more important to teaching quality than immediately observable behaviors (p. 4).

Much of the research on teacher beliefs has focused on the nature of teacher beliefs about knowledge and the acquisition of knowledge (Hofer & Pintrich, 1997) and about the contribution of teachers' pre-existing beliefs to their teaching (Kagan, 1992b). In contrast, disability research has focused on attitudes towards disability (i.e., positive or negative) as opposed to beliefs about the nature of barriers (Antonak & Livneh, 1988). Pajares (1992) says that knowledge is accepted as a component of belief (or vice versa). Although beliefs are theoretically less mutable than knowledge (Nespor, 1987), Kagan (1992b) claims that the pre-existing beliefs of novice teachers can be influenced by experiential knowledge about their students. Borko and Putnam (1996) note that it is difficult to make a distinction between general pedagogical knowledge and knowledge of individual students because they are so intertwined. Knowledge of individual students, along with pedagogical knowledge and teachers' epistemological beliefs likely all contribute to teachers' beliefs about the barriers to learning for students with disabilities. A similar argument was made by Shulman (1987) who emphasizes the importance of content knowledge in a subject area as well as knowledge of individual students. The difference between attitudes and beliefs seems to be a matter of degree and it can be argued that the nature of parent and teacher immersion in the lives of students gives them a knowledge of the individual students which contributes to the deeper construct of "beliefs" rather than simply a positive or negative "attitude" about disability. In this study, beliefs about barriers to learning refers to the assumptions and pre-existing understandings that teachers and parents hold about education for students with disabilities.

Within a school system that has various models of service for students with disabilities, ranging from fully inclusive to completely segregated, it is difficult to understand how the concept of disability is perceived and how it affects students. In addition, the responsibility for individualizing instruction for students with disabilities lies with teachers and parents who have diverse views on the meaning of disability in the context of schools. In the next chapter I will talk about the beliefs held by teachers and parents about disability and conversely ability. Chapters 3 to 7 discuss how these various understandings of disability influence school-based practice. In the end, I hope to draw attention to the students who are at the heart of this discussion and the hope that teachers and parents can work together to provide the very best education that is the right of all students.

Parents

Although few studies were found which examined parent beliefs, a lot of research has linked families to educational experience. Engel's (1993) ethnographic study of parents of children with disabilities found conflicting views between parents, the law, and the language of disability specialists. Engel highlights the importance of co-operative decision making, parent knowledge, and legal empowerment of parents for positive outcomes for children with disabilities. Engel also found that parents generally try to avoid conflict and therefore rarely turn to legal recourse.

Some research on inclusion policy focuses on parent involvement. Hanson, et. al (2001) found that aside from professionals' decisions and the placement options available, family factors, such as the ability to advocate and access information, were integral components in keeping students in inclusive placements.

Since teachers have primary responsibility for classrooms, the collaborative relationship between teachers and parents is important for understanding parent involvement in schools. Aside from the benefits for the students and parents, "teachers in schools with highly involved parents report greater job satisfaction, higher evaluation ratings from both parents and principals, and higher ratings of school effectiveness" (Minke & Vickers, 1999, p. 118). Conversely, collaborative relationships between schools and parents are thought to have a negative effect when schools are too demanding or have the same expectations for all families.

Several types of relationships may exist between teachers and parents. These provide some insight into the variable relationships which may result from divergent beliefs of teachers and parents. Vincent (2000) categorizes these into "parent as consumer", "parent as partner", and "parent as participant". In the first relationship parents, rather than students, are treated as the client of the school and the emphasis is on choice of programming. In this situation, schools become specialized and parents choose the school which best fits their philosophy. In the parent as partner relationship, parents act as volunteers and teachers provide information about how parents can support the education program through homework, etc. In the third relationship, parents as participants have direct input into the decision-making and programming goals for their children. Vincent presents this as the most desirable relationship because participation of parents allows parent views and knowledge to be useful tools in developing programming goals.

In addition to the parents' direct involvement, there are some indirect influences of parents on the educational experience of students. Gross (1996) found that parents who are literate and outspoken are able to secure more resource provisions for their children than other parents. Gross also found that socio-economic status (SES) had an impact on parents' level of advocacy and that "middle-class disabilities" such as learning disability [as opposed to working class disabilities such as behaviour problems] were over-represented in tribunal cases in the UK. Likewise, Hauser-Cram, et al. (2001) show that many studies indicate that SES is a significant factor in child cognitive development for typically achieving children, but that few studies examine this trend for families with children who have disabilities. They also found that many studies indicate that SES alone was indicative of the developmental environment in a family concluding that SES must be examined in conjunction with information about patterns of relationships and operational styles of families. Higher rates of hearing loss, vision loss, speech and mobility impairments and vocabulary development have all been linked to socio-economic status (Ouellete-Kuntz, 2005).

In summary, the literature shows that there have been various trends in how professionals perceive parents' emotional reactions to having a child with a disability. Parent beliefs about the nature of disability have not been studied in great detail but the psychology research indicates that parent beliefs are important for the development of children's self-image. Parent involvement in schools is variable in both the quantity and quality of that involvement. This may be due to family characteristics such as SES or resources for advocacy. The collaborative relationship between teachers and parents is also variable and may be influenced by both teacher and parent beliefs.

The choice of schools to adopt an inclusive model of education is one that recognizes that the challenges of effective teaching belong to the education system as a whole and not just to a "special" group of students (Slee, 1997). Thus, contextual factors that are often considered important to consider in the question of placement for students with disabilities – abilities of teachers, the purposes of the education system – might be regarded as questions that are important for all students in the school system, including students with disabilities.

Individual, Situational and Socio-Political Constructions of Disability

The research that informs this book is based on the Individual, Situational and socio-Political (ISP) beliefs about the nature of barriers in education. I developed this theoretical framework from a combined analysis of the critical disability studies literature and interviews with teachers and parents. This chapter describes the theory and the research that led to the development of this theory. While this chapter is heavy on academic content, it provides support for claims that are made throughout the rest of the book. For those readers who are interested in the outcomes of the research only, summary tables are found in the latter part of the chapter showing the prevalence of these beliefs across a sample of teachers and parents. I begin with an overview of disability theory.

Early research and thinking about disability was firmly rooted in a medical approach to impairment. The focus of medical and psychological research on disability was on identification of impairments, ways to subdue people with disabilities, and occasionally rehabilitation in order to change people from disabled to abled (Oliver, 1996). However, attitudes toward people with disabilities have undergone a significant change over the last twenty years. The development of a Social Model in the United Kingdom, the disability rights movement in the United States, and Human Rights legislation in Canada have forged a dramatic social change in how people with disabilities participate in our society. That is not to say that extreme forms of discrimination do not still exist for people with disabilities but that there is a professional and academic discourse on disability that is based on the goals of full participation and access to human rights for people with disabilities. Tregaskis (2002) credits Finkelstein (1980), Oliver (1990) and the Union of the Physically Impaired Against Segregation (UPIAS, 1976) with the inception of a Social Model of disability in the UK. According to Oliver (1990):

> The issue of disability and the experiences of disabled people have been given scant consideration in academic circles. Both the issue and the experience have been marginalised and only in the disciplines of medicine and psychology has disability been afforded an important place. Unfortunately this has, itself, been counterproductive because it has resulted in the issue of disability as being essentially a medical one and the experience of disability as being contingent upon a variety of psychological adjustment processes. (Oliver, p. x)

The early struggle to recognize the need for an expanded consideration of the condition of disablement led to the Social Model of disability. The Social Model emerged as an alternative to the medical and pathological approaches to disability. Leicester and Lovell (1997) describe it this way:

> Disability is not conceived as a condition of the individual person. The experiences of "disabled people" are of social restrictions in the world around them; the individual's experience of disability is created in interactions with a physical and social world designed for non-disabled living. (p. 116)

The Social Model is a theory of the environmental causes of exclusion of individuals from community structures such as education, housing, employment and social engagement. The environmental causes include the appropriation of autonomy of disabled people by professional practitioners such as doctors, social workers and teachers. The focus on the experience of individuals does not necessarily account for other environmental causes of systemic oppression such as economic, political and cultural bias. The Social Model has been resisted and challenged. In the following section, I discuss the new paradigms of disability that have emerged from challenges to the Social Model and argue for a theoretical framework with three distinct levels of analysis of barriers to learning for children with disabilities. This framework is derived from the medical model view of disability and a division of the Social Model into a theory of Situational and socio-Political beliefs about the nature of barriers to learning.

Barnes, Mercer and Shakespeare (1999) in their book *Exploring Disability*, like most theorists in the disability field, describe a bipolar continuum of disability theory with medical model views on one end of the continuum and Social Model views at the other end. However, Barnes, et. al also describe three levels of sociological analysis for understanding disability: the Individual (experience of disability and impairment); the Social (socio-cultural categories of disability and identity politics); and the Societal (social welfare systems, and politics of disablement) (p. 35). These levels of analysis are the basis for the categories which make-up the ISP beliefs about the nature of barriers to learning. The labels I use for the ISP categories (Individual, Situational, and socio-Political) were renamed and the definitions refined after analysing interviews from both teachers and parents. The definitions of each of the three beliefs were established in Underwood (2002) in which a panel of five expert researchers agreed upon the definitions through coding one pilot interview.

Individual Beliefs

> *The individual belief about the nature of barriers to learning is based in a pathological understanding of disability. Learning problems are perceived to be a result of something being physically, emotionally, or intellectually wrong with the child. The difficulties faced by the child are not considered to be a symptom of their social interactions or the communities to which they belong.*

Barnes, Mercer and Shakespeare (1999) say that for some, "the focus [of disability] is on bodily 'abnormality', disorder or deficiency, and the way in which this in turn 'causes' some degree of 'disability' or functional limitation" (p. 21). They go on to say that:

> The typical emphasis is on helping individuals to pass through a grieving process associated with their 'complex of losses'. In so doing, it sets aside the influence of social material factors, including social policies, in helping an individual disabled person to 'cope' better, or to become more independent. (p. 27)

This belief about disability is traditionally associated with the medical and psychological professions, however, feminist disability theory supports the notion that the individual has a relationship with her/his own body and that the individual nature of impairment shapes a person's own experience (Tregaskis, 2002). Impairments in and of themselves do limit some activities regardless of social structures and attitudes of the people with whom the individual interacts. The omission of discussions of the impaired body (by proponents of the Social Model) has been seen as a barrier to the development of a disability identity. This feminist reaction to the Social Model has mostly examined physical disability, but would also hold true for the experience of intellectual impairment (Morris, 1992). Feminist theorists have further contributed to the discourse on disability by addressing the need for disability to be considered from a more personal perspective including such topics as sexuality, imagery, personal relationships, and parenting (Tregaskis, 2002). As Morris suggests, "such models (Medical Model and Social Model) are problematic because they do not easily allow the space within the research for the absent subject" (p. 159). By focusing on the individual the responsibility for inclusion is in the hands of the person who has the impairment rather than with the people with whom this person interacts. The "subjective reality" of the disabled person is thus preserved, but does not avoid the pathologizing of the disability (Morris, 1992).

An Individual belief about barriers is one that interprets the impairment as the primary cause of disability rather than the situational or systemic factors that restrict the participation of people with disabilities.

Situational Beliefs

> *The situational belief about barriers to learning explains a child's difficulties as a function of interactions with his or her immediate environment. This might include the attitudes of the people with whom the child interacts, or physical barriers, which create difficulties for a child with physical or sensory disabilities. The child's difficulties are not attributed to group attitudes or policy issues, nor are they perceived to be due to impairment.*

People with Situational beliefs accept that individuals who interact with a student on a daily basis create the impetus for inclusion. This means that a parent or a

17

teacher with the will to do so will include the person with an impairment into the family or classroom just as they include other family members or students. This is transferable to any other face-to-face interaction undertaken by persons with disabilities, including in their roles at work, in recreation, and as consumers and citizens. This theoretical position is supported by Kalyanpur and Harry (1999) who describe the attitude of the family as a source of exclusion for disabled family members.

One of the early critiques of the Social Model, according to Tregaskis, was that "role of culture and prejudice" were not accounted for. In other words, a distinction needs to be made between systemic discrimination and individual prejudice. This argument narrows in on the interaction of the individual with the immediate environment (i.e., the community of people with whom individuals interact in their day-to-day lives, such as parents and teachers in the case of a child) as opposed to systemic issues such as institutionalization (or education policy). Kalyanpur and Harry underscore this distinction in their consideration of the culture of special education and the "incorrect" epistemological assumptions about disability. They point out that disability is not an individual phenomenon but a group phenomenon, saying that, "a tacit understanding in all nonphysical explanations for the causes of a disability is that the child is not solely responsible for its (the impairment's) occurrence but that the entire family is implicated" (p. 41). They assert that "on the one hand, the stigma that is attached to a condition affects the entire family. On the other hand, the stigma is mitigated by a holistic view that interprets disability and illness in terms of family rather than individual traits" (p. 41). This view of disability is in keeping with the concern of prejudice as a root cause of disability because the attitudes of the family members (or teachers and classmates) will clearly determine the level of acceptance within the family (or classroom). But the level of community acceptance is determined by pressures outside of the family or school. Thus, there are two levels of consideration in determining the responsibility for the disabling condition. The Situational belief about the nature of barriers defines disability as primarily caused by the behaviours or attitudes of the individuals with whom the person with a disability interacts. For example, a teacher might neglect to adapt curriculum to meet a student's needs because of a prejudice about the student's disability.

Socio-Political Beliefs

> *The socio-Political belief about barriers to learning situates the child's difficulties within their social and political community. That is to say a child's disability is not a function of his or her immediate environment but of the underlying values of the society, education system or educational policy. These values are symptomatic of systemic pressures such as power, economics and political will.*

Under the socio-Political beliefs about barriers, the disabling condition is not present in the interactions of individual people but in the group behaviour of the society.

Legislation, media representation, public policy and funding are all systemic areas of responsibility for the disabling condition which may be primary causes of barriers for students with disabilities. In the educational context, the funding structure for special education, resource allocations for staffing, provincially mandated curriculum, and school norm are all part of the socio-political context of an individual student. Other factors such as policy statements from teachers' federations may also contribute to systemic discrimination. The socio-Political belief addresses the role of these societal factors in the educational experience of students with disabilities.

Oliver (1990) says that the economic oppression of people with disabilities happens through systematic exclusion from the means of production in a society. People with disabilities have traditionally been unemployed or underemployed and kept segregated from society through institutionalization and sheltered workshops; evidence of economic oppression according to Oliver. This argument can easily be adapted for the educational context if we examine the policy of segregating students with disabilities for the purpose of providing specialized programs. People with disabilities have traditionally been educated (or housed) in settings which are separate from other "mainstream" students, including in residential institutions.

In addition to the attitudinal barriers defined in the Social Model of disability, and outlined in the Situational belief category, Tregaskis (2002) notes that the Social Model also defines systemic barriers. The systemic barriers include "cultural images [which] have been used to socially construct disabled people as an unwelcome 'other' whose subjugation is necessary to the continuation or restoration of mainstream society" (p. 461). Thus a social norm shapes our image of "what a disability is ", but it is not an exchange that takes place between an individual and the people with whom s/he interacts in his/her social circle. This is a systemic cultural representation. Tregaskis presses this argument further when she introduces the psychoanalytical approach to disability asserting that, "images of people with impairments (...) are designed to evoke feelings of guilt, pity and sympathy in non-disabled people, as a means of persuading the mainstream population to make donations (for charitable organizations or medical research) " (p. 465). Kalyanpur and Harry (1999) refer to the myth that "disability requires remediation or 'fixing'" which is the result of such cultural portrayals of disability in mainstream society. Disability is thus perpetuated by negative images produced by the larger society making disabled people the object of pity and fear. This can contribute to the lack of participation by the individual in the society.

In summary, Leicester and Lovell's (1997) Social Model definition of disability as an "experience (...) created in *interactions* with a physical and social world *designed* for non-disabled living" (emphasis added), can be divided into two theoretical understandings of barriers: (1) at the level of interaction, barriers are rooted in individual prejudice, (2) at the level of design, barriers are rooted in systemic discrimination where public policy dictates such practices as curriculum design. The linear relationship between pathologically based notions of impaired bodies, and the Social Model concept of constructed barriers to full participation for people labelled with disabilities is ubiquitous in disability theory. Deconstruction of the Social Model theory, however, indicates that there are in fact three theoretical positions evident in the literature. The challenges to the Social Model are thus addressed by separating the experiences of individuals with their immediate environment (their situation) from the experience of individuals with a system (their socio-political experience). The two components of the Social Model remain in contrast to the experience of individuals with their own bodies (individual pathology). These three theoretical positions make up the Individual, Situational, and socio-Political categories of belief which provide the basis for examining disability theory in application.

The application of the ISP theory of beliefs about barriers to learning is the focus of my research. Over the past seven years I have interviewed many teachers and parents about the experience of children with disabilities in schools. In this research I have addressed two key questions. The first research question is whether the Individual, Situational and socio-Political beliefs theory, as designed from the distinctions found in the critical disability studies literature, is a valid represent-ation of the range of beliefs held by teachers and parents. The second question is how these beliefs relate to the things that teachers and parents do in practice. These research questions are illustrated in Figure 2.1.

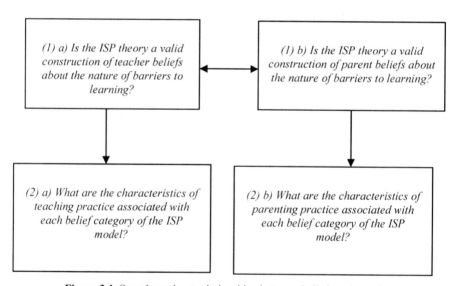

Figure 2.1. Questions about relationships between beliefs and practice.

Questions Answered

The Individual, Situational and socio-Political (ISP) theory of beliefs derived from the critical disability studies literature as described above was refined though analysis of interviews with teachers and parents, using the software analysis packages SPSS 14.0 and NVivo. This process served to validate the constructs derived from the literature and provided preliminary evidence of the prevalence of the belief systems. In addition the interviews provided a means of establishing the relationship between the ISP beliefs and teacher and parent practice.

All of the parents and teachers interviewed for this study were approached through their school principals and asked to volunteer. Teachers were recruited at an informal lunch meeting in each school to discuss the study goals and to request their informed consent. Teacher volunteers then sent home introductory letters to parents asking for their participation. Forty-two parent interviews and thirty-two teacher interviews were conducted with reference to forty-three students. The students were in grades one through eight. Where two parents were present at the interview, the interview is considered as one set of beliefs. In several cases, teachers had more than one student from the sample in their class. The students were drawn from four different school boards: two Catholic school boards and two public school boards. The eleven schools served urban, suburban and rural communities. All of the schools are in Ontario, Canada.

The criterion for including students in the research was that they had Individual Education Plans (IEP). The IEP indicated that within the school setting there was a formal plan for specialized services for these students. The students discussed by their teachers were not selected based on a medical category of their disability, or even the Ministry of Education's (2000b) categories of exceptionality, although these are used for practical purposes in the demographic descriptions of students. From a bio-medical perspective, the students' disabilities covered significant multiple disabilities, behavioural disorders, sensory and physical disabilities, and learning disabilities. Within the context of the Ontario school system, some of the students had been formally identified as exceptional while others had not, depending on the extent of the students' needs and on each school board's policy for eligibility for an Individual Placement and Review Committee (IPRC). Students were recruited from three groups: students who had an Intensive Support Amount (ISA) claim; students who did not have an ISA claim but had been identified through an IPRC; and students who had neither an ISA claim nor an IPRC. These three categories were established because it was anticipated that the categories created by public education policy would have an impact on the beliefs, practices and experiences of both teachers and parents. Further, at the time of the interviews there was a transition in policy taking place which impacted teachers' and parents' understanding of IEPs, ISA claims and IPRCs. Some of the school boards were also shifting to a more inclusive model of service delivery for students with disabilities. Not all of the school boards represented in the study regularly conducted IPRCs and for this reason there was a fourth group of students represented in the sample. Thus the student sample included seventeen students with an IEP only, four students with an IPRC but no ISA claim, eleven students with an ISA claim but no IPRC, and eleven students with both an IPRC and an ISA claim. Supplementary student demographics are shown in Table 2.1 including the type of educational placements.

Table 2.1. Student demographic information.

Variable		N
Total sample:		43
Sex:	Male	30
	Female	13
ISA claim:	Yes	22
	No	21
Disability category based on interview data* and formal identification	Behaviour (including ADHD and ODD)	7
	Communication (Autism spectrum and PDD, Tourette syndrome)	5
	Communication (Hearing loss and deafness)	1
	Communication (Learning disabilities)	16
	Physical (Vision loss and blindness)	1
	Physical	1
	Intellectual (Mild intellectual disability and Developmental disability)	9
	Multiple disabilities (includes physical, intellectual, communication, and behavioural categories)	3
Placement:	Regular class with accommodations	2
	Regular class with E.A. support	6
	Regular class with Resource support	13
	Regular class with E.A. and Resource support	15
	Withdrawal with partial integration	4
	Self-contained class	3

*Note: In one of the four school boards accessed in this study, formal identification through an IPRC was not part of the board practice. Other students were too young to have been formally identified, according to their school boards' policies, but would have an IPRC in the coming year. These board policies explain the large number of students with no IPRC. In this section, the categories that would likely be used had an IPRC been conducted are listed based on information from the IEP and interviews.

Finally, the teachers involved in the study also represented a diverse group ranging from those in their early years of teaching through to veteran teachers, with widely varying professional experience. There were twenty-three females and nine males. The majority of participating teachers had a four-year bachelor's degree plus a Bachelor of Education. Three teachers reported an Ontario Teacher's Certificate as their highest level of education, indicating they had acquired their teaching certificate prior to the requirement to earn a bachelor degree. See Table 2.3 for detailed teacher demographic information. For information about the range of placements taught by the teachers, see Table 2.1 under student placement. Three of the teachers in the sample were Special Education teachers in self-contained special education classes, which accounts for the range in class size from eight to thirty-two students in Table 2.3. The rest of the teachers were teaching in regular education classrooms.

The parents who were interviewed consisted of thirty-four mothers, six two-parent couples, and two fathers. These parents and guardians represented a range of family structures; traditional family units, single parents, same-sex parents, foster parents, adoptive parents, and step-parents. They also represented various socio-economic levels, education levels, and cultural backgrounds. All of the parents spoke English at home at least some of the time with their children. Table 2.2 contains detailed parent demographic information.

Table 2.2. Parent demographic information.

Variable		N
Total sample:		42
Place of birth:	Canada	29
	Outside Canada	9
	No response	4
Highest level of education:	High School	16
	Bachelor Degree	16
	Graduate Degree	8
	No response	3
Annual household income*:	Below $39,999	5
	$44,000-$53,999	5
	$54,000-$66,999	9
	$67,000-up	17
	No response	7
Involvement in a parent organization or support group related to child's disability:	Yes	14
	No	25

*Note: Based on the quartiles for average family income in Canada, census 1996.

Interviewing Teachers and Parents

All teacher interviews took place in quiet locations in the schools. In many cases this was a nurse's room, full of archival boxes and vacated because funding for school nurses has been eliminated. In newer schools, we used an office that was vacant for the afternoon or a corner of the library. Interviews were tape-recorded and transcribed for coding.

Table 2.3. Teacher demographic information.

Variables		N
Total sample:		32
Sex:	Male	9
	Female	23
Highest level of education:	B.Ed./Teaching Certificate	16
	B.Ed. + Early Childhood Education Certificate	1
	No response	3
Additional Qualifications:	Special education part I	5
	Special education part II	5

Variables	Range	Mean	Standard Deviation	N
Years teaching	1 – 30	11.67	8.48	32
Years teaching special education	1 – 13	1.45	3.60	6
Number of students in current class	8 – 32	22.92	4.12	32
Number of students with IEP in current class	1 – 9	4.11	1.97	32
Number of students with IPRC in current class	0 – 8	1.16	1.94	32
Number of students needing remedial support, but without IEP in current class (teacher rated)	0 – 10	3.71	2.25	32

Parents were given the option of being interviewed at home or in the school attended by their children. The majority of parents came into the school. But not all parents were able to come to the school. One interview was conducted in a big farmhouse in the country with the extension cord for the tape recorder stretched across the wide dining room floor to reach the table where we sat, while several children came in from the school bus. Two interviews were conducted by telephone. One with not a sound in the background and the other with the din of construction as the tile floor was replaced in an inner city, publicly funded housing complex. The mother apologized saying the floor had been flooded twice in the last month and she was desperate for them to fix it. Parent interviews were also tape-recorded and transcribed. In two cases, when parents entered the office where the interview was to be conducted, they became very nervous about being tape-recorded. In these cases, the interviews were recorded with note taking during and at the end of the interviews. The interviews lasted between forty-five and sixty minutes each. Copies of the students' IEPs were also collected, and in most cases were available for reference by the both the interviewer and the teachers or parents during the interview.

The ISP Interview

Polkinghorne (1988) says that "narrative meaning consists of more than the events alone; it consists of the significance these events have for the narrator in relation to a particular theme" (p. 160). I have a strong sense that the events or described practices of teachers and parents can only be understood in relation to the commentary about the events as they are interpreted by the teachers and parents. Beliefs are a notoriously difficult construct to measure in research. In research on teacher beliefs, many studies use behaviours as a proxy for beliefs. That is researchers observe what teachers are doing and ask them about their practice and they assume that the behaviours can illuminate the teachers' beliefs. Stanovich (1994) referred to this as beliefs grounded in practice. Other studies use attitudinal checklists to capture the elusive beliefs or values of teachers (Antonak & Larrivee, 1995). The ISP interview on the other hand, asks teachers and parents to describe their experiences and beliefs together, as one organic narrative. It is in the analysis that the beliefs and practices are teased apart in order to understand how the theoretical beliefs of teachers and parents interact with their practice. In the ISP interview, teachers and parents are asked for judgements about the current educational program for the student, attributions about the causes of learning difficulties and explanations of their own decisions and practices. The topics in the teacher interview span the teachers' experiences from when they first learned that the students would be entering their classes to the programs they currently have in place for those students. They were asked to talk about identifying disabilities, assessing student needs, developing IEPs, collaborating with other teachers and parents, and developing teaching strategies in their classes. Teachers were also asked about the resources they have and the resources they need, their training, their frustrations and their successes. The stories that the teachers tell provide the basis for probing about why they did what they did. As described above, teacher beliefs are thought to be an important component of teacher practice. The goal of my research was to honour the relationship between beliefs and practice as described by Muijs and Reynolds (2002):

> Belief systems are dynamic and permeable mental structures, susceptible to change in light of experience. The relationship between beliefs and practice is also not a simple one-way relationship from belief to practice, but a dynamic two-way relationship in which beliefs are influenced by practical experience. (p. 4)

The parent interview questions were first developed by Underwood (2002) and based on Engel's (1993) origin myths which rely on parent descriptions of early experiences with their children to elicit their current beliefs and attitudes about how society views their children with disabilities. The Individual, Situational, socio-Political (ISP) interview schedule uses Engel's (1993) narrative technique that "connect(s) past and present, clarif(ies) the meaning of important events, reaffirm(s) core norms and values, and assert(s) particular understandings of social order and individual identity" (Engel, 1993, p. 785).

The interviews were designed to illuminate school-related decisions and actions of parents associated with each belief category. The parent interview follows a chronological pattern asking parents to describe their early experiences through to their current experience with the education system. Parents were asked to describe their child, to talk about when they first learned that their child had a disability or learning difficulty, and to offer their thoughts on their child's current program in school. Probes were used to encourage parents to describe their beliefs about the things that help their children and the barriers that their children face in school.

Both teachers and parents were also given a questionnaire about the characteristics of the particular child being discussed and their experience with the development of an IEP for that child, and about IEPs in general. Questionnaire data provide participant ratings of student achievement, ratings of the process of developing the IEP, ratings of the IEP document itself, and demographic information. Both teachers and parents were asked to rate their level of personal involvement in program development, monitoring and evaluating progress.

No significant correlations were found between the IEP questionnaire data and the teacher or parent ISP scores. Thus, student characteristics such as level of academic achievement, behavioural ratings, and the level of curriculum adaptation or modification required do not appear to be predictive of ISP beliefs. In addition, teacher and parent satisfaction with the development of the IEP and with their level of involvement in developing the IEP do not appear to predict ISP beliefs. These variables also did not indicate agreement between teachers and parents about the usefulness of the IEPs for the students or the success of the program described in the IEP in meeting the needs of the students. Finally, the general questions about IEP policy, such as who prepares the IEP, are also not predictive of ISP beliefs in this study.

Prevalence of ISP Beliefs

The three ISP categories of belief have a relationship akin to a triangle with interdependence built into the scoring. The ISP interview produces a profile-of-beliefs for each participant, with three scores, rather than a single score on a scale. As described in detail below, the scoring is designed so that a total of six points are allocated to the three categories for each statement. The mean score for each category across all statements for the interview results in profiles that show the relative weighting of each belief category.

The ISP coding consisted of two tasks: statement selection and scoring for beliefs. First one rater selected key statements from the transcribed interviews. The statements were selected if they met the criterion of being opinions about events or non-events (i.e., judgements about the current educational program for the student, attributions about the causes of learning difficulties and explanations of their own decisions and practices). These statements were then scored using a six-point system. The six points are distributed between the three categories of the ISP model. The "Don't Know" category was used to indicate a belief statement that was not represented by the ISP categories. A sample section of the scoring sheet is presented in Figure 2.2.

Reliability of the ISP coding was established through inter-rater reliability scores. Two independent raters coded the early interviews to establish inter-rater reliability for the parent and teacher interviews on the ISP scores. The inter-rater reliability was estimated using Pearson's Correlation coefficient for the first twelve interviews, six parent interviews and six teacher interviews. These twelve interviews scored yielded an estimated correlation of $r = +.83$ (p <.01) for the Individual belief scores, $r = +.81$ (p <.01) for the Situational belief scores, and $r = +.80$ (p <.01) for the Political belief scores. This was deemed to be sufficiently high to continue scoring with just one rater.

The distribution of the six points across the three categories allows for the fact that the participants' beliefs might be a complex combination of belief categories. A mean score for each category was then calculated for a beliefs profile of the participant (e.g. Parent #73 profile = 1.04 (Individual) + 1.74 (Situational) + 3.22 (socio-Political) = 6). It is important to note that the three categories are mutually inter-dependent due to the nature of the coding mechanism. This coding mechanism was selected to force this inter-dependence in order to make the constructs equal in measurement.

Statement Number	Individual	Situational	Socio-Political	Don't Know
Example	0	2	4	0

Figure 2.2. Example of scoring form for ISP coding mechanism.

The ISP categories, developed from the construct distinctions made in the disability studies literature, were evident in the spontaneous statements of the interview participants. The sum of the ISP scores for the total parent and teacher samples are presented in Figure 2.3 as a percentage of all points allocated to beliefs for the sample. The percentage of Individual belief scores ranged from 28% (parents) to 31% (teachers); the Situational belief scores ranged from 43% (teachers) to 52% (parents); and the socio-Political belief scores ranged from 19% (parents) to 25% (teachers). The "don't know" category, which indicated a belief statement that did not fit the ISP categories, made up less than 1% of the scores for both teachers and parents. The frequency of dominant beliefs (the category with the highest score) from the teacher and parent belief profiles is summarized in Figure 2.4 below. The capacity of the ISP categories to explain teacher and parent beliefs is evident.

Teacher ISP Scores

Teacher ISP belief profiles were calculated by finding the mean score for each category of belief for all codeable statements in each interview. A bar graph of the teacher ISP profiles are presented in Figure 2.5 (the raw scores are presented in

Table A1 in the Appendix). Teachers show widely varying ISP scores, with all three of the categories well represented as dominant amongst the sample of interviews.

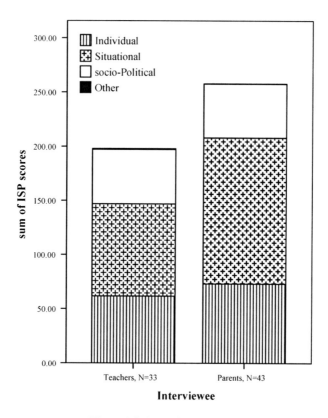

Figure 2.3. *Sum of ISP scores for Total sample.*

Note: "Other" category indicates belief statements that could not be categorized under the ISP construct, and were scored as "Don't Know" in the ISP coding.

Descriptive statistics for teacher belief scores are shown in Table 2.5. The mean scores for each category show that for the overall teacher sample Situational belief scores were more predominant than the other two categories (Skewness and Kurtosis values are shown in Table 2.5). The Individual belief scores include three outliers and the Situational scores predominate across the teacher sample. The maximum score for any of the categories is six.

Correlations between the three ISP constructs are shown in Table 2.4: the Individual with the Situational belief, $r = -.52$ (p<.01, 2-tailed); Individual with the socio-Political belief, $r = -.71$ (p<.01, 2-tailed); and the Situational with the socio-Political belief, $r = -.23$ (not significant). The inverse relationships between the

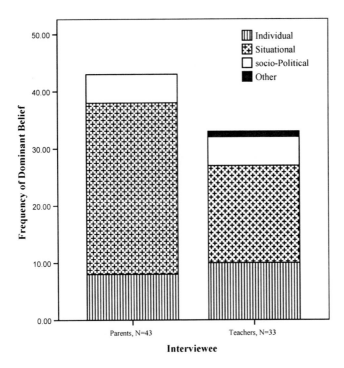

Figure 2.4. *Frequency of dominant ISP belief category, shown as a percentage of the sum of scores for the total sample.*

Note: "Other" indicates no distinct dominant category. In this case one interview had socio-Political and Situational belief scores that were equal.

three belief categories of the ISP coding are partly a result of the inter-dependence inherent in the allocation of points and are not reliably represented in correlation analysis. However, the correlations do suggest that the Situational and socio-Political categories are conceptually closer than either category is with the Individual beliefs.

Table 2.4. *Correlations between teacher belief scores by ISP category and PI scores*

	Individual belief	Situational belief	Socio-Political belief	PI score
Individual belief	1			
Situational belief	-.52**	1		
Socio-Political belief	-.71**	-.23	1	
PI score	-.49**	.54**	.13	1

*** Correlation is significant at the 0.01 level (2-tailed)*

29

The frequency of the dominant belief scores for the teacher sample (as illustrated in Figures 2.4 and 2.5) were as follows: ten dominant Individual belief scores; seventeen dominant Situational belief scores; five dominant socio-Political belief scores; and one teacher interview had equivalent dominant Situational and socio-Political belief scores.

Table 2.5. *Descriptive statistics for three categories of teacher beliefs, based on mean scores for all statements in each interview.*

Statistic	Mean Individual belief score	Mean Situational belief score	Mean socio-Political belief score
N	33	33	33
Mean	1.87	2.58	1.53
Median	1.61	2.47	1.67
Mode	2.00	2.23	1.67*
S.D.	1.13	.84	1.02
Variance	1.28	.70	1.03
Skewness	.80	.29	.19
Kurtosis	.234	-.646	-.729
Range	4.40	3.13	3.83

Note: multiple modes exist. The smallest value is shown.

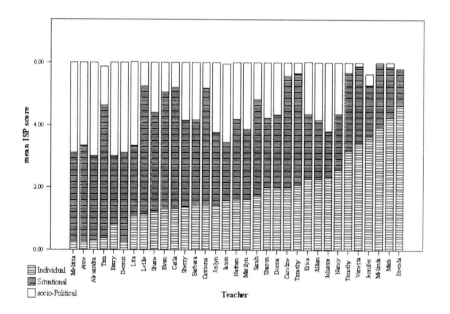

Figure 2.5. *Bar graph of teacher ISP profile scores based on mean score for each category, Rank ordered by Individual score.*

Each teacher interview was also coded using the Pathognomonic-Interventionist (PI) scoring established by Jordan and colleagues. The PI uses the usual two-dimensional continuum found in disability theory. The PI scores for the teacher interviews provide concurrent validation for the teacher ISP scoring while illustrating the differences in the two approaches to coding beliefs. Throughout its long history, the PI scoring has shown good internal reliability (Stanovich & Jordan, 1998). In addition, external validation of the PI scoring through correlations with preference for delivery model (Jordan, Kircaali-Iftar, & Diamond, 1993), relationship to teachers' level of individual engagement with students (Jordan & Stanovich, 2004), and relationship to whole-class teaching practices (Stanovich & Jordan, 1998) provides the basis for using the PI as a concurrent validation measure for the ISP scores. However, it was expected that the PI and the ISP would not directly correspond since the ISP introduces a third dimension of belief, the socio-Political, that is not represented on the PI continuum, and the Individual and Situational beliefs are defined from a different set of literature than the PI.

The PI coding mechanism uses a three-point scale, scored on five topical domains (and a total of twenty items): (a) referral and assessment, (b) programming, (c) review, (d) communication with staff, and (e) communication with parents. For each of the twenty items there is a statement reflecting the P-beliefs and a statement reflecting I-beliefs, with a mid point, on the scale. The interview transcripts are coded by independent raters and produce a mean score between 1 and 3 for each interview, (1 = P-beliefs, 2 = mid-point, and 3 = I-beliefs). Inter-rater reliability has been consistently high across several studies (e.g. $r= +.88$, $p<.01$, in Jordan, Lindsay, & Stanovich, 1997). The teacher interviews were coded by a researcher trained on these earlier studies.

The mean PI score for the teacher sample was 2.10, (S.D. +.53), and showed a slight skew toward the interventionist end of the PI scale (skewness = -.22, kurtosis = -.93). This matches the finding that teachers in this sample scored higher in the Situational category than in the Individual category (Table 2.5), since the interventionist construct of the PI scale is conceptually related to the Situational belief construct of the ISP beliefs. The PI scores and the Situational belief scores correlated at Pearson's $r= +.54$, $p< .01$ (2-tailed), as shown in Table 2.4. In addition there is a significant inverse relationship between Individual belief scores and the PI scores ($r = -.49$, $p<.01$, 2-tailed). This is in keeping with the construct validation outlined above as the higher the PI score the more interventionist the beliefs, correlating with a Situational belief on the ISP score, and the lower the PI score the more pathognomonic the beliefs, correlating inversely with Individual beliefs on the ISP score. The Pearson correlation coefficient for the PI scores and the socio-Political belief score is not significant.

Parent ISP Scores

Descriptive statistics for the parent belief scores are presented in Table 2.7 and each parent participants' ISP scores are presented in the bar graph in Figure 2.6

(raw ISP parent scores are listed in Table A2 in the Appendix). As with the teacher data, the parent Situational belief scores are more predominant than the other two categories across the sample. This is true even though the range for Situational beliefs is the smallest (Table 2.7). The Individual and socio-Political belief scores contain more extreme values than the Social belief scores. One outlier for socio-Political beliefs is evident in the parent data, whereas in the teacher data all three outliers were accounted for in the Individual belief scores.

The frequency of parent belief scores which were dominant (the category with the highest score) were as follows: 8 dominant Individual scores; 30 dominant Situational scores; and 5 dominant socio-Political scores.

The correlations amongst the three ISP constructs for the parent data are shown in Table 2.6: the Individual with the Situational $r = -.55$ (p<.01, 2-tailed); the Individual with the socio-Political $r = -.62$, (p<.01, 2-tailed), and the socio-Political with the Situational $r = -.31$ (p<.01, 2-tailed). The inverse relationships between the three belief categories of the ISP coding are a result of the interdependence inherent in the measure and are not reliably represented by correlation analysis, as was the case with the teacher data. However, the correlations indicate a fairly balanced relationship between the three constructs.

The parent interview data are presented in Figure 2.6 as scored on the ISP beliefs. In some cases, the three belief scores of a profile do not sum to six: This is due to rounding of mean scores and the use of the "don't know" column, where the belief statement did not fit the ISP categories.

Table 2.6. Correlations between parent belief scores by ISP category.

	Individual belief	Situational belief	Socio-Political belief
Individual belief	1		
Situational belief	-.55**	1	
Socio-Political belief	-.62**	-.31	1

** Correlation is significant at the 0.01 level (2-tailed).

Table 2.7. Descriptive statistics for three categories of parent beliefs, based on mean scores for all statements in each interview.

Statistic	Individual belief	Situational belief	Socio-Political belief
N	43	43	43
Mean	1.70	3.14	1.16
Median	1.37	3.22	0.93
Mode	0.37	2.96	0.00
S.D.	1.19	.96	1.09
Variance	1.41	.96	1.09
Skewness	0.67	-.22	1.02
Kurtosis	-0.71	-0.90	0.42
Range	4.16	3.74	4.00

As the PI coding is specific to the classroom experience of teachers, it could not be used to validate the parent interview. A new self-rating questionnaire, the Parent Self-rated questionnaire about the nature of Barriers (PSB) was developed as a concurrent validity measure for the parent interview scores. The PSB was administered to four parents, who were selected because their ISP scores showed predominant beliefs in one of the three belief categories. Although only four parents filled out the questionnaire, this pilot yielded preliminary results. Two parents rated themselves as having the same dominant profile as found in the ISP coding. Two other parents' self-ratings did not agree with the ISP coding. One parent rated him/herself as having a dominant Individual profile, although his/her interview transcript had been coded as having a dominant Situational belief profile. However, this parent used the space provided for comments saying, "I do also agree that teachers can make the difference to how much a child learns in the way the material is presented to them". Another parent whose transcript had been coded as having a predominantly Individual belief profile selected the Situational profile in the PSB. Her comments clearly reflected a Situational belief about teachers: "Another thing to consider is behaviour in children. My child has an EA (Education Assistant) for each subject (now in high school) but because of behavioural problems the EAs are not always able to cope with the situation and my child has been suspended on more than one occasion, not because she intends to be disobedient, but because the school staff does not have the tools or proper education to deal with behavioural problems". Thus, two of the four parents selected PSB descriptions of barriers that matched the dominant category in their ISP profiles, while two did not.

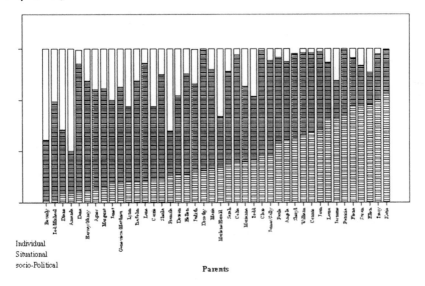

Figure 2.6. Bar graph of parent ISP scores based on mean scores for each category, rank ordered by Individual score.

Summary

This study relies on interview data with a volunteer sample of parent and teacher dyads (in some cases triads, where more than one parent attended the interview) representing forty-three students with IEPs. These parents and teachers present a diverse sample from varying backgrounds and experiences, but they all have the shared experience of working with one student who has an IEP. Interviews were conducted with participants focusing on their experiences of developing, imple-menting and monitoring the individual programs of these students. Questionnaire data also provides additional information about participants and offers opportunities for correlational analysis. The analysis addresses the research questions: 1) Is the ISP belief construct a valid and reliable measure of both teacher and parent beliefs about the nature of barriers in education? (2) What are the characteristics of teaching and parenting practice associated with each belief category of the ISP model? The results of the analyses are presented in Chapters three through five.

The ISP scores generated through this analysis show variance across the study sample for both parents and teachers in all categories of belief. Illustrative cases show the variance amongst profiles of parents and teachers by belief category. Further, reliability of the ISP coding is established through correlation of teacher Situational belief scores and the PI scores. In a small-scale analysis, four parent ISP scores were found to have a 50% with the parent self-rating or PSB. In the next two chapters, the teacher and parent practices associated with each category of belief will be presented. Questionnaire data did not yield any predictive variables for the ISP belief categories.

SCHOOL-BASED PRACTICE AND THE ISP BELIEFS

Chapters 3 through 7 address specific school-based practices and how they are informed by the Individual, Situational and socio-Political beliefs about barriers to learning. Teacher and parent behaviours associated with each of the ISP beliefs were established using a thematic analysis, derived from Grounded Theory (Glaser & Strauss, 1967; Strauss, 1998), of teacher and parent practices as described in interviews.

The characteristics of teacher and parent practice presented in this study are based on a qualitative analysis of the seventy-six interviews conducted in the study. Through the analysis conducted here patterns emerged which are useful in identifying practices related to the coded beliefs of teachers and parents. Using grounded theory, an inductive approach to theory development, the interviews were coded for practices described by the participants. Each description of practice was coded and then thematic groupings were established. Only those practices which were cross-coded with a statement that had been selected for ISP belief scoring were included, i.e., only those descriptions of practice which included judgments, attributions and explanations for the practice were used. This left out the descriptions of practice which did not elicit the participants' own analysis of why they engaged in the practice. This thematic approach provided evidence of the characteristics of teaching and parenting associated with each category of belief. Common practices across the interviews were determined and then grouped by the five interview topics (referral and assessment, programming, monitoring, collaboration, and reporting). Non-academic considerations emerged as an additional topic introduced by the participants but not initially part of the interview topics.

DOMINANT BELIEF CASES

In addition to analysing the ISP beliefs in relationship to practice, I thought it would be useful to present some case studies of teachers and parents who, based on their interviews, were judged to have the most extreme belief systems. I selected the three teachers and three parents with the highest scores in each of the three categories as case studies. These case studies are found at the end of chapters throughout the book and are meant to illustrate how the beliefs inform the practices of individuals. This is different from the analysis on particular practices such as identification (Chapter 3), instruction (Chapter 4), collaboration (Chapter 5), grading and assessment (Chapter 6) and establishing a social environment in the classroom (Chapter 7). In each of these chapters I rely on the collective experience of the teachers and parents I interviewed to get a broad picture of how theory informs practice. The case studies, on the other hand, illustrate the complex and unique ways that belief systems can inform the practice of individuals. The multiple and mixed approaches I use to investigate teacher and parent beliefs and practices is a direct attempt at circumventing the difficulty of measuring and understanding beliefs.

The names used in the profiles, as in the rest of the book are pseudonyms, to protect the identity of all of the people interviewed and those described by the parents and teachers.

Brenda's interview profile was coded with a mean score of 4.62 (Individual), 1.14 (Situational), and 0.05 (socio-Political). This was the highest Individual score in the teacher sample. Brenda teaches in a suburban school that was recently built to accommodate a new housing development. Houses in the area have large backyards and two car garages. The vice principal at the school is particularly interested in inclusive education practice and has been working closely with the special education resource teacher to develop an inclusive model in the school. Overall the school board has a policy of including all students with disabilities in regular classes. However, Karen, a student with multiple complex disabilities, is an exception. Karen is one of Brenda's students, but she spends most of her time in the resource room.

Brenda has been teaching for twelve years in grades four through seven. She has her Special Education Part 2 Additional Qualification (a professional qualification in Ontario). At the time of the interview she taught a regular grade six class with twenty-five students, four of whom had IEPs. The needs of these four students range from accommodations through to modifications, and in the case of one student, Karen, an alternate program.

Brenda's high Individual score can be accounted for by the fact that she takes almost no responsibility for Karen's program. When I met with Brenda she was somewhat nervous but she presented a very professional demeanour. Throughout the interview Brenda's lack of involvement with Karen's educational program is evident. Brenda says that Karen has "been in a situation from kindergarten where she's had a one-to-one Education Assistant with her at all times. She can never be left alone because her disability is that serious ". The effect of Karen being out of the classroom so much is that Brenda actually does not know her very well. In fact, when I asked Brenda to describe Karen, she described what Karen could not do. And there are a lot of things that Karen cannot do: she cannot talk; she cannot walk; and it is not clear how much she is processing of other people's words. But I pressed Brenda to describe Karen as a little girl, instead of as a series of deficits. Brenda describes Karen, saying:

> She loves interaction; she needs eye contact; she likes people. She reminds me of a little baby in some ways. If you make a noise she turns right away. Any time we have choir practice or a marching band or something comes to the gym to perform for the entire school, she's right there and she has the arms going and the head going and the eyes. She just really responds to that kind of stimulus. She loves music. She likes outdoor activities. She goes out all the time for recesses, and she really responds to the primary kids as well. Even though she's in grade six and is in my room, she loves the little kindergartens and the JK's, and if they're watching a video on Franklin or something like that, sometimes they'll say, "Does Karen want to come and watch it? " And she'll go with them. And, you know, even though she's not really watching the video so much, she's watching the other kids. Because

you can see her head turning, and she's keeping an eye on the other ... small kids. And of course they're at her stature, because she's in a wheelchair; we always have to bend down to see her, whereas the small kids are on eye level with her, so of course she connects with them. For adults you have to always bend down and crouch and, if we're in the hallway or whatever, (then...) what's Karen seeing? She's just seeing our backs. Unless you bend down and make that effort to make eye contact with her, she's not going to get it.

Brenda has not really connected with Karen. She is able to give details of Karen's activities but throughout the interview I had the sense that Brenda could not see Karen as a student. Overall Brenda had very little to do with Karen but she did talk about ways in which she tries to include Karen, such as adjusting her desk so she can sit in the class. She also mentions her own efforts to include Karen socially with other students in her class, resulting in a Situational score:

> I try to include her (Karen) – socially more than anything. That she's in the room with us – and even for the other students – that they accept her, and that they see her as part of our class and that she's part of the group.

In addition, Brenda states that she would like to work with Karen more; a statement that is coded as Situational:

> If it was a perfect world, I'd like time ... more time with her alone, with me. And I'd like to be taught more about her (Karen's) condition. I guess I do know what sort of works with her and (what) doesn't, but that maybe I could be pushing the EAs to do more with her.

Brenda says she wants to know more about Karen's condition but she does not say she wants to know more about Karen. This is a distinction that I think is important in understanding Brenda's beliefs. As the following extract from her interview illustrates, Brenda seems to learn from the EAs rather than the EAs taking direction from her. Also, throughout the interview Brenda refers to the twenty-four students in her class, although there are twenty-five including Karen. Karen has seizures throughout the day which Brenda does not feel equipped to deal with. When asked about Karen's progress, Brenda responds:

> In terms of just a year, I haven't seen a big change in her from September. But the EAs tell me that, based upon the last five or six years, there has been growth. That she is making eye contact more, and when someone speaks to her – and if she looks at them and makes eye contact – the EAs will say, "Good, Karen! Good eye contact! " They reinforce that with her. (Interviewer: And do you feel like you're participating in that growth as it develops over that time?) I'm not participating that much ... you see ... because when she's in the room, the Education Assistants are with her, and I can go over and talk to her and do a few little things, but then you know what it's like when there are twenty-four other children in the room. "I need this, (I need that...)", you know, it's constant. So ... you see I would need one-to-one time with her, to be withdrawn, which no one gives me.

Brenda has a fair bit of awareness about the activities that Karen participates in throughout the day, but her knowledge is not first hand and it sounds as if she does not talk to Karen often:

> She loves the water play; she had water activities. She has stimulus like a mat that is beaded; it has different surfaces. There's a beaded one; there's something like sandpaper; different textures that she gets to feel and touch. But water is her favourite. She loves water and splashes in water, and when the Education Assistants remove her from the water, you can see her. She's still reaching, she still wants the water. She loves tactile, touch. Whenever we do talk with her, we bend down and touch her elbows or touch her face or touch her hair, because she needs that, you know, touching.

Brenda's Individual beliefs are evident, yet even though Brenda indicated earlier she would like to work with Karen, she is not taking on the responsibility to do so. Brenda also does not convey a sense of responsibility for communication with Karen's mother:

> Karen's mum brings her every morning. So I see her (the mother) the odd time, because she doesn't arrive at 8:15 with everyone else. Karen comes at about quarter to ten. So she arrives, we'll hear a buzz, "Mrs. So-and-so come downstairs, Karen's arrived". The Education Assistant goes downstairs … But I'm with the other twenty-four students.

Karen needs a lot of physical support. This is done by the Education Assistants:

> One EA takes Karen for the morning, the other for the afternoon. All the lifting is done with two adults. Whenever she's being taken out of the medilift or being put into the wheelchair there are two adults (…) And I've seen them do that.

Brenda describes the need for Karen to use the elevator as a "problem" because it requires assistance. This is despite the fact that the school is brand new and has a very nice elevator. When asked about Karen's communicative abilities, Brenda is clear about the limits caused by Karen's disability:

> She can reach for a stretchy rubber, it's like a hose really. And we hook it onto the handle of the cupboards. And we'll say, "reach for it Karen. Grab it! " And she'll reach for it and grab it. But verbally, if you said, "which is red? Which is green? " she wouldn't be able to point out which one it was.

When I asked if anyone has tried using Augmentative and Alternative Communication (AAC) with Karen, Brenda replied; "that would be nice for Karen – to see if it would work ". But she does not respond in terms of being responsible for the implementation of such a program. In fact, when interviewing Karen's mother, I heard that Karen had been working on an AAC program and was making progress. This was also described in the IEP. Brenda does not view herself as part of the solution to breaking down barriers for Karen's learning; rather the barriers are described as being a result of Karen's individual disabilities.

I also asked if Karen is able to respond to making choices, for example, could she choose if she wanted a glass of milk or juice. Brenda reminded me that Karen does not eat or drink anything at school so she could not ask her such a question. Overall, Brenda seems interested in Karen's program but she is very removed from Karen's activities. Brenda does not view Karen as one of the students in her class and actually describes her in terms of the kindergarten students. Brenda did describe trying to include Karen socially in her class but she did not report any positive results from these efforts. Brenda's Individual beliefs have shaped her image of Karen as a person defined by her disability. Although Karen's communication limitations make it difficult for Brenda to talk with Karen, Brenda has seen that other staff are able to communicate with Karen. I think there are two primary assumptions that Brenda has made that shape her beliefs. First, she assumes that Karen cannot understand what is happening around her and that she does not have any similarities to other grade six students. And second, Brenda assumes that Karen will be better served by Education Assistants than by her, a trained teacher with a special education background.

CHAPTER 3

Labelling, Diagnosing and Streaming

We pass through this world by once. Few tragedies can be more extensive than the stunting of life, few injustices deeper than the denial of opportunity to strive or even to hope, by limits imposed from without, but falsely identified as lying within. (Gould, 1996, pp. 60-61)

As Stephen Gould points out, the effects of misinterpreting human characteristics are monumental. In schools, there is a constant struggle to assess student learning characteristics with the goal of improving instructional practice. However, the process of identifying individual learning characteristics can have some detrimental effects, not the least of which is misidentifying individual characteristics because of the inadequacy of the testing methods. Gould's point is part of his introduction to an exceptional work about the errors in Intelligence testing. Gould's comprehensive examination of intelligence testing concludes that the biggest error in this type of testing is the assumption that there is such a construct as intelligence, which is linear, measurable and an innate characteristic of individuals. Intelligence testing is one of the cornerstones of assessment of learning characteristics in schools, but students are also identified as having special needs through informal and psychoeducational assessments. In fact, even without formal identification of a disability a large number of students are getting "special education" supports. In Ontario, approximately 3% of students are considered to be disabled according to national survey data, but almost 13% are getting special education (Bennett & Wynne, 2006; Statistics Canada, 2001). Thus, formal identification of disability, including learning disabilities, involves psycho-educational tests, medical diagnosis, as well as informal identification of students who are not being served within the regular system and need a "special" program. Within the school system, these children all have the status of being outside the norm, despite the fact that many of them would not be considered to have a disability in other contexts. These students are "labelled" as having "special educational needs" a category constructed within school systems. The construction of this category of students, specific to the school context and which leads to labelling students, is the inspiration for the title of this book.

In practice, all school jurisdictions in which I have ever worked have used some formal procedure for identifying learning characteristics before a systemic program of "intervention" to correct learning problems is funded and implemented. These processes are beguiling for their ease of administering support services, but the question is whether these programs promulgate a particular theoretical orientation to disability. This chapter is about the application of identification processes for use in schools and how they relate to teacher and parent beliefs about disability.

Identification of disabilities, particularly early identification in pre-school or the early primary grades, is one of the central goals of the Ontario school system. This is accepted practice throughout North America. In fact, "assessment and evaluation are central to education reform initiatives all over the world. Not only are countries, provinces and states relying on large-scale assessments as measures of the progress and success of their initiatives, but classroom assessment has become a major part of the agenda for improving student learning" (Earl & LaFleur, 2000, p. 2). Research evidence indicates that with early detection of learning difficulties, most children can dramatically improve their academic skills, particularly early language and math skills. Education policies targeting early identification of learning difficulties and early intervention are now very common. In Ontario, the Ministry of Education has committed large amounts of funding to early intervention programs in language and math. In one publication the Ministry says:

> Effective intervention requires that teachers recognize as early as possible those children who are experiencing reading difficulties, tailor instruction to address their needs, and provide for supplementary instruction when necessary. If adequate screening and assessment procedures are in place, early intervention may begin even before formal instruction in reading. Interventions that are begun when children are very young have a much better chance of success than interventions begun later. (The Report of the Expert Panel on Early Reading in Ontario, 2003, p. 34)

Many of these early identification programs, such as Reading Recovery, have become part of the regular education initiatives in schools and do not require IEPs or formal identification. But other programs continue to require that students' characteristics be documented as different from the norm through IEPs and identification of "exceptionalities". In this chapter the experience of teachers and parents in the process of identifying student learning difficulties are presented in the context of how identification and intervention affect children and influence how teacher and parent beliefs intersect these practices. First, the identification and intervention model is one that uses a rehabilitative focus. Rehabilitation is a red flag in disability theory because of the assumption in rehabilitation that normal ability (physical or intellectual) can be defined, and with hard work can be achieved by people with disabilities. Promoting rehabilitation confirms that not fitting into the norm is considered undesirable and that there is something missing for those who do not fit the norm.

In my research, I talked to teachers about referring students for specialized services and programs, as well as formal and informal assessments of achievement levels and learning characteristics. Teachers usually conducted informal assessment of students' learning characteristics as soon as the student entered their class or even earlier. More formal assessments, such as psycho-educational tests, were conducted later in the school year after teachers had time to learn more about the student. In parent interviews, the focus was usually on formal assessments for diagnosis of learning or other disability.

Diagnostic testing might be initiated by the school or the parent. Based on the information from these formal assessments teachers and parents made decisions about the kind of program a student would get. The most dramatic placement decisions that parents and teachers described involved choosing a school or school system for their child to attend based on the way in which schools delivered learning support. Teachers and parents who considered student characteristics as the determining factor in decisions about placement options had Situational beliefs. Teachers and parents who based decisions about placement on the school or school board model of delivering school support (an inclusive model, a special education model or somewhere in between) had socio-Political beliefs. Teachers and parents who held Individual beliefs described assessments as useful for verification of deficits confirming their belief that there was something "wrong" with a student. Teachers and parents who held Individual beliefs were less likely to describe assessments and identification of disability as useful for informing their own actions. The assessments described as the means to understand student needs and to program accordingly is coded as a Situational belief.

METHODS OF IDENTIFICATION

It is clear from teachers and parents as a whole that formal assessments are conducted in several different ways depending on the school or school board. Although in all of the schools where I conducted interviews there was provision for assessment services, many parents felt that it took too long for assessments to be conducted, leaving students to fall behind while they waited for support. In many cases school staff suggested families pay for private assessments in order to avoid long wait-times through the school board. One teacher told me:

> The testing that they do takes quite a bit of time. It's a long process. You have to get the parent permission; the letter sent which isn't that long. Then Program Support takes them out for half an hour here and there. They can't just run tests all in the same day. So that happens and then we look at the results and then we have a team meeting and honestly by that time we are a couple of months into school, and not too much comes of it anyway.

Three parents told me that they could not afford the private assessment, which was suggested by school staff to avoid the long wait-time for in-school assessments. However, many parents in the study had their children assessed in private facilities sometimes paying several thousand dollars. Parents were forthright about the inequity of private payment for assessment. For parents who had paid there was often a sense of guilt knowing that other parents could not pay, but these parents also felt justified in trying to get support for their children. For parents who could not afford private assessment there was a sense of injustice and guilt about not being able to get support for their children. In either case, the use of private companies for assessments, which are available through publicly funded healthcare and school-based psychologists, speaks to the urgency felt by both parents and teachers for students to be assessed in order to move forward in their education. Teachers and parents find their own ways to get students tested not only because of long-wait times in school, but also because there is a belief that the assessments will either give teachers the answers about how to teach these students, or it will give the justification to move the student to a specialized support classroom.

In the four school boards where I conducted my research, there were multiple approaches to identification of disabilities. Three of the four school boards convened Identification, Placement and Review Committees (IPRC), the process established by the Ministry of Education for identifying students with exceptionalities. The categories of exceptionality used by the Ministry are behaviour, communication (including autism, deafness and hard of hearing, language impairment, speech impairment, and learning disabilities), intellectual (including giftedness, mild intellectual disability (MID) and developmental disability), physical (including any physical limitation and blindness or low-vision), and finally multiple exceptionalities, which is any combination of the above. In different school boards there were different practices for the IPRC. In one school board, school staff held a meeting at which they identified students and made decisions about how much time the students would spend in a regular classroom. These meetings were not called IPRCs because the staff did not want to invite parents to the meetings, a requirement under the legislation governing IPRCs (Education Act, 1998). Instead they would call a staff meeting and later at the IPRC put forth the information prepared in the earlier meeting. In contrast, in another school board, there are no IPRCs called by the school principals. The goal, as described by school staff, is to de-emphasize categories of exceptionality, because in this school board there are no self-contained classes or schools, although they do use separate resource rooms. Instead school staff in these boards focus on the IEP, a program document. So the process for identification varies from a professionalized process that leaves out the families of children being identified, to one that tries to avoid school-based identification altogether. In all cases, students getting additional support were referred to as students with special needs and both the formal and informal methods used to support the students identified them as needing supports. Thus, these students were "labelled" students, a term I use in the title of this book.

All of the school boards in my research used assessment measures to evaluate students' achievement levels, academic skills, developmental levels, adaptive behaviour, intelligence, language and reading skills, and vocabulary. For the forty-three students whose parents and teachers I interviewed, there were twenty-two different assessment measures listed on their IEPs. In addition many of them had notes about psychological, psychiatric and medical assessments. The diagnostic tests that are used in schools provide a range of information including assessment of intellectual, behavioural and language skills, as well as detecting a large number of clinical categories of disability. Sometimes this wide range of information is gleaned from one test. The tests often note that anecdotal assessment be conducted as well but the experiences of students are not part of the diagnostic tool. Most diagnostic tests result in a report about the student that usually ranges from a few to perhaps twenty pages. For simplicity, the information from the report is often summarized in the IEP (or some other format for teachers). The result is that the IEPs are filled with lists of deficits taken from the assessment. While the tests may provide important and specific information about students skills, very little of that information seems to reach teachers. The teachers whom I interviewed had access to most assessments conducted with students, as copies of these assessments were in the students records. However, not one teacher I talked to had read and understood the assessments. The majority of the teachers read summary information about the student found in the IEP. This information was brief and contained very limited recommendations for teaching. As an example, Ryan is a quiet grade seven student with autism. His IEP reads:

Psychological Services Report (District School Board Assessment):
- Significantly below average intellectual functioning
- Academic deficits
- Repetitions and reminders about socially acceptable behaviour
- Education Assistant, one-to-one withdrawal help to focus on academic needs

This is very limited information for an assessment that took several sessions to conduct and involved more than one assessment measure. In addition, these assessments can be stressful for students and their families. In the end, the educational recommendations that are listed are obtuse at best. In order to implement the recommendations, the teacher and Education Assistant will have to do informal assessments of Ryan's behaviour and his academic needs and they will have to prepare appropriate lessons for him. This should be standard teaching practice for all students. Ryan's teacher, Tim, says, "We kind of know ... Even though we lay out expectations in the IEP, we know Ryan as a human being not just as expectations". Tim says of the assessments in Ryan's school record, "Completely out of my realm of understanding. I worked as part of a behavioural services organization for a while so I did know some of these testings, more specifically for behaviour, but I certainly never learned about it in Teacher's College".

No doubt there are teachers who read and understand the diagnostic assessments conducted for students. But there remains a question about how these tests support educational goals and learning. In fact, the validity of these tests has been questioned in the first place. Criticism of Intelligence Quotient (IQ) tests due to bias, particularly cultural and ethnic bias, as well as error in the application of statistical procedures in assessing IQ, are well documented (Gould, 1996). Stephen Gould, however, says that the primary problem with IQ testing is the assumption that there is such a thing as intelligence. The problems with intelligence testing are well known and often acknowledged by those who use them. The Learning Disabilities Association of Ontario, for example, describes many of the documented problems with IQ tests but continues to back the use of these tests in diagnosing learning disabilities. For the purpose of this book, I am interested in how these tests contribute or detract from the experience of students in the classroom. From the perspective of teachers and parents, do these tests in fact appear to improve the experience of students in classrooms?

The underlying assumption of diagnostic tests is that there are measurable characteristics of individual students that can be identified through testing, and that the results of these tests can provide valuable information for teaching. Much of the discussion is relevant to Chapter 4 in which I will discuss instruction. But I will foreshadow here by saying that individual characteristics of students are just one component of good instruction and of learning. For this chapter, I will examine how diagnostic information was interpreted by teachers and parents.

Greg is a grade five student who had what his father describes as a "turnaround year" in grade four. I asked William, Greg's father, what it was about grade four that was so important. William says there were two important components, the first was that his teacher was able to connect with Greg in a way that no one had before. She helped Greg to communicate with concentration and social skill. William says that for Greg, his grade four teacher is the one he will remember when he is thirty or forty as his most influential teacher. But William also credits Greg being diagnosed as having Attention Deficit Disorder (ADD) as being a very positive experience. When Greg was diagnosed, his father William and his younger brother were also diagnosed as having ADD. Greg had an IEP since he was in grade two but there had been no formal diagnosis of a clinical disability. William feels that the diagnosis for both Greg and him has given them some hope and their lives have improved with the confirmation of a clinical cause of their lack of attention. Greg now takes Ritalin and William says this has helped a lot.

Getting a diagnosis can mean that students get help. Certainly school policy favours this avenue for getting support. Many parents described the frustration of their children failing and no one acknowledging that the student might need support. Sheila spent years trying to get an assessment done and met with resistance from teachers:

> (Interviewer: So you requested formal testing in grade two?) Through the teacher. She said, "She doesn't need it. She's fine. She's going to catch up". In grade three the same thing happened. But when she got to grade four, I got a teacher who was concerned and he went to bat for me. (Interviewer: Can you describe what you mean by that?) He arranged all the tests. He called me in and said, "Do you think (your daughter) has a problem?" And I said, "Yes I do. I have for the last three years". He said, "So how about we get her tested?"

A grade three student named Sherman, who is Aboriginal, is bussed to a primarily white suburban school off of the reserve where he lives. As an aboriginal student going to a Catholic school, funding is allocated directly to the Band Council and they provide an Education Assistant for Sherman in his school. This support is partly funded as a result of the assessments. The results of these assessments are summarized in his IEP and followed with the comment, "The results of this assessment were not complete and may not be accurate due to Sherman's behaviour". In this case, Sherman's behaviour is cited by the school psychologist as the barrier to being able to assess Sherman's behaviour. This circular logic leaves me with the thought that if the test was not able to assess the behaviour, then maybe Sherman's behaviour is not a problem. Similar logic is used by teachers assessing students in class.

Several teachers who hold Individual beliefs describe being unable to assess students' individual learning levels because of the students' deficits. Jennifer, a first year teacher who is covering a maternity leave in a grade two class, says that she cannot get to know Neil "because he's popping in and out all the time". Presumably this is because he is going to the Resource room in the school. Jennifer says:

> I try to support him as much as I can. If the EA (Education Assistant) isn't there I'll go to him and make sure he's on task. But I don't really know him well enough to know how much he knows about reading and writing. For instance, we're doing an Easter story right now and I give him a paper and I tell him what he has to write about. He can't write a sentence on his own so he has to tell the EA what his ideas are, and then she writes it for him, and then he'll rewrite it in his handwriting so it's not her work. So he orally tells her, and she writes it down.

Neil, who has been diagnosed as having a global developmental disability, is getting a significant amount of support from an Education Assistant, but this support means that his own teacher does not really know him. His need for the support precludes Jennifer's need to know his skills well.

Melinda, a grade eight teacher in her second year of teaching says:

> Most of the assessment that I do with Robert is a lot of oral quizzes, oral discussion type thing. I'll make up a worksheet, go through that with him. No real tests or anything, really, written or applied, because he has such a difficult time writing.

The fact that Robert has difficulty with writing means that his teacher does not assess is his writing. This teacher is avoiding the skills in which Robert needs the most support. While some teachers see avoiding a student's weakness as a form of accommodation it means that they do not necessarily understand the student's weak areas. This is the opposite of the philosophy behind the goal of early identification of difficulties and intervention. Some teachers also avoid information that is available in student records or through co-workers who know the students because they say they do not want to be biased about the student coming into their class. This seems to leave the teacher at a disadvantage for adapting their teaching early in the school year to meet the needs of their students.

Dennis teaches in a class that has several students who are identified as having behaviour problems. Dennis is the so-called regular teacher and he team-teaches with a special education teacher. He says the IEP has inappropriate information:

> You know, I know what I do when I get report cards of other kids. I want to know specific areas. I want to know if this kid is a runner; I don't want to know another teacher's opinion about a child. I just want to know, are they

allergic to the penicillin, are they a runner or, is the family divorced? Should I know those kind of issues? But I don't want somebody's opinion, 'cause I would love to see that kid fresh. A teacher's just – that's just their opinion. No matter how much it's supposed to be objective it's just their opinion. So I don't read them, generally.

The majority of the teachers I talked to were more comfortable than Jennifer and Melinda with getting to know their students. Many teachers describe getting as much information as they can about a student, a practice usually connected with a Situational belief. Jason is a grade eight teacher and he describes what he did to get to know his student Marcus. Marcus has been diagnosed as having a Pervasive Developmental Delay (PDD). Jason did not really know much about PDD when he learned that Marcus would be in his class. Jason said:

Well I went to read up, and I probably went to his OSR (Ontario School Record) as well, just to find out what level he was at. And when I found out that basically he was at a grade one level for most things, and some kindergarten level, I went on my own time. I approached the grade one teacher after school. And I got some spelling books, some math books, some printing books and things like that, and I passed them on. I think I photocopied some of them and put them into binders; I remember doing that. And then I also passed on some of the resources to the EAs, who had been working with Marcus since he was in grade three. I mean they by far know him better than anybody.

There are two types of identification happening in schools. There are the standardized IQ and ability tests and there are informal diagnostic assessments done by teachers in classrooms to understand student skill levels. The standardized tests are used from a policy standpoint as documentation for the need for specialized support. Standardized tests are also used to identify students with clinical categories of disability, or to label them. Informal assessments, on the other hand, are used so that teachers can get to know their students well. From the standpoint of teachers, the formal assessments are primarily a vehicle for referring students to specialist teachers once the students have been labelled within a category of disability. There is very little information from formal assessments being used in everyday teaching practice. Informal assessments conducted by classroom teachers are much more common, but seem to be unrelated to categories of disability. That is, the information that is used in practice is not the information related to clinical information about students. This is surprising considering the emphasis in policy on identification and early intervention. To put it in the jargon of special education, special education practice is based on clinical analysis of needs and applying the most appropriate service based on those needs. This leads to the question of what purpose diagnostic assessment serves in the school system. I am focusing here on the use of these assessments in school, but it should be understood that assessments used in schools are often used in many other contexts as well, such as for medical information, to make decisions about recreational programming and to plan for the future of children identified with disabilities. Each of these contexts should be considered independently.

PURPOSES OF IDENTIFICATION

Public policy is geared toward early identification or diagnosis of disabilities for the purpose of early intervention or rehabilitation of learning difficulties. But what does this mean for the children who are being identified? For some of them it is a positive experience as described by William and his son Greg, who were both identified as having ADD. But what is it about being identified as having a disability that gives some parents and some children a sense of relief?

For some parents, diagnosis of a disability confirmed their view that there was something "wrong" with their child so that they can deal with the problem like they would a sickness or disease. When asked how she felt about extensive testing done with her daughter, Tracy, the mother of Maria, replied, "I was fine. I just wanted to find out what it is and what we can correct". Maria is in grade eight and has had significant difficulty throughout her school years with social and academic skills. Assessments have resulted in an extensive list of diagnoses. As an example the diagnoses from one of a series of five assessments includes developmental difficulties, reactive attachment disorder, separation anxiety disorder, selective mutism, early onset borderline personality disorder, affective instability, impulse control disorder, visual-spatial dysfunction, dysagraphia and obsessive following disorder. Maria's teacher, Jillian, notes that Maria has difficulty writing and communicating and she seems to phase out for long periods of time. She also has inappropriate sexual behaviours and becomes obsessed with her classmates. The assessments have resulted in many diagnoses, but this has not resulted in finding a "solution" to get Maria to behave like other children. The diagnoses have provided the documentation needed to get an Education Assistant to supervise Maria for the entire school day including at lunch and at recess. But this support is not guaranteed and Maria's teachers are concerned about this support in the coming year at high school. Maria's teachers have suggested she attend a special high school, but her mother has enrolled her at the local high school. Maria's teacher says:

> St. Mary's is a mainstream high school here. They've had meetings with the Program Support teachers there already but as far as her claims, they're not sure what they're even going to get for her next year because she doesn't fit in one category and she doesn't fit in another category. But the behaviour ... the way the Program Support Teacher is trying to do it right now ... that's why she's been documenting everything this year, but she said she's not quite fitting into anything fully so they're really afraid they're not going to get coverage [funding for staff] for her next year.

Susan, a foster parent, adopted her daughter, Jae-Lynne, when she was three years old. I asked Susan what she hoped to get from assessments done at a local children's hospital:

She's going on ten now, and I still don't know what's wrong with her. I'm tired of seeing doctors. I'm tired of seeing psychiatrists with her. And, I mean, I'm tired of going to the hospital, everybody says, "Oh, let's give her an ultrasound. Let's give her this. Let's give her that". Everybody has an opinion. But nobody can actually come to me and say, well, your daughter's autistic, your daughter's epileptic. Nobody can tell me what's wrong with her. And I know there's something wrong with her, 'cause she doesn't watch TV. She hates TV. And we have to watch what she does, because she'll hide knives up her bed, 'cause she wants to hurt one of us. You know, she's different? That's what I'm trying to say. She's different.

In fact, the assessments that I read indicate that Jae-Lynne has Foetal Alcohol Syndrome (FAS). Like many of the children I have described, the many tests and diagnostic assessments have not resulted in the rehabilitation hoped for by their parents. Teachers, like parents, do not necessarily get the answers they hoped for from assessments. Donna describes what she has learned about Christopher:

> Christopher, we've just found out, has, I don't know whether they're calling it a learning disability or not, but he has … definitely got learning difficulties. I think they said he came within one percentile of actually being labelled learning disabled, which is as close as you can get. So I don't know exactly how we're labelling him, so to speak. He has a great deal of difficulty orally. We'll not ask if he's in difficulty, because he never wants to be shown as to be different from anyone else. There seem to be a lot of other family problems. I do not think that he can't learn, I just think that the disabilities get in the way.

Many of the parents I spoke to were discouraged by the diagnosis of a disability. Dorothy and her husband both have professional degrees from their home country in Eastern Europe. She says she felt hurt by the diagnosis that her son had a learning disability because it meant that her son was not like her and her husband, both of whom had been high-achieving students. Dorothy's initial difficulty in accepting her son's learning disabilities and dealing with her own prejudices were barriers to her son's success. But Dorothy found that once she had the assessments she was able to change her earliest feelings and move towards supporting and learning how to help him.

Harvey and Marg, the parents of Stephen who is in grade six, had similar views. Marg describes how she and her husband changed their thinking about Stephen and learning disability in general. She says:

> We started to look at it more closely. But even having the assessment, we never really accepted the fact that he could have a learning disability. We always felt that something got missed, but if he had extra help he would catch up. And you know there's no way he could be that way because when you talk to him and see him you know, there isn't anything. Because we think learning disability means that you're slow. It was a whole learning thing for us as well.

Other parents I spoke to felt right from the beginning that diagnostic assessment would help them to help their children. In response to the question of what the parent hoped to get out of an assessment, Dana responded, "to find out what our next move would be. What would be the best route for Robert in getting him necessary help". Another parent articulates the need to understand the nature of a disability in order to dismantle barriers in educating her daughter:

> (Interviewer: So what kind of information would you like to see, should that assessment be available to you?) Something you can grasp. Something you can do, instead of just jargon. (Interviewer: Some practical suggestions?) Exactly. Because everything has a solution, but you just have to work at the problem.

As described earlier, informal assessments provide opportunities for teachers to learn more about student learning levels and about the students themselves. Teachers' Situational beliefs about barriers are embedded in referral and assessment practices that focus on getting to know students. These teachers describe doing informal assessments, particularly at the beginning of the school year, in order to better understand the individual characteristics of students. Evan, a third year teacher says:

> Well, it's interesting because with the math for the first couple of weeks I usually just get them to do a review of grade three, just because they're coming off vacation and often times you start with numeracy, so, multiplication facts and just addition, subtraction, to get Abigail – to get all the students – back on track as far as being back at school. Abigail was having difficulties with the grade three work ... severe difficulties with the grade three work, so we knew right away that something wasn't clicking.

Leslie is a fourth year teacher and has an additional qualification in Special Education. Leslie also spends the first few weeks getting to know her students:

> What I usually do is for the first week I do a lot of diagnostic testing so I give them multiplication. Basically it's at grade four level and they go right up to as high as grade eight. So I do that for all of them and then we give them some warm up sheets for math and then we do some reading comprehension. Then what I do is I take all that information I have and jot down the levels. I do a spelling test, diagnostic. I make sure they know this isn't on their report card, just to do their best on it. Then from there I look at the needs. So, that'll help me on any academic (issues) and if I notice inconsistencies.

Carla, in contrast to Evan and Leslie, has been teaching for almost twenty years and has a lot of experience working with students with disabilities. She is considered to be an expert in her school. Carla, Leslie and Evan have a similar goal of getting to know the students at the beginning of the year. In this case, Carla is describing working with a student who gets support from an Education Assistant on a daily basis, as well as working in a Resource Room and with specialists who come from the school board:

There were times when I would let the EA stay in the classroom and I would take Naima with the group of six at that point. I would take that group out and I would work with them and that way I got to know really well where they were all at, but specifically Naima. And we played some games and some fun stuff just so I could get a good grasp on their personalities and things like that. And we did for about the first two months actually ... not on a daily basis by any means, but I'd give the rest of the class work to do, novel studies or whatever, and I would take the other group and the Education Assistant would supervise in the class.

Many teachers working with a student like Naima, who is getting so much additional support from other staff, would not take time to know Naima the way Carla has. In my experience this is noteworthy because without knowing Naima the way Carla does, Naima would not be able to participate in the regular class.

Information from the kind of informal assessments described above is used to set up appropriate supports early in the school year for the students. It is interesting to note that some teachers, like Evan and Leslie, described doing diagnostic testing with all students in their classes. This universal approach embraces the notion that tailoring instruction to the needs of each student is good teaching rather than specialized teaching. Evan is explicit about this goal:

The Resource Teacher and I have a relationship where when we identify in the classroom who's having difficulties, every teacher breaks their classroom down into levels as far as grouping and how to group their class, so automatically we started grouping Abigail knowing that she was having difficulties, and then we just made observations from that.

Leslie similarly describes how the universal diagnostic testing is helpful when working with a student who has not had any clinical diagnosis but is struggling in school. In this case, Leslie tries to take a more holistic approach to understanding her students' learning difficulties:

Let's say on the same topic Corinne would write five tests and she would get maybe two Cs, a B+, a B, and then a 30% or 40%. So I was trying to think about what other things were going on during the day. What did she eat for breakfast? What did she do the night before? Because sometimes Corinne seemed extremely tired, extremely inattentive, her focus is just (lost), so it's just constant getting her back to work, especially with tests. I talked to her mum and we tried to look at patterns.

Formal assessments are used to diagnose students within clinical disability categories, but they are also used to get information about students' learning characteristics for instructional purposes. Both formal and informal diagnostic assessments are also used to determine where students will be placed, whether in special education classes or in regular classrooms, and with what kind of support. This use of assessment information has high stakes for students because it can determine how they will be viewed for the rest of their school careers. Some parents do not care which kind of placement or support their child gets, as long as they get some support. Some parents feel that small group settings are the only place for their children to get the attention they need. This usually happens in a resource room outside of their regular class. On the other hand, some parents have serious concerns about the impact of programs which happen outside of the classroom. One of the most often cited concerns is that children in specialized classes will not have positive social role models as compared to a regular class. When students are pulled out of the regular class for specialized support, some parents expressed concern about what their children are missing in their regular class. Lana, said:

> The paediatrician said, "We'll see how it goes. She seems like a happy child". So they continued doing these little programs with her, taking her out of class, but I thought if they're taking her out of class whatever they're learning in class, she's missing. You know how you make reference to certain things after class and things like that.

Some parents are vehemently opposed to their children being in segregated placements of any kind, including withdrawal support programs in Resource Rooms. Many of these parents, holding socio-Political beliefs, view funding as a means for policy makers to focus on identification and reduction of resources in regular classrooms. Diane, a strong parent advocate for inclusive education, describes how identification is used for administrative purposes. In order for the school to get grant money for her son Nigel, Diane is expected to get the assessments needed through her family doctor. In her words:

> Essentially they said to me, "no one qualifies for this funding". And I said, "so what are you telling me?" And they said, "Well Nigel doesn't fit into this category anymore". And I said, "So what?" And they said … initially they didn't tell me that maybe he would fit into this intellectual disability category because they didn't have the scores yet (from a recent assessment) but I knew they were heading that way and I said that to the principal, who was wonderful. The psychometrist (sic) that did the assessment said, "I have a feeling that it's going to be this, just so you know". It was the day before March Break started and she phoned me to tell me the scores so I knew. And I said, "okay, Mr. Frank (the principal), the ISA funding deadline is April 5, and you want a whole new diagnosis documented between now and then? I don't think so".

Lana, the mother of Corinne, points out that Intensive Support Amount (ISA) funding requires labelling of students' disabilities to conform to the categories listed by the Ministry of Education. The number of hours of support allotted to Corinne is tied to the category of disability assigned by the school board:

> The only thing is that the government has tended to cut back, so unless she's completely physically disabled, a threat to other children, or a threat to herself, they'll only cover her to a certain point for funding. I don't know if that's changing over because I keep reading in the paper that they're going to

give more funding. So the teachers have to try to accommodate her for that 20% or actually I think she's only up to 15 hours or something.

Beverly is very knowledgeable about special education policy and has spent a lot of time advocating for her daughter. Beverly described the need for the "right" label for her daughter in order for her to get an appropriate program:

(Interviewer: What's she labelled now?) It's still behaviour because the last principal was not in favour of changing it. The last principal told me that if we changed it she would lose her support, which of course, you know, I don't see how that could happen, because the support isn't, at least, I don't know that they have changed the criteria, but you know a couple of years ago the support amount wasn't dependent on an exceptionality. (...) Because I want her identification changed prior to her going into another school. I want to have the right support set up. I mean, in this school it doesn't matter because everyone knows her so ...

Some parents understand the link between identification and support but feel that this is not working in favour of their children. Fiona who works as an Education Assistant, says of her son's IEP:

I'm happy with the IEP, but the only flaw I see is that children like my son, who don't have a strong disorder or handicap, really aren't guaranteed a lot of the assistance. But the IEP helps me as a parent because I can say, "well okay, he needs his workload modified a bit. We need to do different things".

The three purposes of diagnostic assessment, as described by teachers and parents, are identification of student's learning difficulties, assessment of learning characteristics, and for documentation purposes in order to secure supports, such as Education Assistant time, money to buy computer programs, workbooks and other supplies. These purposes of assessment combined with the complex process of getting an assessment are fraught with tensions between the wish of teachers and parents to adapt instruction for each student's individual characteristics, while minimizing the adverse affects of identification or labelling students. The issue of stigma is an important one with regard to labelling, and I will talk about that in Chapter 7, but there are other issues related to the identification and placement of students that I will discuss in the rest of this chapter.

THE PITFALLS OF IDENTIFICATION:
LABELLING AND REFERRAL

The tensions between identification of student characteristics for the purpose of instructional adaptation and identification for administrative purposes is evident from the teacher and parent accounts already presented in this chapter. The tensions can have repercussions for students, such as misidentification or inappropriate identification of students in a category of disability. Diane does not believe in labelling her child but she allows it because without the labels her son Nigel, who has what is described as a "severe" learning disability as well as a physical disability from cerebral palsy, would not get the support of a speech and language pathologist, occupational therapist, education assistant and resource teacher support. Diane says:

I had to have my child diagnosed as Attention Deficit, and he is, but I didn't have it on file because I didn't believe in it. What's the point? But it's a criteria listed and every year they come out with a change in criteria or they change the wording so you have to go around and you have to find more documentation to support your child's needs.

Diane, like several other parents I spoke, to believes that diagnoses are missed routinely in the school or medical system. According to Diane, Nigel has been getting pushed through the system because his teachers did not recognize that he did not understand the material:

And I still do hold the school accountable for part of this. I do believe that they had not recognized Nigel's needs accurately all along and dealt with them accurately. I do believe they've given him good support around EAs and the physical supports and trying to modify the programs. But I really don't think they fully understood Nigel and still don't. And I think this new, an intelligence test that was done this year which wasn't entirely a surprise to me, although it was devastating, was an eye opener for them and, well, maybe he's not doing as well as we thought.

Amanda had a similar experience with the medical system. She describes her son Alexander's early experiences with clinical diagnosis:

He wasn't saying words yet, he wasn't, "Mum" or "Dad" and his head was off to the side, and they had corrected that, they had said, because one of the muscles was weak in his neck. So we did the muscle exercises that had to be done for Alexander, and his neck was fine. The neurologist said, "Well, some boys are just a little bit late talking. Don't worry about it". We took him to a hearing specialist; we took him to the hospital. And he was fine, so we ended up coming to the school. I will tell you now I have no faith in doctors. Okay, I don't. So he ended up starting in school still not speaking. So we had taken him to Dr. Baker and discovered that Alexander had an 80% hearing loss, which was why there was such a delay. Now, if somebody had seen that at the age of three ... this is why I have no faith whatsoever. So we took it from there.

Both Diane and Amanda are frustrated by misdiagnosis or misidentification because in the early identification, early intervention framework it is paramount that the diagnosis be accurate. An inaccurate diagnosis can result in missing the opportunity for early intervention. Both Diane and Amanda are known at their children's schools as being politically savvy and even overly assertive of their children's rights. However, in their judgements of the problem with identification they seem to focus on the pathological characteristics of their children. In both cases, Diane's and Amanda's interviews were coded as having dominant socio-

Political beliefs about barriers to education, consistent with school staff perceptions of these mothers. But the statements above indicate that both of these mothers are acutely attuned to the Individual barriers their sons have in the educational setting. In both cases there has been a socio-Political barrier, through misidentification, that has compounded the Individual barriers that Nigel and Alexander experience in school.

Another potential outcome of the tensions in the system of identification and intervention is that parents will be asked to participate in interventions that they do not agree with. Dwayne, who is in grade six, came to Canada from Jamaica at the age of seven. His mother had come to Canada ahead of him. When Dwayne arrived he had not seen his mother since he was a baby. Immediately, Clare had concerns that Dwayne was not ready for school. I have written about Clare and Dwayne's experience in much more detail elsewhere, but the experience of reunification is a difficult one faced by many families who migrate for economic reasons, as in their case (Underwood, 2006). Clare describes her experience with identification of Dwayne's needs:

> Well according to the teachers – they had me take him all over the place. I had to get doctors' notes, I had to take him to every specialist there is. He went and got his hearing tested, his speech tested, 'cause they thought he had a learning disability, which on some level I think he did, but when I took him to the doctor, they found nothing wrong with him. One of the doctors thought he had ADHD. So they wanted me to put him on Ritalin but I refused. (Interviewer: Why?) I think he can learn without the medication. And he's proven that – I refused. And one of the teachers, she pushed me on it so hard. She said when she first started teaching she didn't think it would have been a good idea, but she's been teaching for so long, and she's seen that it helps other kids .... And she was on me for a while for me to get him on it, and still ... I said no. You know ... the side effects scared me really, really badly. And they were saying, "Not everybody the side effects will affect", and I said, "How am I going to know that it's not going to affect him. He has to take it for me to realize, for me to know". And I said, "No, I'm not going to take the risk". (Clare and Dwayne)

Ellen, the mother of Dalia, described the effect that her daughter's, diagnosis was having on Dalia's father:

> My husband actually failed a grade in school and he's finding this very difficult to deal with because he's thinking that she's got some sort of gene in her and following his trait because he struggled all through school. He failed grade one. I don't know if you're aware but last July we went to the local children's hospital for genetics testing. There was a program we got involved in and it just happened to come to me through a paediatrician at work and they were doing a genetic study on kids with learning disabilities, mostly reading, which is what she fell in. So we did this eight-hour testing thing at the hospital. (Interviewer: And your husband went as well?) Yes, he had to be there. They mostly tested Dalia. She was in a one-to-one with a

psychologist. They tested her from nine to five with a one hour lunch. She had to give blood. She got twenty dollars for coming in. She wanted to treat mummy and daddy to lunch but we didn't let her. We told her to keep her money. She loved the hospital. The report I just got in January but it gave a lot of the study – what they were looking for and what they found in Dalia – and Dalia was way below average in everything, from the math to the reading to the spelling.

Dalia's father does not participate in meetings or help with homework because he feels that he too has academic deficits like Dalia. Teachers also report disappointment with the identification and intervention system. Evan, whom I described above, does a lot of informal assessment and seems to be very concerned with helping each of his students reach their potential. Yet he feels frustration with the barriers to learning he attributes to a lack of resources in the system to support students. Evan says:

> Well, if I was to share something completely honest, do I feel that the program I'm running even with the Resource Teacher's assistance, do I feel it's meeting all of Abigail's needs? No, and that's probably the hardest thing to deal with knowing that at the public school level with the resources that we have in the classroom setting that I have with twenty-seven students with very diverse needs ... am I giving her the program that she deserves and that she's capable of achieving? No.

Evan's concerns are with his own classroom program and the large class sizes, but many teachers see systemic problems with placement choices for students who are identified as having disabilities. Mark has been teaching for five years. Jeremy, who is in Mark's grade seven class, is working on a modified curriculum at the grade two to three level in all subjects. Jeremy has not been identified in any area of clinical disability or in an area of exceptionality in the school system because assessments have been inconclusive. Jeremy's mother, who spent most of her school years in special education and finally dropped out of school, is extremely worried about the future for her son. Doreen understands that without identification, Jeremy is not eligible for support from specialist teachers in his school board. Mark, like Evan thinks that the school program is inadequate for his student, but unlike Evan, Mark thinks students "like" Jeremy should not be his responsibility. Mark says:

> I've learned over the last little while that as good as inclusion is with Jeremy I try my best to get one-to-one or one-on-four basis. And that's not with me because I've got twenty-two other kids and there are some other IEPs in there and there are gifted people in there. There are a lot of needs so if we can get less people around him and more adults around him it's better.

Dennis has been teaching for twenty-six years in both segregated special education classes like the situation Mark described as well as in regular classrooms. Dennis can compare his special education experience and his current inclusive classroom, and he feels strongly that a policy of including students can make a big difference for them:

> I taught self-contained for many years and looking back now it was a terrible program. You know, it really provoked kids to misbehave, because you put all of those kids in one room. An integrated model, if it works – obviously there are kids it doesn't work for – but we've had enormous success with that program. Ninety per cent of the kids achieve some real successes.

Teachers have very little control over whether the school system has a policy of inclusion or a policy of segregation, unless they change employers, usually involving moving to a different district. Parents are more likely to make this kind of move. Several parents described choosing a school district based on the underlying philosophy or policy for students with disabilities. For parents who held Situational beliefs, the decision was based on which school had staff who understood their child's individual nature and needs and were enthusiastic about supporting the child. For parents who held socio-Political beliefs the choice of school was based on the school board's overall philosophy. Clare describes her choice for Dwayne:

> (Interviewer: Why did you change from the public board to the Catholic board?) You know what? I think somebody told me. I think it was my mother-in-law. She was suggesting to me that the Catholic school would be a better system for him. (Interviewer: Why?) Academically. I think because all her kids went to Catholic school and she was saying they do a lot with kids when they have difficulties learning. And I don't know much, and she's had six kids, and she's been through that, so I figure, she'd probably know a little bit more than I would, so ... I took the chance. (Interviewer: I'm interested because the Public and Catholic Boards have a very different approach to special education services.) It's true. And when Dwayne started going to the Catholic school, we did see a big difference. We did. (Interviewer: Improvement?) Improvement-wise, yes. We did. And my husband said to me, "If we had put him in the Catholic system when he first came, he probably would have been in a better place than he is right now". And I sort of believe that, but then again, you never know, right?

When the school does not address parent concerns, a parent will sometimes change schools in order to avoid the systemic problem. This is also coded as a socio-Political belief:

> This is a touchy issue here because we've had a really good experience in this school and we've had a really bad experience in this school. And last year we left this school for six months because of it and we came back because it is his home school. (Interviewer: Where did you go?) We went back to where he was [to his old school]. It used to be one school and then they divided. So he went back there for the last six months of last year. For us it was to try and help him develop coping skills and to get away from a child that was abusing him, that [the abuse] wasn't dealt with.

Another parent I interviewed had elected to home school her son until he was in grade four, at which point she decided he needed the support the school could offer. Ellen's daughter Dalia goes to a Catholic school which has a policy of including all students in regular classes. However, the school psychologist is suggesting that Ellen move her daughter to a different school board in order to access a specialized program:

> I'm meeting with her paediatrician to go over this report. I sent him a copy but I'd like to touch base with him so he knows what's going on with her in school. So if she needs a different type of schooling (because it) has been put in my head already that she might be struggling. (Interviewer: When you say a different type of schooling, what do you mean?) A specialized school. (Interviewer: You're thinking that maybe she should be put into a different school?) Yes. That he's aware of it. (Interviewer: Your paediatrician is suggesting this?) No, actually, I met with Dr. Lee. I think she's the school psychologist and she went over the whole report from the hospital and basically explained to us what it meant.

Karen, whom I described in the Belief profile of a teacher with individual beliefs, was diagnosed with a rare brain disorder. Karen's mother is well aware that her attitude has affected the experiences Karen has had in her life. She describes her feelings when Karen was diagnosed:

> I got really good grooming at the hospital [where Karen was diagnosed]. I think it depends on the person. Because you can go one way or the other. You can go angry and hold a chip on your shoulder and wait for bad things to happen, or you can just look out for the best for your child ... and I wasn't up for a fight: I'm not fighter. I talked a lot with a counsellor down at the hospital and this condition that Karen has it kills. It kills right off the bat usually or a child usually dies at birth because they don't thrive. They can't feed and their breathing's bad, and most of them are blind. She had different tests done, for hearing and sight, but her hearing's excellent. Her sight – well her sight is kind of iffy; we can't really tell. But she can see. So it's a bonus that she's not blind. Of course having a rare disability, I got as many resources as I could. And then you hear of all the worst cases, and then it's just so depressing.

The early identification, early intervention model in place in schools is not as easy as it seems. The various experiences described in this chapter verify the complexity of identifying and then intervening to correct learning difficulties. The problems that can arise are misidentification or no identification which can lead to inappropriate or inadequate support for students. In addition, identification can be used to justify segregating students when students do not meet the standards for their age. Finally, there is little consensus on the most appropriate intervention. In this chapter I have described parents making choices about which school to attend based on their own beliefs or the advice of school personnel with regard to the best program for their children. In the next chapter I will discuss the many more considerations that are part of instructional choices, or the "intervention" half of the identification and intervention equation. But, it is important to note how choices about intervention are closely linked to identification, despite the fact that the identification process is loaded with problems including questions about the validity of the tests used in assessments, the limitations of these tests for identifying underlying conditions for some students, like Jeremy, and the question of how useful the information gleaned from these tests is for instructional activities. Indeed if the information is incorrect or even lacks function, there is a moral question about labelling people as falling outside the norm, which is exactly what identification does, particularly when it makes use of norm-referenced tests. Barrow (2001) calls it a moral imperative to give students specialized instruction based on disability categories, but categorizing students is not as straightforward as the companies selling diagnostic tests would have you believe. As a teacher, I am a strong believer in teaching to people's weakest areas of learning in order to maximize their potential, but within this framework we need to understand the needs of individual learners, not within the stereotypical categories assigned from norm-referenced tests, or the Ministry of Education, but based on their skills which are observable through prolonged interaction and academic activities. The early identification, early intervention framework can support instruction, but in many cases it also provides a framework to exclude children. The opposing outcomes of the identification process can be understood through the Individual, Situational, and socio-Political barriers.

DIAGNOSTIC ASSESSMENT AND INDIVIDUAL, SITUATIONAL, AND SOCIO-POLITICAL BARRIERS

In general there are two types of assessments conducted in the schools where I met with teachers: norm-referenced formal assessments and informal diagnostic assessments conducted by teachers in classrooms. Teachers' informal assessments can also be norm referenced, albeit without statistical reliability, when they compare students to each other. According to teachers and parents these tests serve several purposes. The first purpose is to diagnose a student's learning difficulties. For some, the diagnosis is a primary goal in and of itself. Confirmation that a student is not in the "norm" justifies blaming the student for their learning difficulties. This is a belief in Individual barriers to learning or the philosophy that there is something wrong with the student and they cannot learn because of this problem. For other teachers and parents, the diagnosis is the first step in finding a solution to a student's learning difficulties. This is the belief in Situational barriers, and teachers and parents who hold these beliefs treat the diagnosis as a guide for their own practice. The problem with this practice is that sometimes there is no solution, or the practices of the teacher and parent do not result in the student becoming "normal" as defined by psycho-educational tests. For other teachers and parents, those who hold socio-Political beliefs, the system of identification itself is a barrier for students. These teachers and parents believe that labelling students using predetermined categories of exceptionality (in the case of the Ministry of

Education) or clinical categories (in the case of psycho-educational testing) as a prerequisite for educational programs actually constructs the category of disability, or defines a group of students who are not "normal". These teachers and parents see student characteristics, and sometimes learning difficulties, as part of the normal range of ability in the student population.

These differing beliefs about barriers to learning result in differences in how teachers and parents behave. Teachers and parents who hold individual beliefs are likely to have much more confidence in norm-referenced tests conducted by specialists than in the observational and anecdotal assessments conducted in the classroom. These teachers and parents are also more likely to focus on the labels that are diagnosed through the assessments rather than trying to use the information from the assessment to support the student. The information gleaned from assessments is often referred to specialist teachers because teachers and parents who hold Individual beliefs are less likely to take responsibility for supporting students who have been identified. Finally, although diagnostic assessments are highly valued by these teachers and parents, the reliability of the tests themselves is sometimes questioned because the students are thought to be unfit to be assessed, as in the case of Sherman whose behaviour invalidated a behavioural assessment.

Teachers and parents who hold Situational beliefs also value diagnostic assessments. However, these teachers and parents describe the identification as part of the information they need to adjust instruction or to plan how to get support for students. Teachers and parents who hold Situational beliefs are concerned with the social ramifications of labelling students, which I will talk about more in Chapter 7, but they are willing to risk the stigma in order to learn more about the student. Parents who hold Situational beliefs are likely to be active in giving teachers information about their children and in trying to support the goals set by the teacher (or the curriculum). Finally, these teachers and parents do not see the labels from diagnostic assessment as fixed. They are constantly reassessing students' learning levels and calibrating their interventions accordingly. I will talk in some depth about adapting instruction in the next chapter.

Teachers and parents who hold socio-Political beliefs about barriers to learning are concerned with the process of identification itself. These teachers and parents are concerned that identification as the primary qualifier for supports creates systemic barriers to learning such as long wait-times for assessment, leading to inequity where some families can afford to pay for private assessments. Other systemic barriers described by these teachers and parents included too few specialist teachers to interpret psycho-educational assessments, large class sizes, and not enough time for specialist teachers to interact with students. These concerns relate to the structure of schooling and many of these teachers and parents see the process of labelling students as primarily serving structural or administrative needs of the school rather than the needs of individual students. Structurally, there is also the question of placement. For many teachers and parents there is a superior model of instruction, either including identified students in a regular class or educating them in a separate location from their peers. In the case of including students, identification does not have a political purpose (specific to placement). However, in the case of segregated classes there is an administrative need to identify those students who will be streamed into special education.

The process of assessing, diagnosing and identifying students within disability categories is pivotal to the procedures in place for teaching students who are determined to need a program that differs from the norm. In most school boards in Ontario the formal system of identification is well entrenched. Even in the one school board where the formal identification process was rarely used, labels from assessments conducted outside the school board were commonly referred to. The experience of students indicates the high stakes associated with the identification process.

The belief profile for Katie's interview yielded a score of 4.23 (Individual), 1.76 (Situational), and 0 (socio-Political). This was the highest Individual score in the parent interview sample. Katie's son David attends a suburban school.

Katie has been a foster parent to David for the last seven years. At the time of the interview, David was in grade four. As a long-time foster parent, Katie has access to support through a social service agency, as well as many years of experience caring for foster children. Although it is not known for certain, there is a likelihood that David has Foetal Alcohol Syndrome or complications due to drug use by his birth mother. David also has a physical disability which has required him to undergo surgery and to use a wheelchair during the school year. Throughout the interview Katie emphasized David's physical and biochemical disabilities as the source of his learning problems, which resulted in the high Individual belief score for her interview. Like other parents and teachers with Individual beliefs, when asked to describe David she begins describing a list of physical, emotional and learning problems.

Katie describes when she first found out that David had traces of drugs in his system when he was born:

> David had traces of drugs ... there were a few concerns ... you know, that that might be a problem later on. But, I've had other children, and I've had problems with that. David, because he's so likeable it's not as easy to ... track him down like the others, even in kindergarten. Some of the things he wasn't catching onto. And before that, you know, reading ... and saying, "Well, what did you think of that story". And some of the things he told me were just the bare ... there was no detail or anything even though we had just read a story or ... told him something. So I found he didn't really recall a lot. And then, trying to get him to print and things like that. He didn't catch onto that ... real fast.

In describing David's learning difficulties, Katie seems resigned to his disabilities and in particular to his lack of drive to work hard. The Situational belief score from Katie's interview comes from her comments about how both she and the teachers try to support David's learning. However, she usually finishes these thoughts with Individual belief statements about how David does not try hard enough or is unable to grasp concepts despite the efforts of the teacher and Katie herself. As an example, Katie describes the problem with providing the school with strategies to incorporate in the IEP:

> Well, different times, if I do something and it seems to work, I'll say, "well, you know what I tried last night?" And I'll tell them what I did (Situational belief). But, there are a lot of things they can't do at school. You know, like if David flatly refuses ... or doesn't get very much done at all (Individual belief).

In another example, Katie says she is no longer putting the same effort into helping David because it seems hopeless:

> I've tried all the ways, and I'm just at the end of my rope. I mean, I help him with homework but I don't put as much time in it as I used to. I can tell you that. I know I don't. I know I don't put as much time in. I don't know if he's learning a whole lot! Like I said, we go over these things, and we'd go over them, and I'll say, "Okay, David, you have to do a chapter". Well the books he brings home from school are for grade four and he … doesn't have a clue to what he's reading anyway, even if he does read it. He reads words not sentences.

David's teacher also says that David needs to be reminded to stay focused, but Donna is clear that David is a "likeable" kid and when he is focused he can learn quite well, especially if it is oral material.

Katie describes her early attempts to support David's reading difficulties. She hints at Situational beliefs when she seems to realize David requires some supports, but her explanation for why these supports are not working lie within David as an individual:

> Well (the teacher) gave me some readers. Especially his reading was poor. We had to focus on one thing or another … and it was reading. I started reading just basic books, and he didn't want to read them. He'd want me to either read one paragraph and then he'd read the next one and he'd made sure that the paragraph he was reading was the smallest one. And then there were a lot of words he didn't know, even simple ones. So I started using flash cards with him, and he got frustrated very easily. Didn't want to do that, didn't want any part of that, or … you know, had to go to the washroom ten times in five minutes and that kind of thing. But he did everything, you know … made a point of trying to get away with any kind of work that way.

When asked about his educational future, Katie seems unsure if David will ever progress. Again she has some Situational beliefs related to interventions as a means of improving David's achievement, but she returns to David as the core problem:

> We had a meeting, and we said there are definitely some problems here, and what can we do about them. (Interviewer: And what did they do?) Did have a couple meetings here, and then they decided, well, we'll … take him out of class and maybe give him some one-to-one or … a smaller group, and see how things … would go from there. (Interviewer: And how did it go?) He's still … far behind in … a lot of things. I don't know. I guess it's helping, because he is … learning some things. I don't know if that's going to come with time anyway. But, it's hard for me to say. Some things he does really quick and some things … he just doesn't have a clue to what's going on.

Within her family, Katie describes the challenges caused by both David and his brother's disabilities as deficits for the family. Although Katie has been a foster parent for many years, she says David and his brother will be the last:

Because (David's brother) and David have been a challenge. You know I'm always at meetings, I'm always ... you know, there's a lot more. Just trying to get them to sit down and do enough, and then if you get one doing it ... if the other one walks in the room, then you're lost. You just start over.

David has had many formal tests done to assess his learning difficulties. From Katie's explanation of these tests, she sees them as a means of confirming his deficits. He was put on the drug Ritalin in order to "see if it was necessarily ADD or anything associated with that". But this was inconclusive and Katie speculates that, "his problems are a little bit more than that".

Beyond concerns about David's academic achievement, Katie has concerns about David's self-esteem. Again, her statements about programs helping him to do better are coded as Situational, but she always returns to David's inability to stay focused:

> I think, ideally ... David would be better one-to-one. (Interviewer: All day.) Yes. I mean, somebody mentions one thing to him and ... he's gone. And, you know, you've lost him, and you've got to get him back on track again. It's the same thing at home. Somebody comes in the house, he has to stand up to see who's coming in. ... Or somebody knocks on the door. He's out the door before I have time to get out of the chair because, any disruptions, and then he's gone, and then you have get him back and get him ... situated again. I think it would help him, and I think he'd certainly have more self-esteem if he did do better in school. Because every once in a while he'll say to me, "Mum, I'm the stupidest one in my class". You know, and, "Mum, you know I got the worst report card. How come I'm *always* getting the worst report card?"

It takes a lot of probing to get Katie to talk about David as a person. Throughout the interview, Katie seems almost harsh in her judgement of David's difficulties, but when she talks about his self-esteem, her compassion is evident:

> I'll say, "You're not stupid". I'll say, "You know, there are other things that you can do better than other people". And maybe reading's not one of them. I don't usually say that to him, but, you know, ... if he says he's stupid I'll say, "You're not stupid".

Although Katie talks about support by teachers and by her as important for David, she reports that no improvement has taken place. She attributes this failure to David's lack of motivation and to his medical conditions, and she is in the process of giving up trying to find new solutions. In fact, Katie is so discouraged she says she will not take in any more foster children after David and his brother leave. David's brother and sister are described by Katie as being big supports despite the fact that they fight sometimes. Katie's Individual beliefs are premised on the assumption that David's learning difficulties are a result of Foetal Alcohol Syndrome but she does not consider that David's experiences of foster care and hospitalization may have impacted his ability to focus. In addition, Katie does not have the optimism that David's teacher has about his capacity to learn, especially when she uses oral rather than written materials.

CHAPTER 4

Do You Need Teaching To Learn?

And Other Instructional Considerations

As described in the previous chapter, the early identification, early intervention model of teaching is prevalent in the schools where I interviewed teachers and parents. This chapter addresses the issues connected to intervention and instruction. As discussed in the previous chapter, the notion of intervention is built on a principle of rehabilitation. Intervention is done in order to modify the outcome of a circumstance, and it is somehow thought of as qualitatively different from other forms of instruction. However, the vast majority of teaching strategies used in intervention are just intensive forms of good instruction used elsewhere. In the case of education, intervention is intended to improve the achievement of students who are identified as at-risk of failure sometimes due to disability. The implication is that there is a normal level of achievement that all students should aspire to meet, and that teachers are obliged to consider. Oliver (1996) describes how rehabilitation is dependant on the notion of normality, which sets up a power struggle between those who are normal and those who do not fit the parameters of normal and who are subject to rehabilitation. When rehabilitation fails, Oliver explains, professionals are apt to continue trying to find an intervention that works, or that makes the individual as normal as possible. These approaches are based on definitions of success that are fixed to a notion of normality and deny the value of diversity in ability of all kinds. At its worst a rehabilitation model perpetuates the hegemony of normality that saturates all aspects of education and society. Chapter 6 explores the ambiguity of academic achievement as the measure of school success. In this chapter, the relationship between teaching (instruction, intervention and other related concepts) and learning are scrutinized. Teaching and learning, as described by teachers and parents, involves three predominant considerations: who is responsible for teaching; the method of instruction; and whether the instruction is in fact working.

RESPONSIBILITY FOR TEACHING

One of the primary concerns about teaching discussed by parents and teachers is about who is responsible for teaching students. With classification of students as having disabilities and learning difficulties, there is the opportunity to defer responsibility to other professionals. From a pedagogical standpoint there is tension in the literature about whether students identified with disabilities are better served by teachers with specialized skills and training or if classroom teachers have adequate skills to teach students with disabilities.

Special education research has traditionally focused on understanding the nature of disabling conditions and the development of specialized programs to address these conditions. This research has taught us a lot about intensive teaching techniques and direct instruction designed to meet the needs of students with particular disabling conditions such as learning disabilities (Kauffman, 1999). With the shift to inclusive education, there has been a concern that these teaching techniques are no longer being used. Kauffman (1999) says that current education researchers:

> Emphasize indirect, discovery-oriented, radical constructivist teaching. Furthermore, much of the research in special education today is not about teaching and learning, and many special educators do little or no direct, intensive instruction using the best teaching procedures we have to offer. (p. 247)

He goes on to say that, "we cannot continue to avoid focusing on instruction suited to the special needs of students with disabilities" (p. 247). The implication of this stance is that there are teaching strategies that are suitable for students with disabilities, which target the student deficits identified through clinical assessment, that are not the best teaching strategies for students who do not have disabilities. Barrow (2001) says that:

> One can only say that the questions, once one has arrived at a proper and thorough understanding of the characteristics in question [i.e. Defined the disability], are whether it will be better (in the sense of more effective) for the individual with that characteristic (deafness, dyslexia) to be included in the classroom with those without it and whether it will be better for the latter. In seeking to answer these questions one must place them in the context of relevant factors such as the abilities of teachers and the purpose of the exercise (namely to educate people). (p. 241)

Both Kauffman (1999) and Barrow (2001) argue that the teaching strategies that are most effective for students with disabilities are not the same as the teaching strategies that are most effective for all students. However, Larrivee (1986) found that teachers who were effective at including students with disabilities in regular classrooms were also effective general educators. Further, Fuchs, Fuchs, Hamlett, Phillips and Karns (1995) found that, "when special educators adjust the nature of students' programs in response to individual, objective assessment information, their students learn reliably and dramatically more" (p. 440). This indicates that knowledge of the student as an individual is pertinent to effective teaching, not just specialized knowledge of disabling conditions as Barrow asserts.

Several teachers suggest that students with particular characteristics need to have one-to-one support. In Jeremy's case, his teacher Mark has determined that he needs lots of repetition and support to stay motivated. These teaching strategies in technical terms are called practice opportunities and student engagement, and they are good teaching practices for all students regardless of ability level. Mark, however, sees these teaching practices as extraneous to his regular practice and he defers responsibility to Education Assistants:

> Jeremy's willing to work ... he's a bit moody with the EAs and can be a bit moody at times, but overall he's willing to do what needs to be done in order to learn. It's just that it takes so much longer; everything is repetition, repetition, repetition. And it's hard to teach Jeremy at the same level as the other kids when he needs to do a lot more repetition and he does forget things very quickly. It's a big challenge for him so he just needs lots of one-to-one, lots of support and motivating and he can't waste much time because he doesn't have as much luxury time to waste, so to speak.

Catriona also thinks that one-to-one instruction would benefit her student Owen. Owen is in kindergarten, but Catriona has already determined that, Owen cannot function well with his peer group. Her belief that a one-to-one placement will benefit Owen is not changed by her experience:

> I really see him as a child who needs a lot more one-to-one than we have the people to give him. I'm not saying that a regular classroom situation is wrong for him, because I think he needs to see the other children as role models, but I think he needs to have time in a totally non-stimulating environment, where there's nothing on the walls and where you're working on incredibly specific activities. And this is what I was hoping for when we had a one-to-one with the special ed assistant put in place for Owen. Unfortunately the one-to-one arrangement has not been working well. It's a person who's well meaning and I think very keen for Owen to like him, but as soon as Owen's realized that he has the upper hand, he's just walking circles around this person. In fact, I'm finding his behaviour is escalating in a negative way since this person's been working with him one-to-one.

So despite the fact that Owen's behaviour is worse with the one-to-one intervention, Catriona continues to be unwilling to deliver the kind of instruction Owen needs within her own program. Some teachers use the EA to do the programming independently. These teachers are keeping the student busy without assuming the responsibility for the student's work. Jennifer takes advantage of the work done by EAs when Neil is in her class. The work Jennifer assigns for Neil keeps him busy but she is not engaged in understanding Neil's skill level:

> The EA has a little logbook that she writes things down for me to know about Neil. That's there for me. He has a big binder of all of his worksheets and he has math and language ... it's very basic JK, Kindergarten work and it's grade two. So if we're doing math then I'll go into his binder and I'll grab a sheet for him to do.

Giangreco (2003) points out that using Education Assistants can decrease student engagement by isolating the student from their teacher and classmates. Teachers, like Mark, expect that instruction, supervision and planning for students labelled with disabilities will be done by EAs. The social benefits of inclusion can be undermined in this circumstance. In addition, teachers who think they do not have the training to carry out a "specialized" program may defer to an EA who has even less training.

When there is no EA in the classroom some teachers expect students who are working on curriculum from a different grade level to work independently. When Jason was teaching the American civil war in his grade seven class, he struggled with preparing appropriate materials for Marcus. Marcus was then expected to use skills he had already mastered, rather than moving on to new skills and new instruction from his teacher:

> So Marcus would have to find, first of all, the correct soldier, and then match the colour of the coat, the colour of the shoes. And he would do this independently. I'd just give him a stack of the photocopies, maybe five, in a fifty-minute class. He'd do one in about ten minutes. And he would, on his own, independently, find the soldier and match the colours, … to some detail, too. Like the buckles on their wrists, the buckles on their shoes. Things like that. He's very quick. He colours everything quickly. And he cuts – you're constantly telling him to slow down. But he was able to observe the details. He was very proud of them. I stuck them up on my wall; if you want to stick your head in when you go by my room, you'll see … what he did there. Yeah, they're British and American revolutionary soldiers, so, that was a little modification I did, and that worked for a little while. Unfortunately, there's only so much colouring you can do over a course of the second term, and then when we moved on to the Loyalists and other things like that I didn't have … I couldn't think of another modification that he could do independently because he has to be able to do it independently.

Mark has similar difficulties figuring out how to teach Jeremy when there is no EA in his class:

> He's an intermediate student; he's in grade seven. His level is a little bit lower than the average in the class unfortunately. Jeremy's been included but because he's at quite a low level in some of the core subjects it's kind of difficult to include without extra support. When I don't have any support he's a constant challenge because he really just doesn't get it unless I constantly help him out [which he later says he is unable to do]. So that's Jeremy and he's included at all times but he's being modified on a constant basis in every subject.

Melinda, teaching grade eight, has little responsibility for Robert's education, but when he is in her class, she feels her primary responsibility is to the other students:

> It's really difficult to get a lesson planned out for him. He can't really do anything independently. So I need to be there all the time, and he's out with (the EA) most of the time, but if I'm doing, let's say Science, Geography, or History with him, I have the rest of the class as well.

In some cases, parents take on the responsibility for instruction when they do not agree with the program in place at the school. Laura was not satisfied with the level of support for her daughter so she got more support:

> I talked to the family doctor about it and he suggested a doctor that I could take her to and that's when they ran these tests, but they couldn't find anything. Then they put her into a speech program ... I did privately through my husband's work. She was getting speech at school but it wasn't very much and I wanted her to get more so that's when I put her in privately. It was funded by my husband's work so I didn't have to worry about it.

More commonly parents get itinerant support through local service agencies. In addition, many parents hire private tutors. Of course, the use of private services creates inequity amongst families with the financial means or insurance coverage and those who do not have the means to get support.

In all of the cases where teachers deferred responsibility for teaching to Education Assistants or other specialized staff the practice was associated with an Individual belief about barriers to learning. It is evident that teachers and parents with Individual beliefs do not consider regular classroom teachers to have the ability or responsibility for students with disabilities. This deferral of responsibility is predicated by the belief that being separated from their peers will either benefit students with disabilities or benefit their peers. In an examination of "effective" teaching strategies, it is evident that this is not the case.

INSTRUCTIONAL PRACTICE

There is a large and continually developing literature on effective teaching, or those teaching behaviours that produce the best results in student achievement. The evaluation of teaching practices is contingent on the outcomes of education which again are norm-based. However, this literature has some interesting findings about good teaching.

For the most part, advocates for special education, like Kauffman and Sasso (2006) and Barrow (2001) presuppose that teachers will be less effective if they are expected to master a wide range of teaching strategies. Stanovich and Jordan (2004), however, found that teaching in inclusive classrooms was an effective form of professional development since it encourages teachers to expand their teaching repertoire and leads to more effective teaching for all students in the class. Berliner (1994) also found that flexibility and opportunism (i.e., using a wide range of teaching strategies) were characteristics of "expert" teachers. Thus, the teaching strategies found to be effective by special education researchers are actually important for regular classroom educators as well. Barrow (2001) says that we cannot expect all classroom teachers to be expert teachers, but this logic must also hold true for special education teachers in segregated classes. There are many good teaching practices that have been derived from work done in special education classes. A few of the best practices that are commonly used in special education classes include:

– Explicit instruction giving detailed directions, step-by-step instructions and modelling tasks. This has been found to be effective in math instruction (Fuchs, Fuchs, Prentice, Burch, & Paulsen, 2002), in language instruction (Snider, 2006) and in overall teaching practice.
– Student engagement involving dialogue between the teacher and student with frequent questioning and error correction (Brophy, 2002; McGhie-Richmond, Underwood, & Jordan, 2007).
– Good pacing with ample classroom time for instruction rather than for procedural activities (Jordan & Stanovich, 2004).
– Developing self-regulating practices in students for independent mastery of skills. This does not mean students work independently from the outset but are guided toward independent work. Again this has been found to be effective in math instruction (Fuchs, Fuchs, Prentice, Burch, & Paulsen, 2002; Uberti Zrebiec, Mastropieri, & Scruggs, 2004) and in language instruction (Harris & Graham, 1996).

In all of the examples described above, the techniques have been found to be effective across ability levels and in both special education and regular classes. Just as special education research has made a positive contribution to understanding "best practices" for regular classroom teachers, the literature on teaching in regular classrooms has contributed to the discourse on "best practices" for teaching students with disabilities. Trent, Artiles and Englert (1998), argue that special education should be informed by the principles of social constructivism. They state that:

> Special education has relied too heavily on deficit thinking and must now enhance existing practices with alternative approaches that consider the sociocultural contexts in which children with disabilities learn. (p. 277)

Vygotsky (1978) introduced the notion of social constructivism in psychological studies of learning. Social constructivism shifted the focus of cognitive development from traditional learning as a series of steps (a transmissive approach) to an understanding of learning as a process within individual students of constructing knowledge (a social constructivist approach). Brophy (2002) clarifies the use of social constructivist theory in education:

> Social constructivism is primarily a theory of learning rather than a theory of teaching, so educators who identify themselves as social constructivists can and do advocate a range of teaching approaches. However, these approaches tend to share the key assumptions that, ideally, learning involves negotiating understandings through dialogue or discourse between two or more members of a community of people who are pursuing shared goals. (p. ix)

The implication that learning involves dialogue is in keeping with the Situational theory of barriers in education. Since learning involves more than one person (members of a community) engaged in dialogue, learning does not take place within the individual, but within the social interactions between individuals.

Brophy (2002) warns of the risks in oversimplifying the relationship between transmissive teaching and social constructivist theory:

(1) reducing discussions of teaching to this single dimension, when teaching has other important components that do not fit easily into a transmission vs. Social constructivist comparison; (2) implying that one must choose between the two approaches, when logic and some data indicate the need for a judicious blend; and (3) implying that a particular choice or blend will have universal applicability, when there is good reason to believe that what constitutes optimal teaching varies with grade level, instructional goals, and other contextual factors. (p. ix-x)

The complexity of the teacher-learner roles as described by Brophy above is consistent with the findings of Swanson and Hoskyn (1998) in their meta-analysis of 180 studies on teaching intervention for students with learning disabilities. They found that both "cognitive strategies", which includes dialogue with the teacher, and "direct instruction" strategies, which includes transmission of information but focuses on how that information is presented, were effective for students with learning disabilities. This significant change in thinking about learning has initiated a new focus in research on the role of teachers in the educational outcomes of students with disabilities. Interestingly, one of the key assertions of this research field is that teachers' beliefs have been shown to be integral to their teaching (Kagan, 1992a, 1992b; Kaplan & Owings, 2001; Muijs & Reynolds, 2002; Pajares, 1992; Schraw & Olafson, 2002).

Although there is a symbiosis in the special education and effective teaching research, there is also tension. This tension is evident in the policy debate set up between those who support inclusion and those who do not. The effects of education policy on teaching practice are central to teacher and parent discussions of instructional practice.

Situational beliefs in the teacher interviews are associated with descriptions of teachers' efforts to be flexible, creatively using resources, designing lessons for all students in the class, and gearing lessons toward student success. Evan was especially interested in talking about adapting instruction for all student ability levels:

Sometimes, we actually get to sit down, whether it's after school, or well, I'm here very early in the mornings so sometimes we can do it then. Often times it's at the end of the day, or (the Resource Teacher) says, "You know what? I have a great idea. I'll do this and then we'll meet up in the morning and talk about it". Or "I have this great idea...trust me". And I have no problems with that either. I'll show up and say, "All right, what's the lesson?" She'll teach my class as a whole lesson, she'll teach the entire class...a grammar lesson, and it's geared for (the student in the study)'s needs. It's geared for everyone's needs. It may even be review of a concept. So she'll teach the whole lesson, break them into groups, and may take the students who have higher needs. Or she may take the group with the lowest needs and give an extra push to do extensions. I have mode students (students identified as gifted) in my class as well, so we don't necessarily treat a lesson geared towards… "Okay, you're working at a grade two-level, so we'll concentrate here". It works at all levels.

Melinda, who described her responsibility as primarily toward the majority of her class, is concerned that the work she gives to Robert is meaningful. She makes a distinction between "busy" work and doing meaningful work that shows some awareness about the relationship between teaching and learning:

> I've got twenty-two in the class this year. I'm lucky. Yes, just twenty-two. I had thirty-one last year in this place. But, I am trying to develop activities that he can actually learn from, do some of it independently, and get something out of it. Not just a time waster. I think that happens a lot, you know, just give them something to do to keep them busy.

Thus some teachers are working to engage their student regardless of ability level in meaningful work. Other teachers described working toward all students participating in the class, but not necessarily in a way that furthers the skills of the individual students. Tim describes how he ensures that Ryan is participating, with the help of an EA:

> They (lessons) happen in my class and (the EA) comes in and offers support and sometimes will take him out to work on an assignment but he stays and listens to the instructions. It's the same as in music and drama and things like that. So he would stay in the class and listen to the instructions and then he and I and (the EA) would usually talk about, "What do you think we can do here?" So for the river assignment they had to orally present it and they had to have elements of rivers like draining patterns. We talked about language and (the EA) said, "Well I can help with the labels. I'll write the labels up but when he's standing up he can describe what the things are". So (we think) what can he do? What is he going to have trouble with? And how can we change that so he can still participate as one of the class? So that seems to be working pretty successfully so far.

Finally, Marlene is concerned about the relationship between the program she is providing for Jacqueline and the requirements for documenting the program in order to secure funding and implement the program. The impact of resource support on the student's program is evident and the embedded belief is coded as socio-Political:

> We had to ask the parents to go to the doctor to get this note saying she has down's syndrome. So all the doctor did was, "Jacqueline has down's syndrome", and signed his name. Put that in the file, "Oh, it's acceptable now". And it's just … the petty little things I'm finding. And I understand, because they have to go through hundreds of these. But they (the auditors who grant the funds) sent it back and said, "We want a day in the life of Jacqueline. I said to the Resource Teacher, "I could write a day in the life of Jacqueline, with myself and the Education Assistant in the classroom and it would come across like the majority of other children in my class". I said,

"Or even better than quite a few!" I said, "Or we could do a day in the life of Jacqueline, with no Education Assistant, and a teacher who Jacqueline has no idea who it is, and it's I can get away from … I can get away with *everything* with her.

So Marlene sees teaching and her relationship with the student as pivotal in Jacqueline's achievement, in essence teaching and learning are closely related. For parents, the expectations for instruction are more structural in nature. Parents are unlikely to comment on the instruction that takes place when they are not present, but they have opinions about the relationship between teaching and learning. Some parents, like Lana, describe learning difficulties as a motivational problem for her children: "My son, he's one of the kids who knows how to do the work but he doesn't want to do the work". But many parents feel some sense of responsibility to support the relationship between teacher and learner. One of the ways parents try to supplement the school program is to hire private tutors. Many parents view a tutor as similar to their own support but less taxing on their time. One of the problems with tutoring is that it costs money and several parents said they could not afford private tutoring. Fiona, an Education Assistant herself, also did not see it as an appropriate intervention because this was in fact a responsibility of the school system itself. Thus tutoring allowed the school to maintain a systemic barrier for students:

> Well I suppose if parents want one-to-one, you hire a tutor. But, the ideal program would be if we (were able to) keep the classrooms from getting too large. I know they can't always have two classes (per grade), sometimes the numbers are just a bit over, and it's just that we can't split a class. We can't have two classes. We can't have one and a half; we have to put them all in one room. It just becomes very difficult for the teacher, and I sympathize with them because they have a large class. Then the parents aren't going to sympathize. The parents want their child, and I want Caleb to get the help that he needs. But I just can't see that happening with the funding formula and the fact that EAs are just … (not available).

Another concern for parents is students failing their year. Several parents expressed concerns about school board policy to pass students on to the next grade level, despite their lack of skill mastery at the current grade level. One of these concerns was about the long-term impact if students were pushed through from elementary school. Susan said:

> Keep her. Keep her until she gets the grade. And no, that doesn't sound good, but, well, how's she going to get anywhere in life if they're going to keep passing her to these grades. And when she gets to grade twelve and she doesn't know anything, … that's why a lot of kids are found on welfare and getting pregnant, because they're not getting the proper education that they should be getting. The teacher should say to the board – 'cause it's not the teachers, it's the educational board – should say, "Listen, these kids don't

know grade seven so why should they go to grade eight. (if they haven't) got the concept of grade seven".

Aside from the long-term implications of pushing students through the system, parents are concerned that students are passing from grade to grade without support. They feel that a student not being able to complete the work of one grade should be a flag for intervention. Diane was concerned that Nigel, who has physical impairments from cerebral palsy, was also struggling in school. She wanted Nigel to be assessed for a learning disability because she felt that the instruction was not meeting Nigel's needs:

> They fought me on it. I noticed they were pushing him through and he wasn't getting things and I just thought, "This isn't working". They would have him doing this and I would go, "but what is he doing this for". He can't even read this. He didn't know his sight words. He still can't read. I just know from working with him that this isn't appropriate. Something's wrong here.

Another parent, Lana, focuses on the program benefits for her daughter, Corinne. Lana describes the school's reservations about holding Corinne back a grade, but she believes that the intervention has helped her daughter:

> If she had went ahead to grade three she would have been the lowest in the class and always needing help, and she was okay with being held back. It was the school that wasn't going along with it. So I held her back and she attended grade two. There were still some problems but it wasn't as bad as it was. And I've noticed as the year goes by that her reading is more developed, so I think it just takes practice.

But repeating a grade, like Corinne, does not always result in the student achieving the norm. Despite her belief that Maria should be held back a grade, Maria's mother does not believe that Maria will ever catch up to her peers:

> I have to forget about school, academic skills, because she'll never graduate. She'll have to get a certificate instead of a diploma. She'll never do the math in high school and she's exempt from French. (...) Because she'll never graduate, I don't know what she'll do when she leaves school. I don't know if she'll go on to college or not. That's a big concern. What's going to happen to her?

Most of the parents have some hope that with more teachers, better staffing ratios, more funding, better programs and more Education Assistants, there children can be successful, in the traditional sense, in school. Dana says:

> If there were more teachers available to help, you know, for speech too especially. Well it's just he gets the one-to-one but sometimes it's just not enough, because he forgets a lot of the stuff he's learned. And if there's someone there – I mean if there was more funding, then they'd be a lot more help. And next thing they can offer more programs they can offer to everybody.

Harvey says, as his wife Marg nods in agreement:

Yes, get more teachers. Get more people, because with the classes getting bigger and the teachers not being able to look after the kids the way they used to, (we) definitely need more. You cannot just have one support teacher for three hundred kids or four hundred, five hundred kids because I'm sure there are more than one or two kids that need help.

Marg then adds:

I wish that there was a program support person totally committed, that that's all they did. And when I say that I mean if a teacher is away, that program support teacher is not relieving the teacher. (Interviewer: She shouldn't become the supply teacher for the day.) Exactly. It happened, I just discovered that for two weeks he hasn't gone to his special reading class and he's quite protective of his program support teacher. "Oh, she's really busy, she's helping out. She doesn't have time for me all the time mum. Don't go there and get mad!" I don't want to get mad but no, I expect that if you have a program support person, and not only for my kid, there are other kids that are probably experiencing or suffering because that person is so worn thin you know. Maybe not one, maybe two or three, that if something happens, at least there's one person there to pick up the slack.

Beverly is so concerned about her daughter having adequate supervision she tried to come up with a creative solution, but with little success:

I remember going in and trying to say, "Look, I'd like to keep her in school". At first I talked to the principal, "Could the school have somebody come in and stay with her"? "No, we don't have the money for that". "Okay, so can I hire somebody to come in and stay with her in school"? "No, we don't allow non-union people in". "Okay, can I come and stay with her". "No non-union people. No outside people are allowed to hang around in the school".

The parents' concerns about instruction are predominantly to do with staffing and having adequate coverage, but they do not talk in depth about the nature of the interactions between teachers and learners. For teachers, the research indicates that instructional practices such as flexibility and adaptability, student engagement, use of direct instruction, and use of a large repertoire of teaching strategies are considered best practices for both special education teachers and regular classroom teachers. However, there is a policy debate about whether students with disabilities are best served in regular or "special" settings. Teachers and parents who hold Individual beliefs are influenced by notions of normal and students who fall outside the category of normal are considered to be best served in specialized settings. However, it is evident from talking to teachers and from the research literature that the best teachers in special education and in regular classes employ similar techniques.

For teachers and parents who hold Situational beliefs, there is a focus on intervention. These teachers and parents are concerned with what they can do to improve the outcomes for students, through instruction, getting tutors, and increasing the level of support. Support is a broad term, but there was a belief that if students had more time with teachers, and the teachers had fewer students, students would do better in school. Snider (2006) sees this as one of the myths of teaching. She suggests that it is not just the amount of time or the student to teacher ratios that are important, but what is being taught and how it is being taught. Snider says that we are using un-tested curriculum with haphazard teaching strategies and many students are failing as a result. Snider implicates the early intervention model in her criticism saying that simply identifying learning difficulties early does not make a difference unless the student gets effective teaching. She says the lack of effective teaching has resulted in the myth of disability, blaming students for a problem that is in fact poor teaching.

The socio-Political belief about barriers to learning is not present in the interviews I conducted with teachers and parents in reference to instruction. This is probably because the nature of the topic is situational and refers to the individual. But I think there is a socio-Political perspective here. While I agree with Snider (2006) that some student failure can be attributed to lack of teaching (you can't be expected to know something that no one has ever told you), there is another component to instruction. As long as we are using norm-referenced standards, there will always be students who are not "normal". This is a product of the policy not the individuals. Good instruction involves many well researched practices, some of which I have described here, but unless these practices are geared toward the standard of the individual student, always pushing the student to do better than they did yesterday or last week, while maintaining respect for the differences between students and within students, schools will continue to be disabling.

OUTCOMES OF TEACHING AND LEARNING

Maintaining high standards is a common goal for schools but this usually relates to the overall standard of the school. One of the criticisms of grouping students into classes by ability is that the expectations for the whole class are lower in the low-achieving classes and the expectations for the class are higher in the high-achieving classes (Boaler, William, & Brown, 2005). Streaming students sets up expectations based on the relative achievement of students rather than assessment of their individual skills. Stereotypical characteristics of disability categories can have a similar outcome, lowering expectations for students identified as having a disability. The effects of low expectations are well documented in the literature on over-representation of students from ethnic minorities in special education programs. Losen and Orfield (2002), in their overview of the findings from several large-scale studies on ethnic minority students in special education conclude that low expectations are perhaps the greatest challenge faced by students from ethnic minority groups in the United States. They say the most damning racism is the "soft racism of low expectations" (Losen & Orfield, 2002). The risks from identification are that instructional practice will be influenced by norm-referenced assumptions rather than by deep understanding of student characteristics. However, teachers use information about students in many different ways. A common comment I have heard from teachers is "I don't read the IEP or the school records because I don't want to be biased about the student". It is my belief that this is a cop-out. The more information a teacher has about the student the quicker they can get to know them. It is how the teacher filters that information that leads to prejudgement.

The overall expectations for students in special education programs are generally lower than in regular classrooms. Information from the 2001 Participation and Activity Limitation Survey indicates that students who are in special education programs are far less likely to earn a high school diploma or higher than their disabled peers who are not in special education or their non-disabled peers, even when taking into account the severity of the disability (Statistics Canada, 2001).

Many teachers give the impression that they have determined the ability level of students before they have engaged in instruction. Jason discouraged the inclusion of Marcus in grade seven subjects that are extremely important for secondary education. Jason does not make any attempt to accommodate Marcus in these courses but makes a judgement about Marcus's abilities before giving Marcus the opportunity to try academic subjects:

> (Interviewer: And I just noticed that he's not going to the rotary subjects: history, geography, science. Is this the first year they've had rotary subjects?) Yes. And this is the first year … actually I pushed for that because I said I didn't think he needed that for life skills and only because I live with a child that's at a grade one level, so I know what I've done for my own child in the school system who's in grade nine now. So I went in and said, "What does he need history, geography and science for?" Yes, he could sit and listen but he can't do the work, he can't do the writing. He doesn't really remember it from day to day to do a test. I said, "Couldn't we put him into something that he could really use?"

The life skills program Jason refers to is in fact a course that focuses on everyday activities like going to the store, personal hygiene, and taking public transit. These courses require the integration of analytical skills, literacy and numeracy skills, geography, and arithmetic skills. In addition, these activities involve interaction with peers and community members, which happens naturally in the classroom. The content of life skills courses is learned by most students through experiences outside the classroom. For example, a common activity in life skills is going to a community store. Most children learn how to go to the store by going to the store with their families, with parents, grandparents and older siblings modelling behaviours. The fact that some children are expected to learn these skills in school suggests that only trained professionals can teach some people about everyday living activities. However the specialized skills of literacy, numeracy, analytical thinking, etc. that are taught in school to other children are supposed to be taught at home for children identified as needing "life skills". Jason continues:

> What you would like for Marcus would be a specialist who was working with him. I don't know. I don't know whether Marcus would be better served learning more life skills as well, to accommodate him. Again, I think about the fact that we're learning the seigneurial system, or we're doing the Revolutionary War, and things that he may or may not be picking up. But regardless of whether or not he's picking them up, there are other things that he hasn't picked up that are more important.

The expectation for Marcus is that he is "picking up" information that is being "taught" to other students. Leslie is explicit about her difficulty in teaching a student who does not fit the "norm". Leslie believes that her usual teaching strategies cannot work for Corinne:

> And if there was just one subject area, then this is the area of needs and her strengths. So really, to be honest, these are done after everything's said and done. I mean we look at strategies and just with experience I say, "Okay" … but it's not like Corinne comes with a set of instructions … the average student, the average class, kind of does. I know strategies, I can name you a million strategies to teach math to the average student. I can tell you about teaching any subject in that case. But then you bring someone here that doesn't fit into that area … well someone could tell me … I guess the teacher beforehand could say she needs extra time or I could read that on a piece of paper.

Mark takes a similar approach. He does not modify his expectations for Jeremy who is working below grade level and he does not place the same value on the modified work in relation to the work of the rest of the class:

> Well the easiest way is just to look at him and to see what he's up to and if he's happy he's learning usually … unless he's up to something silly and he's really happy then. But you can usually just tell by the way he's acting if he's learning something. And he always shows me things when he's proud of them. And I'm glad he's proud of them but they're not the expectations of the grade seven, they're the expectations that were set by the EA. And I'll thank him for showing me and tell him he's done a really good job.

Mark does not evaluate the work itself but uses Jeremy's behaviour to evaluate whether he is learning. Using his experience with Jeremy, Mark made some more global comments about how funding should be allocated based on the criteria of disability category as well as family characteristics. Mark clearly holds Individual beliefs but it is interesting that he includes family characteristics as part of student pathology. While Mark is explicit about his views on family characteristics I believe that this is a more common perspective than most teachers are willing to discuss. Certainly family characteristics have a relationship to school failure, and like disability this a socially constructed category:

> I guess the other thing is if the student isn't behavioural and if the parents are on board then it makes sense to give that student a little bit more of the

support. I don't know if that would be discriminating but it would put the people in place for a better reason (and) you definitely get a better product out of it. Whereas giving someone who doesn't have the support at home or is behavioural the same sort ... if they get the same sort of support then it wouldn't be ... (Interviewer: They would probably get more support.) It would waste time for a lot of people and for the student himself. For someone like Jeremy, he is a good boy, he has a good attitude, he's got these learning disabilities, and he's got good support at home. They're trying their best as well and it's a shame that he's going to be struggling in grade nine without something changing.

Several teachers who held Individual beliefs never initiated responsibility for teaching students they had pre-judged would not "benefit" from their teaching. For these teachers, the students' ability is fixed, that is they will not ever improve and so the teacher does not see value in their own teaching to this student. Melinda says:

Robert will make small progress throughout the year, and then he comes back in September, and it's starting back from scratch again. He just forgets everything. Just everything. But I think also there's a lack of motivation. He's not really that interested in schoolwork.

Similarly Jennifer has very little information about Neil. She has received a short summary of the information in his IEP but she has not taken any initiative to learn more about him:

(Interviewer: Have you seen the IEP?) Briefly ... not too much of it really. (Interviewer: Okay. So this hasn't really served a purpose for you that much, the IEP?) Not really because the EA comes in and she's with him a lot and then the resource teacher, she takes him out a lot. (Interviewer: What kind of information was in that blurb that you got about him?) That he's on an IEP, that he can act silly sometimes in class, that he has an EA, that he has Program Support. That's about it ... not too much.

In contrast to the teachers who have predetermined the outcomes for identified students, Teachers who hold Situational beliefs are likely to use the interaction that takes place in the teaching and learning process in order to continually reassess student skill level and to recalibrate their teaching accordingly. These teachers describe reassessing goals throughout the school year and improved student achievement. Marlene provides a good explanation of this approach:

I usually set up at the beginning of the term, saying the objectives I want, (and) expectations for Jacqueline by the end of the term". So, I have a lot of them (objectives and expectations) in there. They're not at the grade level; they're at the grade one level, so I have to go through the grade one expectations and see what she's working at and put those down. Now, I know just this past week, I was updating, because there are some things that I did end up doing this term, that I didn't think I would have a chance to because I didn't know if she was going to be able to get to that step, but it turned out she *was* able to get to this step. So I have to *add* those to the IEP for this term.

Carla has requested that Noah continue in her class in the coming school year because she feels that she can carry over her work from the previous year. She feels that knowing the student well has benefited him as evidenced by his learning progress:

Well probably March/April is when you start thinking about what you're going to do the next year. Are you going to change? And I had to take my qualifications to teach grade seven because I wasn't qualified. So when I decided to take my qualifications I talked to the EA who was in my classroom and said, "What do you think if I kept him for another year, just carrying on the programming?" It's actually been disappointing not working with him, but I was hoping to see a lot more progress so I feel badly that we haven't been able to see that. So in the third term I decided that there were some that I would like to keep and hopefully because they didn't have to get to know a new classroom teacher, they didn't have to get to know how that classroom teacher works and his or her expectations.

The work teachers do to support students by monitoring their progress through the teaching and learning process is not always successful. Leslie is concerned that she has not figured out how to help Corinne to progress. For Leslie this means that she must continue to try to connect with Corinne:

I wish I could help Corinne to her full potential and I don't know if I'm doing that. If we figured out what the problem was that could help too.

For some teachers, their own success is tied to the achievements of their students. This is supported by policies that use standardized test scores to evaluate teachers and schools. Jason says:

And for all the ways that Jason brings life to the classroom, or all the fun things that he does, I don't know how much he's learning. And every teacher wants to know that each of their students is learning.

Similarly both Melinda and Evan use as much information as they can get about each student. They both described doing a lot of one-to-one interaction with students in order to evaluate their progress. Both teachers also read the IEP but they find this standardized form less useful than their own experience with students. Melinda says:

I don't know if it's just the way that I teach, but you get to know the kids, and you just know internally where to go and what to do with them. Why do you need to have something down on paper? I think the IEP is good to have as a document. It's good for somebody else who's coming in to be able to look into detail … what's been going on with this child exactly, what expectations were looked at. I think that the last IEP wasn't so detailed. It was more general, didn't really give you as good an idea as this one does…in my opinion, anyway.

Evan takes a similar view of the IEP:

I think it's effective in the sense that it's constantly making me aware of her needs, whether I'm able to do that on a consistent basis...no. That's where I would stand as far as IEPs.

Jason is less positive about how the information in the IEP can help his teaching:

If I actually believed that in writing an IEP things would change, that I would see that student then getting resources, people coming in, experts helping them ... me getting support to do my job better, I'd be the first one to write one. But it doesn't change anything. A student with an IEP that says that they're four years behind, and a student with an IEP who ... without an IEP who is four years behind are receiving the same level of support. So all you're really doing is creating extra work for yourself when you go to a program support teacher or a principal and say, "I've got a student who's way behind. What should I do?"

The connection between the act of teaching and the process of learning is so tightly bound it is difficult to separate. That is why the quality of teaching is usually assessed through the outcomes of learning. For teachers who hold Individual beliefs, they usually do not even begin the teaching process for students who they do not believe can learn. For these teachers, the identification of a disability or learning difficulty is the signal for them that the student cannot be taught. For these teachers, early identification means that intervention must be undertaken by someone else. In my experience talking to these teachers, the deferral of responsibility to specialists is not because they believe that the student will actually do well in another type of program, but that they do not belong in the regular classroom. When I teach courses in the teacher preparation program at the University level, there are always some students who say, "it is better for some students to be out of the regular classroom". My question to these teacher candidates is, "What do you think is happening in the other class"? They usually have no idea. The answer is teaching, just like, one would hope, is happening in your regular class.

For teachers who hold Situational beliefs, they do not predetermine the outcomes for students based on identification. Instead these teachers continuously re-evaluate student goals based on information from gleaned from the teaching and learning process. For these teachers, the IEP and other standardized documents are of minimal use because they do not provide detailed information about the everyday learning of each student.

TEACHING, LEARNING AND INDIVIDUAL, SITUATIONAL, AND SOCIO-POLITICAL BARRIERS

The myth of process is based on the idea that learning will occur naturally if teachers give children the tools for learning. There is no need to impart information. This assumption presumes that critical thinking can be isolated from facts and information, which is questionable. It further presumes that academic learning is natural and that natural learning is preferable to the alternative, which I suppose is artificial learning. Both of these faulty premises are based on the misapplication of research in cognitive psychology. (Snider, 2006, p. 29)

The title of this section reflects the distinction that I see between the approach of teachers who hold Individual beliefs and the approach of teachers who hold Situational beliefs. That is that teachers who hold Individual beliefs do not accept their own role as a teacher for students who have been identified. This results in practices such as referring students to specialists, thereby relieving themselves of responsibility, and expecting labelled students to work on their own. This leads to the phenomenon described by Snider above, where critical thinking and academic skills are separated from facts and experience as in "Life Skills" programs. For these students, there is a presumption that they do not have the "natural" capacity to learn and thus the focus should be on experiences. A US study found that for many girls in special education classes science education is one of the first content areas that gets pre-empted in favour of remediation and life skills programs (Hamrich, Price, & Nourse, 2002). Under these circumstances the identification process undermines teaching. Identification and classification of students into categories of "exceptionality" precludes their access to the common curriculum and thus predetermines what they can learn. Snider (2006) is critical of the popular Head Start programs in North America, an early intervention program, because she says, these programs presume that simply identifying students at-risk of failure will result in improved outcomes. Instead, Snider says, we must address the shortcomings in teaching practice. In Ontario, students with learning difficulties are often taken out of French programs, and in fact most French immersion programs do not offer any special education supports. If students are failing they are encouraged to go the English stream to get help. This practice assumes that students who have learning difficulties cannot learn a second language, when in fact learning a second language may be very beneficial.

For teachers who hold Situational beliefs, there is an acceptance of responsibility for instruction. Identification of student disabilities and learning difficulties is just another piece of information that contributes to the process of knowing students. Interestingly, the information contained in school records and IEPs, that is the information from standards-based assessments, is usually considered to be of far less value to these teachers than the information they get from actually interacting with students in their class. These teachers are practicing the early identification, early intervention model that is the policy imperative behind expensive and time-consuming identification procedures, but they are much less likely to use the information from identification than the teachers described above.

There is also a socio-Political perspective about instruction, which was an undercurrent to the discussions I had with teachers and parents. There are presumptions within provincial education policy about normality based on age and grade level. These presumptions are evident in the standardized curriculum, in standardized provincial tests (which many students do not write because the available accommodations do not meet their needs), and in the classification of some instructional supports as "special" while others are considered to be "regular". In fact, I use the term regular to refer to classes that are anything other than special education. This term is less than ideal, but I have yet to find an alternative that retains the clarity of this term while circumventing its connotation of "normal". All of these policies cater to a norm, creating a category of students who do not fit the curriculum, who do fit the test, who do not fit the teacher; in other words constructing the category of disability. In contrast one might take the view that students of all abilities are an asset to the instructional experience of the class as a whole. That teachers who accommodate the needs of one student are introducing a wider range of teaching practices to the whole class, and that the presence of each student in the class expands the experience of the other students, as some parents noted in a study by Giangreco and others (Giangreco, Edelman, Cloninger, & Dennis, 1993). In another study, non-disabled students were found to have greater academic progress in inclusive school settings than in non-inclusive settings, while the disabled students in inclusive settings did not have significantly improved academic progress but the authors concluded that the overall effects of inclusive schools were of academic benefit to students with disabilities (Cole, Waldron, & Majd, 2004). The socio-Political considerations in education highlight the tensions between a curriculum designed for the collective student body and practice of differentiating instruction to match the differences between students. Nilholm refers to this tension as the dilemma of the education context (Nilholm, 2006).

Some final comments on the discussion of the early identification, early intervention policy that I have explored in this and the previous chapter are warranted. First, many of the parents with whom I talked, as well as people I have known in my personal life, experience a sense of relief when they receive a disability diagnosis, either for themselves or for their children, particularly when they have had a period of uncertainty leading up to the diagnosis. For these people identification of a disability can mean "knowing what they are dealing with". For many, identification of a disability leads to membership in a unique cultural community, as is the case for people who use American Sign Language, or for a growing number of people with autism. My concern is with the use of disability labels in schools and the way these labels can effect instruction and in turn learning opportunities for students. If used appropriately, the information from formal assessments can provide support for the instructional and learning experiences of students and teachers.

Tim's interview received a profile score of 0.38 (Individual), 4.24 (Situational) and 1.24 (socio-Political). This was the highest Situational score in the teacher sample. Tim teaches in a small rural school that has just been built. The Special Education Resource teacher in the school is very supportive of all of her students and takes the initiative to write all of the IEPs. This model does not support teachers using IEPs as a tool for individual planning in their classes but it does provide an atmosphere in which the emphasis is on teachers teaching rather than doing paperwork. As a rural school, there are few supports for students with disabilities outside of the school. The principal explains that several families get counselling through the school because there are no social workers available from elsewhere. In addition, although there is itinerant support from the school board if there is a snow storm or other bad weather these support staff will not come to the small community.

Tim has been teaching for four years. Before he was a teacher he worked in social services in a residential care centre for youth with disabilities. Tim has no Additional Special Education Qualifications. He has taught grades four through seven and at the time of the interview was teaching a grade seven class with twenty-seven students. Only Ryan, the student in this study, has an IEP, although there are five students in the class whom Tim reports as at risk for school failure.

Throughout the interview, Tim focuses on Ryan's strengths and how he can build on these strengths in his teaching. The high Situational score on Tim's interview comes from his consistent descriptions of support for Ryan to build on these strengths. Tim does report some barriers for Ryan due to policy problems, a socio-Political belief, but his own responsibility for Ryan's education, a Situational belief, seems to trump the socio-Political perspective throughout the interview.

In a description of Ryan, Tim includes an example of how his own teaching instructions can affect Ryan. Tim describes Ryan as:

A really, really, neat kid. He's very quiet. He's developing more in his verbal skills but he's very withdrawn, very quiet. If he's confronted at all or if there's an issue or something that they want to talk about, he shuts right down ... that's the worst time. If he's relaxed and with his friends then he's much more vocal, but if I say, "Ryan, pull out your math book" then he freezes and shuts down and won't talk about it. So there's some of that there. But he's a really neat kid.

Tim has seen a change in Ryan's reliance on the EA this year. Despite the fact that the EA works with Ryan one-to-one for about 50% of the day, Tim is very involved in Ryan's program. He sees this as an added support to what he already does as a teacher, unlike teachers with an Individual belief who often report EA support as being in lieu of their own role:

Yes. And even approaching him ... it used to be more (the EA) ... if he was acting angry or something, (the EA) would be the one that would approach him and talk with him and now it's more "well now we need to transfer that" and "Ryan, (the EA)'s not here right now. We're having a problem. Let's talk about it. What's wrong"? And there are a lot of pauses and looking around and coaxing and he's starting to be able to articulate, "I'm mad because (another student) wrote on my desk". So it's starting to be able to come out.

The foundation of Tim's teaching is in his knowledge of individual students. In contrast to Brenda's deferral to the EAs, Tim takes responsibility for his role in getting to know students, a Situational belief in which his own actions are central to his teaching. In discussing the role of an IEP for a student like Ryan, Tim recalls the results of an in-school team meeting at which Ryan's case was discussed with his mother:

> There was a team meeting in September that I was ill for. I was away that day so (the program support teacher) did fill me in and gave me the minutes of the meeting and we talked about everything that had been discussed. Ryan's mum's really good and she's really supportive so there were no real issues. A lot of it was just we'll carry on from last year.

On the other hand, Tim does see the importance of documenting an education plan. Tim describes an incident where Ryan became quite upset about a book that the school wanted to remove from the curriculum. Tim was amazed at Ryan's ability to verbally express his anger over the censorship:

> I think the IEP does reflect him academically but it doesn't necessarily encompass all the emotional and social barriers that are part of Ryan too. And that one incident [the censorship] was certainly a shock and we were surprised he could vocalize all of that but it's not completely out of Ryan's realm. He's able to talk and discuss issues. There were other issues from his home life. Sometimes he'll be acting angry and he'll slam his books down so we know that there's something up. And (the Education Assistant) can sit and talk with him about it and he is more and more able to verbalize connections ... "I was mad at my mum because she didn't set our alarm clock this morning" ... Some of those sort of insignificant issues that we couldn't track before, we're starting to track some more.

Tim's description of the IEP shows both his Situational and his socio-Political beliefs. He notes that the Program Support Teacher takes lead responsibility for writing IEPs in his school and although, "it's great for me because it saves me some time. It also makes me less familiar with the IEP. I have to go through it and it's not my language so that's kind of a drawback". The real problem with the IEP, for Tim, is in its relationship to ISA funding. Tim describes this barrier to his teaching as a systemic problem:

> It would be interesting to know about the ISA claims and exactly what the government ... I mean I certainly have a perception of the IEP being about money and not necessarily being about the kid and how he works in the classroom. It seems that the wording and things involved in the IEP are much

more about how can we get support for this kid than actually what are we going to do with this kid everyday.

Yes. Even for reporting, when you do report cards you change language and you change gears. But I sometimes find that the IEP is too wordy and you spend too much time trying to find the right way to say it rather than actually saying what you're doing.

In describing the program he has put in place, Tim has many teaching strategies. This is in direct contrast to Brenda, the teacher with an Individual profile, who describes few strategies of her own, but can occasionally talk about what the EAs do. Tim says:

We're actually changing the grade level. So for a teacher it's really doing a grade one/seven split. (Interviewer: So what kinds of things do you do?) A lot more one-to-one stuff: repeating the instructions and giving one-to-one; making sure there's eye contact; trying to put it into simplistic language; using more examples; trying to give more visuals; that kind of thing.

Tim also has found that one particular student, Aiden, has really been successful in doing peer tutoring with Ryan:

So I try to know where to seat him and there's always a concern with Aiden. I'm always aware of not burdening Aiden with Ryan because he's such a wonderful resource but he's a kid too and deserves to have a life outside of Ryan, although in discussions with Aiden he's always saying, "Oh I can do that". So we change the seating arrangements regularly in class and I did have him sitting with somebody different but it just didn't work as well as with Aiden, and Aiden was willing to move back so we arranged that. As far as having him closer to the front – not so much. I like to have him closer to me and to an exit because he leaves the classroom. So not to disrupt the other kids, we keep him close to me and close to a door.

Some teachers rely on other students in the classroom to give peer support to students who are struggling. While peer learning is a good practice for teaching, there is some question about the impact of the helping relationship on true friendships (Male, 2007). Tim relies on Ryan's relationship with Aiden:

(Interviewer: When the IEP was being designed you didn't have too much to do with the design but when you were planning what you did in the classroom, what sort of things did you do for setting up your classroom?) Well first of all, Aiden is such a wonderful resource because we sit there together and when I give instructions to the class; Aiden whispers to Ryan and lets him know what he needs to be doing. So having that peer resource has been amazing and if Aiden's not there then there's Gavin and Liam who are ready to step right up to the plate. (Interviewer: So these kids have probably been going to school with him since Kindergarten.) Since kindergarten – and they have developed that social skill with him. I think seeing Aiden recognized for it too was a big incentive for some of the kids (the student was given an inclusion award from the school board). Getting that award last year made the kids look around and think, "I like Ryan a lot too". I could be a help here. And this network of friends that's been set up too … Ryan has lots of connections, lots of kids who are willing to defend him and help him out if he needs it. So that's been a huge help as a teacher in the classroom.

The Situational beliefs that Tim holds are perhaps best understood by his continual description of Ryan as a part of his class. Despite the fact that, "He (Ryan) can't do any written work, he can't read, and he can't understand complicated math concepts" Tim clearly views Ryan as an integral part of his class. He reports having regular contact with Ryan's mother and he is involved in designing the activities which the EA uses.

CHAPTER 5

Voices That Are Heard and the Politics of Collaboration

Collaboration is now considered to be an integral part of inclusive education practice (Evans, Lunt, Wedell, & Dyson, 2000; Stanovich, 1996; Thousand, Villa, & Nevin, 2006). In fact, almost any text on inclusive education includes at least one chapter on collaboration, with one recent text putting collaboration before inclusion as the key to successful teaching practice (Walther-Thomas, Korinek, McLaughlin, & Williams, 2000). Collaboration is so pervasive in the literature on inclusive education, I wondered if it was more important than the beliefs of the individual teachers and parents involved. One of the early hypotheses of my research was that students would have more academic progress if their teacher and parents had similar belief systems, regardless of what those belief systems might be, than if their belief systems were disparate. I did not find any statistical evidence of this hypothesis but I am reluctant to abandon it altogether because I think, regardless of the effect it has on student progress, teachers and parents who share belief systems are likely to be more successful in their collaboration than if they do not share belief systems. From an empirical standpoint further research is warranted, but my hunch is that collaboration is more likely to be successful for teachers working with each other, and with administrators as well, if they share belief systems. Certainly, administrators' belief systems have an impact on the practices of teachers working in their schools (Leithwood & Janitzi, 1999; Stanovich & Jordan, 1998). The collective beliefs of administrators and teachers are sometimes referred to as the school climate or school culture.

The literature on collaborative practice shows that many different types of collaboration are found in schools. These include collaboration between teachers and other school staff such as Special Educators or Resource Teachers, between teachers and Education Assistants, between teachers and parents, and between teachers and students. There can also be collaborative relationships amongst students in a class, and amongst all teachers in a school. In this chapter I will focus on collaborative relationships amongst school staff and between parents and teachers. I have selected these relationships simply because they are the relationships that teachers and parents talked about the most in my research. The relationships amongst students were discussed but mostly in the context of socializing, and they are thus included in Chapter 7, on the social climate in the classroom.

TEACHERS WORKING WITH TEACHERS AND OTHER SCHOOL STAFF

The teachers I spoke with described many important collaborative relationships in their practice. The emphasis in our discussions, however, was usually on their relationship with Resource or Special Education teachers, Itinerant Support Teachers such as Speech and Language pathologists from the school board offices, and other trained staff such as the school principal. There was also a significant amount of collaboration between teachers and Education Assistants (EAs) in their classrooms.

In Chapter 4, there was some discussion of how collaborative relationships affected teachers' instructional practice. For example, Evan described how he and the Resource Teacher in his class would sometimes switch roles, with Evan supporting individual students while the Resource Teacher led the whole group lesson. Evan noted that this teaching arrangement gave him the opportunity to learn new instructional techniques from the Resource Teacher and the opportunity to have additional one-to-one time with students. Thousand, Villa and Nevin (2006) describe this type of co-teaching as "supportive teaching", but they note that co-teaching can take on many forms. They also describe "parallel teaching" where teachers work in the same class with different groups of students. This type of co-teaching was described in Chapter 3 by Carla, who at the beginning of the school year, takes a small group of students aside each day while the Education Assistant teaches the other students. This gives Carla the opportunity to assess the skills and level of learning of each child in her class. Carla describes how she coordinates instruction with the EA:

> We usually sit down on a regular basis, could be weekly or bi-weekly, and we look at what the rest of the class is looking at in terms of language or math and then we take all of that and we bring it right back down to the grade one level ... if we're doing a novel study then Noah'll do a novel study, it just will be a different one. If we're working on measurement in math then so is Noah. We do that so that if the terms come out during homework time and we're doing our agendas, he's understanding that he's working on the same type of subject that we are.

Noah has low vision, and so Carla also works with an Itinerant Support teacher. Carla explains how this collaborative relationship has improved:

> We've had a lot more input this year with the low vision teacher in terms of her expectations of Noah than we did last year. Last year, she would just come in and say things, tell us to do things, and lots of times we would know that we'd already tried something and it didn't work but she insisted that it would work. So we found a lot more, "I know better than you because I'm the expert" kind of feeling but now something happened and she came in here with the idea that ... maybe someone's told her something, I don't know, but she's working much more closely ...

The other two types of co-teaching described by Thousand, Villa and Nevin (2006) are "complementary teaching", two teachers giving instruction together with separate roles, and "team teaching" where two teachers share all of the traditional teaching roles including planning and responsibility for all students. In my study only one teacher described this type of relationship. Dennis, who had worked for many years as a special education teacher, now works in a team-taught class. Dennis and a teacher who is designated as a "behavioural specialist" teach a regular class, which has three students designated as having "behaviour exceptionalities". Leading up to the interview, Dennis protested that he was not the correct person to be interviewed about the "behavioural student". However, in the interview it was clear that Dennis shared the responsibility with his co-teacher for Catherine, a student with Asperger's syndrome. Dennis describes how the relationship works:

> The way we split it up is I am responsible for the classroom, the overall classroom. And, the other teacher is responsible for the details. Now the details, most of the time, meaning children who need special attention that might be behavioural but might not be, depending what the area is…because it could be a social situation. If it's an academic situation, in Catherine's case, she often doesn't need help. So, at the beginning, because we had heard things about her, we made sure we were with her from the time she got off the bus 'til the time she went home.

The teaching roles in Dennis' class changed over the year and I will describe Dennis and Catherine in much more detail in one of the case studies. So, I heard from teachers about co-teaching, but it was the exception. Most of the collaborative relationships described to me were consultative and drop-in support (Thousand, Villa, & Nevin, 2006). Vanessa described how consultation with other teachers has really helped her to individualize her instruction for Paul:

> Last year, probably mid-year, I knew my grade placement – that Paul would be coming to my classroom. I gave full credit to the previous year's teacher. She's very thorough. She sat down with me … at the end of the year to discuss Paul because he is a higher priority. She is wonderful, and just before school started, we sat down to talk about all the students so that they can come back and I know exactly where to start off with them. At least I know where she found them as a starting point and different strategies. With Paul, I knew that he was working at a kindergarten level (he is grade two now) and it was important to start getting his sounds to break down words. I knew that being able to communicate through some form of writing, that he was still writing long letter strings, and no formation of words, so I knew that that's where I needed to start, and building his confidence too. (Interviewer: But you had to find your own strategies, or she had some ideas?) She had, well, the IEP from the previous year it gives some strategies, and I conference with her if I have any particular concerns.

As I described in the chapter on instruction, teachers who hold Situational beliefs are likely to see collaboration as central to teaching practice. Several teachers describe the Resource teachers and other staff as having important information and knowledge about students that they see as a resource for their own teaching. The most common relationships that I heard about from teachers who hold Situational beliefs were based on the classroom teacher maintaining responsibility for the students while relying on other staff for support. This was true even for teachers who were co-teaching. Evan says:

> Ultimately, it's my responsibility. At least that's the way I feel. Ultimately when it comes down to it, I'm on the line as far as consequences and everything else. The resource teacher and I work well together…extremely well…so we communicate quite a bit before the school year even starts. We talked about how we're going to implement strategies … she's been at the school longer than I have so she knows the students coming up as far as profiles. We'll keep an eye on those students and see how they do. The resource teacher and I really worked on this (the IEP) together and developed it. So we looked at expectations that we wanted to cover, and we talked with the EA as well to see what she was going to be doing.

Marlene describes how she uses the Resource Teacher to share the workload and to help her generate ideas:

> The Resource Teacher helped me write the IEP. We found different things that we felt would work with Jacqueline. I searched through whatever we had here, and … along with the Resource Teacher – I'll use the Resource Teacher as a sounding board – and the two of us have sat down, but then I've put it under my own name.

Teacher statements that characterize collaboration as a process by which the responsibility for student learning is transferred to someone else reflect the Individual beliefs held by some teachers. In these cases, teachers describe student deficits as being best dealt with by specialized staff. For example, Brenda describes her involvement with itinerant support for Karen, who has a rare brain disorder and spends most of her time out of the regular class:

> I don't talk to them (itinerant support) … briefly, the occupational therapist ordered a desk that is designed so that Karen's wheelchair can pull right up under it. So she can sit in the group with the class. So she's part of that group.

Brenda continues describing how she works with the EAs:

> (Interviewer: Who guides the EAs in what they're doing?) Mainly the program support teacher, and then a little bit from me. But I'm trusting that what she's telling them is what's right … I'm not doing a lot with her and yet I'm the one that has to sign this IEP. Well I don't sign it, the principal does.

But the program support teacher has done most of the work with writing all this up. But I was told, "Don't worry about that IEP: we're doing that one".

So some teachers transfer responsibility to specialists, and the result is that these teachers have less opportunity to get to know the students. The goal of including students in a regular class is clearly undermined when the use of Resource Teachers and Education Assistants to provide a program for students leads to the classroom teacher losing a connection with the student. This is the case for Melinda and her relationship with Robert:

Sometimes he's unmotivated about schoolwork, and he'd rather be doing something else, but for the most part he's okay. Because he's out of the class so much ... I have a rapport with Robert and a certain way ... that I talk to him, but I don't know about teaching strategies so much.

Jason describes how his lack of familiarity with Marcus put him in a difficult situation in a meeting with parents and the Special Education staff at his school:

I was in the team meeting. But these things take place early in the year and you really ... don't know Marcus that well. Team meetings are always a scary thing because the first thing a team meeting always starts with (is) let's speak ... the classroom teacher. And everyone turns and looks at you. Meanwhile, you don't know the student very well. You're just getting to know him, and really, when you think about the fact that the EAs have been working with him one-to-one, he used to be, I think, at 100% EA support when he started school. So they've been working with him since maybe grade two to grade seven.

Jason also describes what would happen if the EA were not supporting Marcus:

If it wasn't for them (the EAs), I can't say how much attention Marcus would be getting. Because I'm at the front doing compound sentences and things like that, and if it wasn't for someone being with Marcus, he'd just be basically sitting there or logged in on the computer, that kind of thing. So they basically work with him on some language and some math and some spelling every morning, and he does religion with us, just listens.

Parents often feel that EA support is optimal. In fact many of the parents I spoke to equated instructional support with EA support. This was the case for Laura:

Naima's lucky and the reason she's lucky is there's another boy in her class. She's lucky that she's getting all this attention because of the budget problems. The other boy needs an EA all the time. Now if Naima wasn't in the same class as that boy she'd have a heck of a problem. So what's been happening through the years is the teachers have been making sure that those two are always together so that when that boy gets the EA so does my daughter. That's how she's lucked out. And if that wasn't the case we would have had a big problem probably because of the budget constraints.

There is also the element of school culture in collaborative relationships. Some teachers described an overall feeling at a school where teachers supported each other to help students succeed. The research evidence suggests that a positive school culture can cultivate collaborative relationships (Thousand, Villa, & Nevin, 2006). For teachers who held socio-Political beliefs, collaboration was influenced by the systemic atmosphere in a school. Marlene, in addition to a Situational perspective described above, also had these socio-Political beliefs. She described why it was important for teachers to communicate with each other:

> Now, the teacher from the previous year had given me some information. However, over the summer, things changed. You know, you have setbacks, so you've got to feel through what's best for Jacqueline. So trying to set up her program, along with … all the rest of the class … It's a difficult thing. So, now that we have a very good program set in place for her, when she goes on to the next grade at the end of the year, it's going to be easier to say, "This is where … the flow is…".

Further, systemic problems hinder some collaboration particularly with Education Assistants. Carla sees a problem with the duties assigned to EAs. Carla describes this as a school level policy problem but in fact it stems from the collective agreement with the Education Assistants union:

> Basically what we do in team meetings is we sit down and, because they usually take place well into September/October, I'll basically discuss where the student is at that time, what we've done in the classroom, what different resources we're using with him and our teaching strategies. One thing is the EA should be required to be at all those meetings and they're not. In this school, they're used to cover the classes when the teachers go to the meetings.

Additionally, the attitude of other professionals can hinder the collaborative goals of teachers. For example, Nancy is a veteran grade one teacher, who has Charlotte in her class. Charlotte has been diagnosed as having Oppositional Defiance Disorder. Nancy says:

> I think what would really help with these children is a video or modelling by other people. But they'll come in and observe and tell you to do a few things and the child isn't doing … the psychologist said he won't come in to the teachers' rooms and observe the children because he said, "When I come I won't see the behaviour. That child will thrive that a stranger is in here and they'll be mesmerized by that and won't act out".

Nancy cannot get the specialists to help her within her class. Collaborative practices between classroom teachers and other school staff show the tension between the individual differences amongst the players in the collaborative relationship and the differences in how collaborative practice is designed in each school. For collaboration to work it is necessary to have time allotted for meetings, support for co-teaching, and a balance of power amongst the individuals involved in the collaboration. Sherry describes Nicole's involvement in planning for Jawad. It is evident that Nicole's involvement is constrained by the culture of involvement in Sherry's school:

Mum is not involved with the programming ... (she says), "Okay, yes, you know, he will have his own education plan. I agree to that; I agree to what you're saying". So she's just on the verge of agreeing to the process, but she's not involved in (it), "Well I think he should be knowing this". She doesn't get involved with that. Now, I don't know at other schools or areas ... maybe parents are more involved. But usually it's the teachers and the people that are going to be delivering the program that ... determine what's going to be taught.

Itinerant Support Teachers sometimes use their professional status as experts to subvert the role of classroom teachers. This professional "expertism" can "silence or discourage participation" when the other person in the collaborative relationship feels intimidated (MacArthur, 2004). Acceptance of expertism can lead to deferral of responsibility to the expert when the teacher holds Individual beliefs. On the other hand, teachers who hold Situational beliefs are likely to resent this expertism, and prefer a model where each member of the collaborative team has a role in supporting the student. The benefits of good collaborative practice are evident for parents. Carrie described the difference for her daughter Karen when a collaborative team was formed:

The first year was probably the worst. Junior kindergarten. It was the teacher and the EA at the time. The EA was maybe just not really meant for that position, and so I was caught in the middle. And, because of the fact that Karen couldn't communicate ... My older sister, she teaches special ed, and she said, "Well, a communication book is very good, because the teacher or the EA – (if) the teacher's very busy, the EA can fill in the book". So I suggested this. Well the teacher didn't have time and the EA is not qualified and the principal said no". ... So it took until senior kindergarten, and things came around. ... It just started getting better. The teachers, the system and whatever. And I was new and I didn't know. I didn't fight it because I thought well maybe this is the best that that can be.

PARENTS WORKING WITH TEACHERS

Aside from the IEP document itself, the reporting process for parents of children with IEPs is different than it is for other students. These parents are expected to participate in many more meetings than other parents. Provincial education policy requires schools to have both report card meetings and IEP review meetings. Some parents are happy with this level of reporting, others are not getting as much support from the schools, and still others find the number of meetings onerous. One of the differences in how parents react to reporting from the school seems to stem from their perceptions of how the school responds to their inquiries and suggestions. Other parents describe the importance of sharing information about their children at meetings. Some of the schools encourage this participation. This is coded as a Situational belief when the parents describe their contribution to the meetings as important for their children, as Clare does:

> I do (feel comfortable in meetings) because basically when they talk to me about what they have noticed, and I tell that they want to know from my point of view how he is at home. And we basically share how he is at school compared to how he is at home. And it is a big difference between home and school behaviour. And I think it came down to that ... every meeting we go to it comes down to the behaviour. If he settles down in class, he can get his work done, and he can do the work, because he's got the potential.

Tracy also felt good about meeting with Maria's teachers:

> (Interviewer: When do you think about the IEP meetings that you've gone to over the years starting in grade three-ish, can you remember how you felt in those meetings?) I felt pretty good. I felt that they were helping and they were doing their best. I never felt that they were not helping me.

Other parents felt that school staff were intimidating or did not listen to them. Or they were simply not given information. Amanda's socio-Political beliefs are evident when she describes the impact of the meetings in which her son is described in negative terms:

> Sometimes the meetings go pretty good, and sometimes I will leave in tears. You know, I will. I will leave in tears. I don't let them see that. It's just ... it gets to be a little ... I don't know if it's because it's been so many years, and ... it seems like I hear the same things every time I go.

In fact, teachers do not always see parents as an important source of information. Brenda, in an interview, was almost surprised by the suggestion that parents might have meaningful input:

> (Interviewer: Do her parents ever provide you with those kinds of tips for working with her?) No, no, no, we don't talk with mum and dad that much about programming or about what she's doing. Any discussion with them is more (about) seizures, and medication ....

Teachers who emphasize the partnership with parents as important for their instructional practice and who treat the parent as part of a solution to barriers are coded as having Situational beliefs, as Melinda does:

> I was in contact with her a lot in the fall (when) we were getting the whole program set up for his transition between grade eight and high school. So they've been making visits to the high school affiliated here, where he's going to be going. They've been having visits and meeting with guidance counsellors there, so they're getting used to the school surrounding, and I think they have a buddy system set up. We're working on that transition plan,

so we met a few times in the fall … to explain that, get that underway, and just get everything settled. I haven't talked to her so much now, but she is always available, so I call her. If ever there's a problem or whatever, I can just give her a call and she'll come right over.

In many texts on collaboration in schools, the relationships with parents are treated as separate from the relationships with other school staff. However, collaboration is characterized by the team approach and parents should be part of that team, by law and by logic. Parents, like teachers, have specialized knowledge. While teachers know about content and pedagogy, parents know their children and, as described in Chapter 4, intimate knowledge of the individual characteristics of students are central to effective teaching.

The parents I spoke with had very little understanding of the collaborative relationships taking place within schools. For them, collaboration was all about the relationship they had with their child's teacher or with a special education teacher. Not surprisingly these relationships were extremely important for families. In fact, the collaboration or lack of collaboration between teachers and parents was perhaps the most important factor for parents as they described their own behaviours. For this reason, I will begin this section with some context from the literature on parent roles in education. I will then consider issues related to homework separately, because homework was the practice most often cited in descriptions by parents about how they supported their children in school.

While ample evidence exists for the relationship between teachers' belief systems and how they teach, there is relatively little work done to examine parents' beliefs and their behaviours associated with educating their children, particularly children with disabilities. However, several studies examine the emotional state of families who have children with disabilities. As the primary developmental environment for children, the family is central to putting adaptive strategies in place for children with disabilities. According to Ferguson (2002) in the nineteenth century, disability was regarded as a moral deficit of the family because it brought economic hardship. This resulted in reform schools, asylums, and residential schools with the goal of requiring professionals to assume the role of the parent. More recently, Hauser-Cram, Warfield, Shonkoff, and Krauss (2001) identified three categories of research on the adaptation of families of children with disabilities. The first category of studies uses the "social ecology theory" which examines the quality of family environment and support systems which contribute to the family environment. William, who was diagnosed with ADHD at the same time as his son Greg, described to me how the school blamed the family for Greg's difficulties before his diagnosis:

Any problems that Greg was having in school … were ours, and even though she was the teacher, and we were the parent, we shouldn't be working together to resolve them. And "you should sort them out at home, and then send him, perfectly fine, to school, so I don't have to do anything. And I can just sit back and just relax and…" you know. And it just got to the point where we were going, "Look, just ... stroke off another day in the calendar, he'll be out of that area soon enough [because they were moving]".

The second category of studies described by Hauser-Cram et al. (2002) use "family systems theory" which characterize individuals within the family as interactive with all members contributing to the family environment. The third area of research identified by Hauser-Cram et. al (2001) as "family stress theory" is characterized by the assumption that multiple factors contribute to how families adapt to having a child with a disability and that it will change the pattern of the family:

> [Early work in this area drew] attention to how children with disabilities inevitably damage the families to which they are born. Whether they preferred to use primarily attitudinal (guilt, denial, displaced anger, grief) categories or behavioural ones (role disruption, marital cohesiveness, social withdrawal), most researchers assumed a connection that was both intrinsic and harmful" (Ferguson, 2002, p. 125).

Hauser-Cram et al. (2001) found that behaviour problems and communication difficulties did result in higher stress levels amongst families with disabled children, but that these stress levels were not clinically significant in comparison to families of children without disabilities. Similarly, Ferguson found that recent literature has shown that stress and well-being are similar across families with and without disabilities, and that many parents report benefits to having a child with a disability. The research on parent coping and emotional reactions to having children with disabilities could impact teachers' assessments of parents' emotional states and also the social acceptance of parents who have children with disabilities. In fact parents report that professionals blame difficulty in parent–teacher relationships on parents' poor adjustment to or denial of a child's disability (Engel, 1993). Ferguson says that denial is usually a rejection of a label or terminology rather than naïveté about the nature of a child's characteristics. Several parents who I talked to also rejected labelling of their children, as I described in Chapter 3, however, they often set aside their objections because of the need for identification in the school system.

In addition to the literature on parents' emotional reactions to their children's disabilities, the psychology literature examines parent beliefs in general. Both Goodnow (1997) and Lightfoot and Valisner (1992) found that parent beliefs and values have a direct effect on the beliefs and values held by their children. Thus parents likely directly influence how children understand their own identity, including their identities as persons with disabilities. Besides the effect on children's own belief systems, it is hypothesized that beliefs affect how parents participate in the education system. In earlier research, I found that amongst six parents of children with IEPs, their beliefs spanned the three categories of belief described in the framework for this study (Individual, Situational, and socio-Political beliefs) and that these beliefs appeared to influence the level and type of involvement these parents engaged in at their children's schools (Underwood,

2002). Pivik, McComas, and LaFlamme (2002) similarly found that that parents of children with mobility limitations reported several sources of barriers to inclusion: physical barriers, intentional attitudinal barriers, unintentional attitudinal barriers, and physical limitations.

Thus there are inconsistent claims about the nature of parents' emotional reactions to having a child with a disability. Nevertheless, recent research indicates that these emotional reactions do not significantly vary from the emotional state of parents of non-disabled children. The beliefs parents hold, however, may influence both the beliefs of the children themselves and the level and quality of parent involvement in schools. Research on the effects of parent involvement is inconclusive. While most school districts now have policies in place to engage parents in the education process, there is little evidence that links this practice to improvements in student outcomes (Corter & Pelletier, 2004). However, the effect may not be on student academic achievement but on the general atmosphere of collaboration in the school. Inclusion advocates are clear that parent participation and consultation is central to the philosophy of inclusive practice. The logic is that families know the student better than teachers and that family knowledge is fundamental to the instructional process. But, when talking to parents, even those parents who feel that they have a good relationship with schools, there is very limited use of parent perspectives in the instructional practice of teachers.

Dana characterizes her relationship with school staff as good despite the fact that she seems to respond to the school's needs rather than the other way around. This parent's description of her own contribution to the educational process is positive, yet her role is really a support role rather than the engaged role of a participant (Vincent, 2000):

> We worked together ... If there was a problem, they'd phone me or have a meeting. Meetings, and meetings, and ... pretty much everything I have input on. You know, what does he like, or what's his best subject: He's on the computer all the time; he listens to music; he reads his books; he watches movies. If you interview the program support teacher she'll tell you, I'm pretty involved. Even for volunteering, I do everything, pretty much.

Diane would like to make suggestions for the goals on Nigel's IEP but she notes, "it just looks so obvious that the IEP is something computer-generated, that none of what I suggested fit into their computer program". A typical consultation for the IEP, which is governed by policy that mandates consultation with parents, involves teachers informing parents of the education plan rather than parents giving information to teachers. Patricia, the mother of Paul described the process this way:

> (Interviewer: So when they set up the IEP, they write up all those goals. Do you remember them consulting you about those goals?) They asked me if I agreed with them. (Interviewer: Okay, they didn't ask you in the development stages, after they had set the goals they asked you then?) No they did them, and I read them after. (Interviewer: And once these goals are set up, how do they implement those goals? Do they consult you about that at all?)

They asked me if I agree with it, and if there are any changes or anything they haven't covered that we'd like to add. (Interviewer: Okay, and do you contribute at that point?) The last time, no, I don't think I did. I think everything was fine.

Clearly, Patricia's input is limited, despite the fact that throughout the interview, she had very clear ideas about Paul's needs. Teachers are also interested in the relationship with teachers. As William described above, sometimes teachers blame the parents for the difficulties students experience at school. Jillian (Maria's teacher) describes how Maria behaves at home:

She can't write a properly formed paragraph on her own. And this is another thing though that she's had so much guidance that there's a lot of learned helplessness ... she's very smart in the sense that she knows that if she's helpless she won't have to do it on her own. And that's very evident to me. (Interviewer: Do you find that frustrating?) Very much so and there's really no self-motivation there at all. She won't do homework. (Interviewer: At all?) No. It's a real struggle and usually it ends up getting done here. Her mum is just tired and doesn't know what to do with her and dealing with the behaviour so the homework gets put on the back burner and usually it's not done. (Interviewer: You talk to the parents pretty regularly?) Yes. We have quite a few meetings, mostly behavioural though. Unfortunate too is the academics usually get pushed aside because the behaviour is the prominent factor. We're fearing she's putting herself in a lot of unsafe positions right now and mostly all of our meetings this year have been getting her ready for high school, what we're going to do with her in high school.

Maria's mother, Tracy, does not see academics as important for Maria. Tracy leaves the school planning up to the "professionals" as she describes it, with the exception of her push to have Maria in a life skills program. However, Tracy says, "unfortunately Maria doesn't always get it", meaning she does not always learn the life skills content. Tracy holds Individual beliefs and she expects the school to deal with Maria's behavioural and learning difficulties.

For the most part parents were very knowledgeable about their children's abilities. This knowledge was gained through monitoring of their children's progress. The responsibility parents take for understanding their children's learning needs is associated with a Situational belief. In addition to homework, Sheila monitors Fatima's work at home:

Her reading is still very behind even at this point. I notice (this) in her writing (too). (Interviewer: How do you assess that? Where are you getting that information from?) Just from me. (Interviewer: From reading with her at home.) And from reading her assignments and her spelling ... it's words she should know how to spell.

Through monitoring their children at home, several parents described seeing different behaviours and skills at home than were reported by the school. Amanda describes Alexander's behaviour at home:

I could be wrong. It could just be because I'm his mum and, you know, maybe I see things at home that they don't see at school. It's a different atmosphere as well. Alexander will do more things at home; they see him as not being able to do them at school which confuses me. You know, this is the one thing that does confuse me, why is he able to do this at home, but once he is in school maybe it's because ... disruption from the other students or ... it could be anything.

Similarly, Dorothy finds her son Christopher is different at home than at school:

I think Christopher is different at home and at school. I think he feels much more comfortable at home than he feels at school. I think he feels the home is more familiar. Because I remember I came with him once when he started grade four, and he saw his teacher – his previous, his former teacher in grade three – and he was so uncomfortable, and he didn't feel ... well. He wasn't happy. I notice he is a different boy. He was ... uncomfortable and a little bit ... terrified, coming to school. No, he wasn't happy.

Susan also monitors Jae-Lynne's abilities at home, but finds that her daughter has deficits not recognized by the school:

I'm getting frustrated, because Jae-Lynne's ... it's just so hard to explain. The school's doing what they would do with any other child. Normally, reading is best for a child. I agree 100% with the school, when it comes to a normal child. But I tell the school something totally different about Jae-Lynne. What I see, because I'm raising her, the school sees something different.

Aside from seeing differences at home compared with what is reported by the school, parents frequently described an intuitive knowledge about their own children which no one else would have. Patricia would like teachers at the school to know about her son:

He's a very sweet little boy, very caring, always goes to hug somebody; he can be a little shy I find, just with new situations. But you see it in his face when he gets confused, you can see it when he's confused because he does this thing and I just know that whatever he's doing is just way too complicated or he's just had enough or he's tired....

On the other hand, parents sometimes feel that they do not understand their children as well as the school staff. Lana acknowledges that she is uncertain about Corinne's needs:

I know things about her but at the same time there are certain things I don't know about her, like how she can learn to do certain things.

Diane (a parent) also acknowledges the separate roles of teachers and parents.

They argue that they don't have the educational background and so on to support what needs to be done, the programming and everything. Well neither do I and I'm here. I'm a parent. But the teacher has a good idea of what's going on and she always has a good understanding of what Nigel's learning habits are, what he can grasp maybe, and what he may not grasp, what may help, what may work better, that kind of thing better than I would because she's there all day. So that's why I demand that.

The information that parents share with school staff is for the purpose of staff gaining insight into the experience of students. There is a fine balance between this being important for instructional purposes and violating the privacy of families. Nicole described to me some of the circumstances that have led to her son Jawad's behaviours. Jawad witnessed his father abuse his mother, and he has had run-ins with other children in his neighbourhood who are stealing from the local shopping centre. Nicole says, "I have wonderful communication with the school". But in one instance she felt judged by the school psychologist and the principal:

I don't like assumptions and I don't like criticism or being told on what to do at home. You know what I mean? And I found that maybe the school just had enough with him. And they were – the principle and the psychologist – sarcastic a little, (that's) how I took it, about what was happening at home and they even come on about my personal life. About maybe Jawad is not seeing enough of his dad, or maybe his dad is a negative influence on him ... like, wait a minute here. He has a father; he has every right to see his dad, unless there was something wrong. I'm sure that I would see it. So that was the thing. But it's too bad that it got to that extent, because I have a wonderful communication with the school. It's just that situation that I wasn't too comfortable with.

Similarly in their interviews some teachers judged parents harshly. Catriona describes her thoughts about Owen's situation at home:

I don't know how much time they actually have with Owen. He's dropped off at daycare at 7:30 in the morning, they tell me he wakes up at 6:45, and I said, "Well, would it be possible to work some quiet reading time in with him at home", and they said, "That sounds like a good idea". It happened once. In the second day he was back to daycare by 7:30. Two days a week he goes to a special intensive language program. So he's taken to daycare at 7:30. At 8:20, I think it is, he's picked up, Wednesday morning and Friday morning, to be driven to another school where he takes this other program. It's a group of eight children working with two adults in a very intensive one-to-one language enhancement program. And then he gets brought back, to lunch at the daycare, and then after lunch he's brought to me, and then after me he goes back to daycare, and after daycare he goes home. And I think on a good night he might have an hour. And it sounds as if one dad works late two nights a week so the dads sort of spell each other off. And he's in bed, you know, by eight o'clock at night. One parent is completely new to parenting. The other has a twenty-two-year-old son by a former marriage. So for the one I think it's just a whole exciting new thing to have a child. But I really wonder how much knowledge he has about what children need, and specifically this little guy. They're also applying to adopt a second child. They've put the papers in. They say they are not going to go about it aggressively, should it happen in the next two years, but my reading of what the father had to say to me was that basically they're looking for another child because Owen reports he doesn't have friends. I think they're trying to find a friend for Owen.

Interestingly in this case, the parents reported in their interview that Owen read with them every night and that he was quite verbal. Catriona says that Owen is non-verbal and this is one of the reasons she thinks he needs to be in a one-to-one program. In reflection, on Catriona's criticism that Owen's parents would adopt in order for him to have a friend, I am reminded of how often I have been told that I should have a second child because my son needs to have a playmate. I wonder if Catriona would consider this to be an acceptable reason to have a biological child in light of her thoughts on Owen's parents' reasons for adoption.

Parents collaborate with teachers in other ways than through input on planning. One significant way in which parents collaborate with school staff is through volunteering in their children's classrooms and schools. This has mixed results for the students, as reported by the parents, because it can be distracting to have their own parents in the classroom. Amanda describes how her son Alexander responded to her presence in his class:

> I try not to volunteer in the class. I was for kindergarten. I used to come in, volunteer twice a week, and then … it is true, Alexander was starting to get a little bit too dependent on Mummy. It got to the point, "Well, why aren't you there everyday".

Other parents I spoke to volunteer in the lunchroom or in different areas of the school. One of the parents, Fiona, is an EA in her son's school and she said that she makes a special effort not to be too demanding of his teacher.

Although direct collaboration is not always possible, many parents actively advocate on behalf of their children. For the most part, the advocacy role of parents is informed by socio-Political beliefs because they reflect parents' use of the system to get support for their children, rather than interfering in the day-to-day relationships of their children. All of these parents say that if they did not advocate for their children, their children would not have the supports they have now. Dana, who has a very good relationship with school staff, is clear about the importance of her role:

> (Interviewer: You said you were dedicated to this job (supporting her). What do you think would happen if you weren't? Like, if a parent weren't there for Robert). He'd be a lot worse off than where he is.

Sheila has a similar view:

> If I don't hear anything I'm not shy. I come in and ask. (Interviewer: So you're Fatima's advocate. You make sure that things are in place for her).

> Yes, you have to be like that though when you're child needs extra help in school. If you just sit back and don't do anything nothing will be done. They'll just push them through the system. I'm not saying that they're bad teachers or anything but that's just the way it is. You have to have a voice and you have to speak up and you have to fight.

Amanda is also not shy to advocate for her son Alexander, when she feels there is a problem. The mechanism for addressing issues at school is not clear so Amanda has developed a strategy:

> You just need to go. You need to get everybody. You just do not go to one person. I have found, over the years, that if I have something that I feel is important, I'll go talk to the teacher; I will talk to the program support teacher; I will talk to the principal; actually, I will talk to anybody who has an ear, in this school – the Education Assistant, the librarian – I will speak to anybody because the more people that know, then it's not just going to get ... If one person knows, it might get shoved under the rug, but if everybody knows it's a little bit harder to shove it underneath the rug ...

Sometimes, the advocacy role can have tensions because parents are not always in agreement with school policy or with the opinions of school staff. Teachers are sometimes very open about how they view parents. While interviewing teachers and parents I spent time in the staff room of most schools. In these cases the teachers would ask which parents I was interviewing that day. In all cases, if the parent had taken up the advocacy role the teachers would warn me that these parents could be "trouble". This was not always said maliciously, but it was clear that this role for parents was not embraced by teachers. Interestingly, the parents sometimes felt that their advocacy was appreciated by school staff. One parent told me that the principal had asked her to advocate for better staffing in the school because the principal did not want to stick her own neck out at the school board. Diane describes how she thinks she is received at her son's school:

> They're cautious on the information they give me but they know that if there's anything out there that I should know, they make sure I know it – because if I find out from somewhere else, God help them. And they've learned that. The communication between Program Support and myself in this instance is excellent. The Program's (Program Support Teacher) very good that way. She's very open and very honest. She speaks her mind. We've had a few arguments. We've agreed to disagree a few times but she does make you feel like you're heard. But on the other hand, if I don't agree with her I let her know.

Parent and teacher collaboration can also have a transformational effect. Nancy described how working with Charlotte, who is in grade one and has now been diagnosed with Asperger's syndrome, has changed her understanding of inclusive practice. Nancy credits Charlotte's mother, Paula, with Charlotte's transformation.

I think when inclusion came in you just had this idea that the people they were hiring to look after these children would be trained specifically to deal with that problem and your job was to provide the programming but they would know how to deal with that child and be able to cope. And that's what's hard, when the people that are there to help the child don't know what to do with them either and I'm supposed to be telling them, but I'm not trained either. This was how I felt when Charlotte first came into my class. I had never seen a child like her. She was an MID (mild intellectual disability) and ADHD. In thirty-five years of teaching I had never seen anything like her.

But I have learned a lot. Her mum has given me information and I have gone to workshops to learn about how to deal with the behaviour. I have had to change my thinking.

But her mum has been a really big help. I'll send home any extra work that she somehow refuses to do in class or couldn't get done because she's been out of class because of her behaviour. And her mum is really, really great about returning that with feedback. She'll say, "Charlotte took two hours to do this with much temper tantrum". She tells you exactly how she reacted – Charlotte could do this part by herself but had trouble with this. Or, I had to help her with this. So she gives excellent feedback.

Beverly is very active in advocating for her daughter's rights in school as well as in the community. Beverly has given Catherine's teachers books about Asperger's syndrome and spends many hours re-writing Catherine's IEP. However, Beverly thinks this should be done by school personnel:

(Interviewer: Do you feel that you have an educational role? You're educating the educators about this particular disability?) Oh yes, you are definitely. And, you know, it's too bad, because if they're one kid in a class of thirty, and the teacher has to learn this wealth of information to deal with one kid. I don't think they'd be very motivated, necessarily. They shouldn't have to. There should be more support, more specialists, rather than the teacher having to read textbooks and textbooks on asperger's or tourette's or whatever. There should be people within the school system that are really working with the teacher.

Not all parents have the confidence of Diane and Beverly. Many parents became advocates because they were forced into the role. Celia is the mother of twins who have both been identified as having behavioural and learning disabilities. She says she has just started to understand what her children need:

I'm so glad I'm aware of it (how to get support) now, so that by the time they get in grade nine, I'm going to be informed and already have them in the door.

Fiona sympathizes with parents who do not have knowledge of the system and how to effect change for their children:

A parent couldn't do it on their own. You really need to be involved with all the other support resource people, whether it's occupational therapist, speech therapist, or if it were a CYC counsellor, anybody who is involved with your child, you really have to have the big picture, otherwise this (the IEP) doesn't mean a lot because it's a lot of words and I don't know that a lot of parents understand it because it's all short little statements, little phrases, …develop visual motor perceptual skills.

Collaboration between parents and school staff varies greatly. In this study the three dominant ways in which parents reported collaborating was through input on IEP goals, volunteering in schools, and direct advocacy for their children's educational needs. Parents own goals for their children were associated with both Individual and Situational beliefs depending on whether they focused on student deficits or interventions for educational attainment. Volunteering was associated with Situational beliefs because it was reported as a means of parents taking a direct role in supporting students' educational needs, or as a barrier if the student became distracted by their parent. Advocacy was related to socio-Political beliefs about barriers because it involved trying to make systemic changes in schools. As in collaborative relationships amongst school staff, parents experienced power imbalances related to expertism. While parents had valuable information about their children, they were sometimes reluctant to share this information, or were discouraged from sharing.

HOMEWORK

For most parents in the study their most direct role in supporting instruction for their children was through homework. Research on the effects of homework indicate that doing homework can improve student achievement but how homework supports students is not clear (Epstein, 2001). The most appropriate amount of homework, the amount of support expected from parents, and the nature of the assignments are variable amongst the parents and teachers I spoke to. For some teachers, there is an expectation that parents will actually teach their children. I once observed a class where a student asked the teacher to explain a homework problem from the night before. The teacher could not answer the question and he said, "well how did your parents explain it"! This is an extreme case but from speaking to parents it is clear that homework is a big concern.

Many parents experienced frustration with the work habits their children had around homework. Tracy describes the routine when Maria gets home from school:

When Maria comes home, she goes straight downstairs and she usually goes to sleep. I cannot get her to do anything. I used to try and get her to do homework. They'd send home certain books and get her to do certain things in them and I would sit with her but she didn't want to do it. You can't explain to her that you have to do your homework. This is what you have to do. She doesn't care and she doesn't understand the consequences of it.

Celia spent more time trying to help her children, and she can see the improvement when her children do their work. But, the homework routine also led to frustration for Celia:

> I'm fairly literate, so I can help you there. (But) because I helped them so much it was like I was actually doing their homework. If they complete their assignments, they can go from a D to a C. So I was starting to do a lot of that and then after so many months it was, "do it yourself". I'll help you with the punctuation, the spelling, etc, but you put your own thoughts down there and you get your own material and you do it yourself. And if it doesn't work and they don't do it, oh well.

Patricia had a similar experience to Celia. She starts homework with Paul but almost right away he starts to get frustrated which leads to Patricia getting frustrated:

> Oh he knows and he'll scratch his face and, "Oh, come on. It's early. We just started! You can do this". He knows where to play his cards. Where mummy will do this, if I do this, she'll help me.

In discussions of homework, many parents focused on the academic goals they had set for their children. These parents describe helping their children to overcome barriers by making accommodations and supporting them. This practice is associated with Situational beliefs. Dana takes her instructional role very seriously, even buying educational supplies. She says:

> If I can do anything at home, I'll do it. They bring speech home, they bring math home, or suggest programs for the computer. And I will go out and get it, or have an idea where to get it and what my next move will be.

Harvey also has seen improvement since he learned that Stephen had a learning disability and he began reading with him at home:

> He's slowly coming along, and he's really improving because I've been reading with Stephen, Marg's (his mother) been reading with him, and I've seen the improvement in his reading since he's been in the program (has an IEP).

Clare comes up with her own activities at home to support Dwayne's learning:

> Well I have some little books. It's basically on handwriting, and he's trying that out every evening. He comes home; he gets a paper; and he tries. And he shows me, "mummy is this how it's done?" And it's like you have to take your time. What I do too, I make sure he gets a little reading done everyday.

The parents I spoke to often described getting inadequate support from teachers in order to work on learning goals at home. For example, Lana tried to get information about the upcoming lesson content for her daughter Corinne:

Well, I said to the teacher, "Can you give me a heads up on things before they come up? Like if you know next month, you're doing cats, dogs, and birds and you're studying geometry, can we just go over that beforehand?" And I don't think she clicked in on it.

Lana also helps Corinne with her homework, and she is confused by the feedback from Corinne's teacher:

I looked (at her homework) and I thought, well she's answered who she was (the homework question) but it wasn't how the teacher wanted it. But she just wrote "Who is she?" But didn't explain it. They just hand the paper back and you say, "We spent a lot of time on that. We did a lot of work". And then to get it back and that is (disappointing).

Beverly had similar difficulty interpreting the homework instructions while helping her daughter Catherine:

And the teacher, even if she would just write, "such and such is due". And the teacher thought that because she was sending home the description of the homework, ... a photocopy home – It didn't make sense to me because I wasn't there to hear it. And I couldn't interpret from the sheet what they really wanted Catherine to do. And Catherine couldn't understand it. So she would have her homework in her bag for days and she'd be telling the teacher, "I left it at home", and it would be right there.

Aside from the difficulties in completing homework, Fiona noted that homework is a well-established part of the instructional program in schools and that not all students are able to get the support they need to complete their homework. This is a systemic problem, although she describes it in the context of her son, which she believes creates a socio-Political barrier for him:

It's amazing. They have a lot of homework now, and that's a good thing, but ... it takes a lot of time, and I'm lucky that I have the time. But I could see parents leaving the child on his own, and if he's a strong student, yes, he should be able to do this homework on their own. But Caleb can't do it on his own and if I left him to do his homework on his own, it would be incomplete every week.

Many of the parents I spoke with felt that they should be doing more to help their children with homework and in collaborating with the school in general. Just a few of the circumstances that were described to me included parents who worked more than one job, or shift work where parents struggled to provide homework support. Ellen explained how this effected her in one meeting:

When I had this one meeting with the school psychologist and the teacher and the EA and the principal, that was the only meeting that I broke down in tears because you were hearing all the problems and that and yes there were good things that were coming out, but the problems were more overwhelming than the good and that scares you. And I had just come off a twelve-hour night shift.

Several parents I spoke to were in school themselves. Dana had been a student but she says she had to drop out of University in order to help her three stepchildren with schoolwork. Several parents described changing jobs, quitting jobs, or going to part-time work in order to support their children in school. Parents also reported that they had several children with learning difficulties in their families and they were overwhelmed with helping all of them. In addition, several parents described demands on their time through interactions with social service agencies. Parents of children who accessed other services related to the child's disabilities, particularly students with medical complications, described not being able to remember who said what and what advice had been given due to the plethora of professionals in their lives.

Another barrier for parents was their own past experience in schools. Ellen describes how her husband's school experience has affected his participation in Dalia's schooling. Dalia's father failed grade one and he suspects that he has a learning disability:

I just know what my husband went through ... I've informed them of that and that's why he's not at the meetings. I mean a) he can't physically be here because of work and b) he can't understand all the terminology up to now. I tell him when I go home, "I had a meeting today and this is what happened".

From another perspective, parents who have been very successful in school can be overwhelmed by their children's difficulties in education. Dorothy went to school under a communist government and academic achievement was very important to her throughout her life:

I learned all my life – maybe I have a special situation, because I learned all my life, I was very good in school. My husband learned, and both me and my husband, we have university degrees and specializations. And it's very hard as a parent when you are told your kid has a learning disability and you don't know if he will be able to learn or what (will happen) with his future.

Both parents and teachers see homework help as a key responsibility for parents in supporting the instructional practices of the teacher at home. This role, however, is not a simple one. Parents sometimes are frustrated by their own children, in the same ways that teachers are frustrated by them. The tensions created at home around homework can lead some parents to conclude that problems with homework are caused by the attitude of their children. Other parents conclude that teachers do not provide enough information or clear enough instructions to parents to help their children. On the other hand, often parents spend many hours each week collecting resources and helping their children with their homework. This process happens within the context of the busy lives of families where each individual has their own responsibilities, activities and goals.

WORKING TOGETHER THROUGH INDIVIDUAL, SITUATIONAL, AND SOCIO-POLITICAL BARRIERS

Collaboration amongst teachers and support staff, and between teachers and parents is thought to have several positive outcomes. Claims about the positive impact of collaborative practice include improved academic achievement; fewer referrals to special education programs; improved job satisfaction and professional development for teachers; and improved satisfaction with school programs for parents; as well as an equalizing effect for achievement amongst different social groups (Evans, Lunt, Wedell, & Dyson, 2000; MacArthur, 2004; Thousand, Villa, & Nevin, 2006; Walther-Thomas, Korinek, McLaughlin, & Williams, 2000). However, in listening to teachers and parents, not all types of collaboration are created equal. For one thing, there is often a power imbalance where parent knowledge is regarded as less valuable than teacher knowledge. Teacher knowledge is similarly considered superior to parent knowledge but less valuable than the knowledge of Itinerant support teachers. These values are reinforced through the amount of time and resources that are allocated to hearing the voices of teachers and parents. The system favours some types of knowledge over others.

The power imbalance leads to considerations of democracy in education or who gets the power to make decisions in the education context (Nilholm, 2006). This question is central to understanding why it is important to establish the theoretical differences between the Individual, Situational, and socio-Political beliefs. The identification of different positions can allow policy makers, teachers, parents and other power brokers in education to make democratic choices about how we educate our children. At the moment, Ontario education policy mandates that parents be consulted in the education process but there is no mechanism for the findings from the consultation to be implemented. Consultation is interpreted in many schools to mean that teachers must inform parents of the program plan, while in fact parents have important information that could help teachers. Additionally, while parents and teachers alike are calling for better resources in classrooms, these resources usually take the form of more Education Assistants and more time with Itinerant support workers. However, these resources do not always improve the instructional climate for students. In addition, collaboration alone does not create an inclusive environment. For example, school staff can collaborate to have a student excluded from the school, or parents can collaborate in order to promote special education programs, as has happened with some parent advocacy groups in Ontario. Collaboration, like all other school practices is informed by the belief systems held by the individuals in the collaborative relationship.

The belief profile for Dana yielded a score of 0.42 (Individual), 5.01 (Situational), and 0.54 (socio-Political). The Situational score in this profile is one of the highest across all interviews.

Dana is Robert's stepmother. She moved in with Robert's father when Robert was a baby. At the time of the interview Robert was in grade eight. Dana's focus throughout the interview is almost entirely on her empathy for his circumstances and helping him to have a positive future. She does not emphasize his learning problems but when she talks about them she attributes them to his family circumstances, taking much of the responsibility on herself. Dana also speculates that Robert's December birthday has caused him to develop more slowly than his peers. When Robert entered school, the principal suggested he wait one year, but Dana felt that he needed stimulation as early as possible to help him catch up to his peers. Dana clearly feels a close bond with Robert, indicating that even when others could not understand him she could:

> When he was about a year old, his speech wasn't very good … he'd make a noise and, (makes a grunting noise), point. And … whenever he'd talk, you didn't really understand him, but I knew what he wanted. Like a mother, you know. He was having a hard time communicating, and I knew.

Dana's goals for Robert are both academic and social, again focusing on the causes of his difficulties located in his social interactions, including peers and teachers. In contrast to Katie's Individual beliefs, Dana sees Robert's potential as being contingent on these social interactions:

> Well I don't want him centred, because then the kids could be cruel. I want him to be with his friends, learn what they're learning, but at his own pace. And have someone that … could teach him that. And … not feel frustrated … if he's got to go slow, that's fine too! And by the end of the year, he'll be caught up too! I know they're doing what they can, but … everyone's human.

Like Katie, Dana has experienced frustration at her son's short attention span, particularly while trying to provide support at home. However, when Robert is unable to concentrate she views this as a shortcoming in herself rather than in her son:

> We did everything we were capable of … renting all these movies, and getting books for him, and … his attention span was very short. He'd sit, (his father) would read him a book, within two minutes he'd be gone, playing something else or doing whatever. And … that's frustrating, when you're trying to help him and he just … didn't want it. So … that's what … *our problem* was (emphasis added).

In working with the school, again Dana's Situational beliefs are evident. She uses the IEP as a tool to understand what interventions are in place, but is also very committed to her own role in her children's education. With regard to the IEP, Dana says:

> Well, I like them (the IEPs) because they tell you what your kid's doing, and what they're going to focus on. What their strength is, what their weakness (is), and what's their next move. And it tells me what they're thinking. And then if I have any comments, I'll put the comments down, or I'll come in here and I'll say, "Okay, what's our next move?" You know. I'm not afraid to come in, and they know me. If I have a problem, I'm here, and I'm very dedicated to my children.

Dana is happy to have any information about her son. She sees this as part of her responsibilities as a parent. Also like Katie, Dana must attend many meetings at the school to discuss her son's difficulties. In order to be available, Dana quit school and work and the family now lives on one income generated by her husband. She does not report this with any regret but she sees it as her responsibility as part of a family:

> Meetings ... they'll phone me if they need me here. Well, I'm here within two minutes. I'm dependable so it's not a problem. (…) If there's a problem, well we deal with it. And that's how I've learned to deal with it now. Lay it on the table, let's go ... you know, talk to me! Let me know what my kid's doing, because I'm not here. And they're the ones that can tell me what my kid's doing. But I'm not worried because I know they're (the teachers) doing their job. You know they're doing an exceptional job for what they're given.

With regard to formal assessment, a physician tested Robert before school age and Dana was told that he was "delayed". When asked what she hoped to gain from the assessment, Dana says, "To find out what our next move would be. What would be the best route *for him* in getting him necessary help". The focus here is on what other people can do, a Situational belief, in contrast to an Individual belief that assessments will confirm the deficit. Dana also uses the IEP to understand what teachers are doing in Robert's classrooms and to monitor his program. She also looks to the school for strategies she can implement at home. Dana, unlike some parents, reads the IEP thoroughly. When asked about what changes could be made at the school to better support Robert's needs, Dana focuses on Robert's social integration. In many of the interviews, this question generated socio-Political belief responses because it focuses on policy reform. Dana, in contrast, continued to focus on the direct interactions with Robert, and how the people who see him everyday could support him, generating a predominantly Situational belief response with an element of the socio-Political:

> (Interviewer: If money was no object, is there any program for Robert ... what would be on your wish list?) (Dana sighs) ... well ... the one thing maybe, because he likes to be with his teachers, you know, have more help. And setting more programs, like after school programs or something for him to just be part of ... but they used to have that, but then the funding (ran out).

Throughout the interview, Dana focuses on Robert's potential. Ultimately, Dana's focus never waivers from trying to find the supports for Robert to be independent. Dana's hopes for Robert capture the aspirations that any parent can relate to for their children:

> I want him to be somebody. And I want him to have a family, and be proud ... and have a job, and go to work, and have a family, and ... meet your old grandma. You know, I just want him to ... how do you say, be ... you know, oh ... (Interviewer: The best he can be.) "I'm me", "I can do this". (Interviewer: Proud of himself the way you're proud of him.) Oh ... I'm tickled. (Laughs)

CHAPTER 6

Outcomes, Achievement and Accountability

Amartya Sen, the Nobel Prize winning economist, has articulated the relationship between education for individuals and benefits for societies. Sen's central thesis is that opportunities are inter-related:

> [There is a] remarkable empirical connection that links freedoms of different kinds with one another. Political freedoms (in the form of free speech and elections) help to promote economic security. Social opportunities (in the form of education and health facilities) facilitate opportunities for participation in trade and production. Economic facilities (in the form of opportunities for participation in trade and production) can help to generate personal abundance as well as public resources for social facilities. Freedoms of different kinds can strengthen one another. (Sen, 1999, p. 11)

According to Sen, education gives social opportunities to individuals. I believe that education permeates not only social opportunities but also provides the means (through literacy, numeracy and analytical skills) to attain political and economic opportunities. Thus the outcomes of education are of the utmost importance for the integration of individuals in democratic society. Further, these outcomes are reflected in public attitudes toward the desired outcomes of education systems in Ontario. In a provincial public survey, respondents indicated that the first priorities for the Ontario education system should be preparing youth for work (20%), preparing youth to make ethical and moral judgments (19%), and preparing youth for their responsibilities as citizens (16%) (Livingstone, Hart, & Davie, 2002). For individuals with disabilities, these educational outcomes may be particularly important as there is some evidence that education can have a mitigating influence on the social disadvantages long associated with disablement in society (Underwood, 2007).

It is, however, rare that personal freedom or engaged citizenship is measured as the mark of individual attainment in school or as an outcome of school systems. Through several of the earlier chapters I have briefly described some of the target outcomes for teachers and parents. For example, the desired outcome of instruction is learning, one desired outcome of collaboration is improved instruction, and the desired outcome of early intervention is remediation of learning difficulties. Outcomes, achievement and accountability are strong forces in the current education climate in Ontario (McGlaughlin & Jordan, 2005) and indeed around the world (Apple, 2001). International standards in education are closely aligned with goals for competitiveness in global markets. Governments are increasingly being pressured to provide accountability to voters through public policy. In Ontario, one of the ways that educational accountability has been addressed politically is through the establishment of the Education Equality and Accountability Office (EQAO). The primary purpose of this office is to conduct and analyse province wide standardized tests. When EQAO testing began in the mid 1990s, most students with disabilities were excluded from taking the tests, thereby maintaining the "validity" of the findings. Interestingly, a study in the United States indicates that there was no statistically significant difference in validity of state-wide assessments when accommodations were made for some students with learning difficulties (Karkee, Lewis, Barton, & Haug, 2003). With pressure for equity, EQAO now has guidelines for accommodations in the tests. However, many students are still excluded, including several of the students in my study. There is some question about how equity can be achieved on standardized tests. Exclusion of students from tests can be considered discriminatory because it by-passes the mechanism for accountability for students with disabilities (Browder, Wakeman, & Flowers, 2006). This means that there is no way of knowing if students who have been excluded from the test are getting good quality education. It may also indicate a presumption that students with disabilities will not be contributing members of the economic and social community. On the other hand, inclusion in standardized tests can lead to narrow interpretations of achievement, ability and good teaching (Hall, Collins, Benjamin, Nind, & Sheehy, 2004). That is, if appropriate accommodations are not in place, and the test does not assess relative gains for individual students, it may falsely indicate that the students are not improving. The interpretation of achievement, ability and good teaching are central to understanding the issues that teachers and parents described with regard to educational outcomes. The first part of this chapter addresses teachers and parents perspectives on achievement and assessment of achievement. The second half of the chapter addresses the policy issues that drive the evaluation of achievement.

WHAT COUNTS AS ACHIEVEMENT?

Many of the issues raised in Chapter 3 about identification and diagnosis of disabling conditions are similar to the issues faced by teachers, parents and students in evaluating classroom achievement. All of the students in this study have IEPs . For this reason, the IEP is one of the mechanisms for reporting to parents along with the regular report card. Most of the parents described IEP meetings as the primary time for formal reporting (as opposed to regular parent-teacher meetings at report card times). For this reason, both teachers and parents explain how the report card and the IEP are used to assess students. Harvey explains how the IEP gives him information about achievement for his son Stephen:

> The IEP's not something that we ... I don't know if it's something that we should refer to all the time. We don't. We sit down; we go through what's written there, whether we agree, disagree, you know. We talk about what we plan to do at home. We talk about what types of activities he's going to be doing in his special class, and that's about it. If he gets tests or assessments I

guess it would be at the beginning to see, so you have a benchmark. You know ... he's improved over the six months, or whatever so this is working.

Lock and Wilson (2000) point out that in research that focuses on classroom assessment with an instructional purpose the validity and reliability of the testing methods are not usually reported. This is often portrayed as a problem with classroom assessment. However, these studies do incorporate analysis of the classroom context and knowledge of individual students, which is an important factor for instruction as reported in Chapter 4. While the principles of psychometric assessment are considered to be "best practices" for both identification of disabilities related to learning environments and for general classroom assessment, it seems that there is a conflict between the professional goals of teachers and test makers (Lock & Wilson, 2000). Katz and Earl (2000), using a distinction that reflects the work of Fenstermacher (1994), differentiate between classroom assessment that focuses on the "known" or fact-based knowledge and assessment of the "knower" or evaluating the learner. In the latter, individual goals are defined based on the effort put forth by the student as well as progress that is defined by the student's individual level. Assessment of the "known" on the other hand focuses on norm-based assessment that is consistent with rigid curriculum standards and the expectations of students by age. The latter fits with the norms established through the EQAO testing described above. If achievement is equated with standardized assessment and does not allow for accommodations or assessment, achievement measures do not work for many children. One of the most common assumptions is that accommodations in assessment lower standards of achievement (Rieck & Wadsworth, 2005). Donald, a grade five teacher, has the same expectations for everyone in his class, including Cooper, who has a history of being suspended from school:

> My way is – no matter what happens, no matter what disease – if you have a disease or whatever, because the mother used to play the "Oh my kid has ADHD and my kid has this, my kid (has that)" then they gave me Cooper. Well the thing is it doesn't make any difference. If you say, "I'm a diabetic", when inclusion it still means I have to stop at a red light. So the idea is no matter what happens, you still have to follow the rules of the classroom. And therefore, as far as rewarding, I reward the effort, but I try not to do it too much, because if he gets up to the class level, that's fine, that's where he should be, and I don't want to reward him just for getting to the class level. Maybe I'll let a few things go, less if he's at class level and slips and turns around and turns around very quick and gets back to work. But I won't get on his case, if he's behaving, fine – Cooper pat on the back – sort of deal.

For Cooper, who has had a lot of difficulty interacting with his peers and school staff, behaving at "the class level" is a real challenge. Donald's belief is that regardless of the individual circumstances, he will not give Cooper praise based on his individual achievements, despite the fact that achieving the "class level" would represent a much greater relative gain for Cooper than for other students in the class. However, many teachers I spoke to did view individual achievement as central to fair assessment. Paul's teacher, Vanessa, has spent a lot of time trying to find ways to evaluate Paul on an individual basis:

> They do have portfolios in the classroom that contain their writing and their responses to reading. Whereas for Paul's, his file perhaps isn't as big in the way that...I mean he communicates in different ways ... sometimes it is through the scribing and sometimes it's through ... (for example) they did a play the other day so it's (his portfolio) not as big as probably some of the other ones but there's still probably a writing sample and a reading response for each month.
>
> I would say that he talks at an average grade two level (Paul is in grade two). I've had children on IEPs with extensive vocabulary but it's not that as much as to say that when you want to find out what Paul knows or the connections that he can make, his strongest format is through oral communication and his ability to listen and be perceptive to what is going on in the classroom or to the story, or he'll pick up clues. In fact, he's the one to sit back and quietly observe and you don't think he's paying attention and all of a sudden, his hand's up and he has something to share that's right on topic. He'll occasionally show that too. But his reading and writing is where he struggles immensely and his coping skills through being able to listen and being able to express. He shows such capability and ...orally, through tape recording or through listening to his ideas, he does show great strengths and yet pencil and paper and the normal curriculum bound expectations are very difficult for Paul to achieve.

For many teachers, assessment was an ongoing formative process. This means that the teacher used information she gleaned from in-class activities to adjust her teaching as the student showed gains. Marlene uses this approach with Jacqueline:

> Gradually, over the first month or two, I found myself seeing how she behaved in class, talking with the mum, saying, "I'm looking at doing this with Jacqueline. How she's reacting to it; how comfortable are you with it?" I was ... asking the mum quite a few things, just so I had an idea of what it was like. I talked to the teacher who had taught her the previous year, and she found it was more of a hit and miss. See how this program works, how this works, and go from there.

Several parents indicated they expect teachers to get to know their children and assess the learning levels of each child individually. Sheila says that some teachers don't take her daughter Fatima's individual needs into account:

> The next year I come in to whoever she has as a teacher and I say, "Are you aware she's on an IEP? Have you read her file?" And then go from there. (Interviewer: So you alert the teacher to the fact that she has an IEP.) I did one year have a teacher that wasn't aware of it. They're supposed to read the files. She hadn't had a chance or whatever and that's important.

For many teachers it was as important to reward student effort as it was to reward measurable skills. This is because effort indicated that students were building good study habits and because teachers wanted to encourage students. This is consistent with evaluating the "knower" as well as the "known". Marlene described this approach, which differs from teachers who do not assign grades when a student is working on modified curriculum goals:

But the thing is I feel that's not fair to a parent (to see report cards with no marks). The child puts a lot of effort into their work in the classroom, they need to know. I mean, another child might put little effort into the work, working at the grade one, but sits there and goes, "I don't care". They're in grade three but aren't putting in any effort. Whereas I know Jacqueline's putting the effort in and that she deserves to see that she's getting a B in her things; and feels good about it. So I – we don't know how this fits. We're not sure, but I put this on (graded report card modified for the grade level at which she is working) for the parents' sake. And the mum was surprised because when talking to the others, she said, they all received report cards with no marks, and she said, "Well, Jacqueline got marks. Jacqueline gets the IEP and she gets a report card". And they were shocked at ... what she's getting.

Students' grades are dependant on whether grades are reported for work at grade level or for a modified grade level. This can be very confusing for students and parents. Sheila explains how important it is for teachers to clarify how their children are being graded. Nathan told Sheila that he was going to move her daughter from a modified program (at a lower grade level) up to a program at grade level with accommodations (supports):

"If I give Fatima the grade eight work and accommodate her and if her marks are Cs instead of Bs ... they're going to fall because it's harder. She has to realize that and you have to realize that", Nathan said to me. (Interviewer: How did you feel about that?) I was okay with it probably because he called me in and explained it all. Because if he had just gone ahead and done it, then I would have gotten her report card and gone, "Oh my god, what's happening?" Those marks do mean something.

Parents sometimes use the reporting process to influence instructional practices of teachers. Diane describes how she uses the IEP to influence the way in which her son Nigel's teacher, Marilyn, accommodates him:

I follow [the IEP] to the letter. And I've submitted this. I'll go over the IEP five or six times, rewrite stuff, change stuff. They don't have to accept it but at least here they've been fairly good about accommodating my petty needs. (Interviewer: What kind of stuff do you scribble about?) Sometimes it's the terminology they use, sometimes it's they haven't recognized the need in a manner that I feel is appropriate for Nigel.

Beverly similarly expects her daughter, Catherine, to be evaluated based on her individual abilities. Beverly described how she uses the IEP to inform Catherine's teacher, Dennis, about what she considers to be appropriate accommodations:

> I gave it (the IEP with revisions) to Dennis and I got something back that was pretty much the same as before. And when I look at it I see things like, "Catherine will be able to develop strategies for entering a group situation in a positive manner", which means that she needs to be able to learn the social skill of how to *join* a group of students who are doing something, because she doesn't know how to do that. And the strategies and resources are "Set clear and consistent expectations". What are they? What are the expectations? I just said, "If they're set, what are the expectations". It's important to know what they are so that you can implement them. If they aren't written down, they're going to think the expectations are one thing one day and then tomorrow they'll be in a different mood and think the expectations are something else. Verbal and non-verbal reminders in other places it tends to say, "Verbal and non-verbal cues". Well she doesn't understand non-verbal and verbal cues very well, so what are the cues going to be. How do they know she's going to understand them?

Amanda also would like to see individual goals on her son Alexander's IEP. Amanda expresses the emotional impact it has on her when Alexander's effort and relative achievement are not reported:

> It doesn't seem to be they're changing it (the IEP) very much but … from what I'm reading, what I'm understanding, I'm not sure if it's because I'm the mum, and … I would like to see *more*, but I feel that there should be more in his IEP, from year to year. He's improved so much … I'll sit there in a meeting and talk about, forty-five minutes, about Alexander and the improvements that he's made, because somebody has to. (Interviewer: Do you see that come out in the IEP after you sit in the meeting and say that?) Not really.

Celia, the mother of twins Isabel and Dylan says, the IEP is helpful because "I need it in black and white this way so I can use [the IEP] as a back up from this paper to the previous one to the previous one to see what the changes are. So yes, I find them very informative".

In the interviews that I conducted, it was fairly common for teachers and parents to have a different understanding of achievement. Melinda, Robert's grade six teacher, describes how Robert's mother reacted to the fact that Robert's older brother has been placed in a stream that will not lead to him getting a high school diploma:

> I don't think that the IEP has really been looked at in depth by the mum. She was surprised. She has another son who has some difficulties too. He's a bit higher level than Robert, but he's still very low. And he's not working for credit. He's working on the certificate program at the high school. So he's not working for credits; he's not going to come out with a diploma; he'll have a certificate. Well, she was surprised. Well he's been working with EAs on a completely different program doing grade four level things last year. So she

hasn't really read the IEP. We've gone through it with her at the team meeting when it was developed; she signed it. But I don't think it's been explained to her in simple terms. I know it's important not to go on about … using all these big words and talking about educational jargon that she doesn't understand. It's been explained in simple terms, I just don't think she really understands … how needy he is. You know, how serious his difficulties are.

Some teachers are attuned to the importance of meaningful reporting not only for the benefit of parents, but also in order to teach well. Barry emphasizes using meaningful tracking rather than simply a system which is easy to use, such as computer pull-down menus designed to speed up the time it takes to develop an IEP or report card:

What it (the computer program for the IEP) probably serves that way of thinking (simplifying the process), certainly filing and reporting and so on. I think also the same with general reporting; once you're on to it it's a faster system. This is an easy thing; it's just that the meaning has to be questioned of the whole report. I can now do classroom reports far more quickly than I did when I was writing anecdotal records all long hand and each one individualized. It's much easier to click, click, click but they're certainly less meaningful. (Interviewer: Do you still keep anecdotal notes?) For myself, yes, they're right there.

Teachers who took the time to learn about their students and used this information to create individualized goals for students held Situational beliefs. However, some teachers see individual characteristics as limiting in terms of goals. This is coded as holding Individual beliefs, particularly where the student's individual ability is blamed for their lack of progress on the standardized curriculum. Carla has this view for her student Naima:

I think for kids like Naima who … it sounds awful and I don't mean to put limitations on her … but chances are she's going to need to know the basic computation skills rather than all the abstract for her life skills … But at the same time we need to meet certain requirements from the government that aren't necessary for Naima or that I don't feel are necessary at this time for Naima. (Interviewer: You're saying inappropriate for her learning.) Yes, in terms of saying that yes, we have covered measurement. I mean we're required to cover a certain amount …

Individual beliefs are also associated with teachers who avoid responsibility for reporting. Jason indicates that his role in communicating with Marcus's mother is strictly about administrative activities, and he leaves reporting of instructional assessment up to the Education Assistants:

They say it's too bad poor Marcus has three mothers, right? He's got the two EAs and his own mother, and they're all writing back and forth about things. And sometimes if there's a message that is pertinent to me, like a scholastic book order or a class trip, and the EAs don't know how to respond to it, they'll bring up the communication book and show it to me and say, you know, "Hellen's (Marcus's mother) wondering about this".

Jennifer's interview indicated that she had very high Individual beliefs. However, Situational beliefs were indicated when she describes how she might learn more from Neil's parents through the process of reporting to Neil's parents. Although it is late in the school year, Jennifer has only been teaching the class for a few months, because she was hired to cover a teacher on leave:

> The report cards are going out end of next week before Easter break. So it's up to me to schedule appointments with parents that I think I should talk with about whatever issues. It's not mandatory but it's up to me to decide who to talk with. (Interviewer: Do you think you will meet with Neil's parents?) Yes, I think I'd like to get to know more. That I should know about him. (Interviewer: Do you think that they can provide you with some information?) Yes, just more support ... I just need to know more about Neil. I don't know him very well.

It is also possible for teachers to allow students to contribute to their record of achievement. Marlene includes comments from both Jacqueline and her mother in the anecdotal records that are kept in Jacqueline's file:

> The behaviour logs are part of the IEP, but what we do is we have them written up, and they're kept in a folder, and then we send them on for the ISA claim. Now, I don't send the behaviour logs home to the parents. I talk to the mum about some of the situations, but ... we feel, I guess because it being a small school, I'm not sure in a larger school if there's no interaction with the parent, you might need to. But if there's a real situation that I feel the parent needs to know, often what I do is Jacqueline will sit down and fill out a little conflict resolution paper. Just putting her little information, then I will add to it, and the parents will sign it and send it back.

While many teachers and parents see collaboration as an important part of assessing student achievement, not all parents agree. Susan does not think that parents should be consulted when teachers decide if their children should be evaluated based on modified or accommodated standards. Susan's Individual beliefs are apparent:

> But say I never went along with the IEP. They can't put her on an IEP unless a parent goes along with it. I don't agree with that. If say, I didn't want to go along with the IEP, I think the school has the right to say, "Okay, the mother doesn't understand if a child needs this". Do you understand what I'm saying? A lot of the mothers don't want their kid to lose self-esteem. Because if they fail them, it's going to hurt their self-esteem.

Many teachers see the assessment as a way to inform their teaching practice and they use the process of reporting achievement to parents as a way to communicate with parents and students. Teachers who engage in this type of "formative assessment" have practices associated with Situational beliefs. Parents who hold Situational beliefs are also likely to support teachers who get to know students individually and who evaluate relative gains and effort for each student. Teachers who hold Individual beliefs, however, are more likely to evaluate students based on standard levels of achievement for the class or for the grade level. These teachers do not give students credit for relative gains and they see accommodations in evaluation as diminishing the standards. So these teachers are likely to view accommodations such as giving additional time, as unfair (Rieck & Wadsworth, 2005). It is only unfair if test accommodation alters the goal of the test, i.e., changes the content of skill proficiency required. If the test accommodation does alter the goal of the test, the test becomes unfair to the students who will not be able to accurately demonstrate their skills. Other test accommodations that may be used include using a scribe to write answers for the student, orally reading or giving the test on tape, alternate forms of presenting, and changing the setting of the test to name just a few (Hutchinson, 2007; Rieck & Wadsworth, 2005).

Some parents also hold Individual beliefs about assessment and they feel that the educational standard should not be adapted for their children. There are also significant systemic factors to consider in relation to assessment. The next section examines the policies that govern assessment.

GRADING FOR DOLLARS AND OTHER POLICY ISSUES

Teachers use informal mechanisms to evaluate their students, as described above, but their evaluation of students is also governed by two formal processes. These are the Ontario Report Card and the IEP. The IEP, while technically a document that guides instructional practice, was described by both teachers and parents as a mechanism for reporting. In many cases it was considered to be more relevant in determining student achievement than the report card. Confusion about the difference between IEPs and report cards was pervasive. The IEP as a mechanism for evaluating student achievement had many problems as described by teachers and parents. Tim describes his own confusion about what he is supposed to be putting in the IEP:

> I always get confused ... I've only been teaching for four years now and in my first year of teaching I had three IEPs (referring to students with IEPs) in my class because there were more IEPs around then. I had to try and write them and work through them and no one was really sure what we were supposed to be doing: if we were supposed to be modifying the grade level expectations or if we were supposed to be looking at different grade expectations. So I'm still confused about that.

Parents were also unclear about the distinction between report cards and IEPs. In one case, the parents did not even know that the IEP was specific to their child. In fact Lana learned about the IEP through the interview:

They came up with the idea (of putting her daughter in a resource support program run by the Special Education Teacher in the Resource Support Room). I just thought it was a program that came into the school to see where kids were at. It could have been anyone; it could have been any child who was picked at random. (Interviewer: Well it's an IEP. It's a program specially designed for your daughter by the school and with the parent if the parent wishes to be involved. And so it's very specific to your own child's needs and it's not random.) No one's ever said, "This means this and this means that". (Interviewer: Did you have an initial meeting around the IEP?) No.

Tim is more likely to use the report card as a mechanism for reporting although he acknowledges that the IEP and report are sent home together. Tim describes the difference in how he uses the report card and the IEP to inform his teaching:

I know we send the IEP home with the report card so the parents can see both and peruse both, but I'm certainly not pulling out the IEP on a daily basis and referring to it. I'm dealing with Ryan in class. So that's one of the fallbacks or the weaknesses of the IEP because I don't refer to the IEP when I'm doing the report card. I report on what I see Ryan doing in class. (Interviewer: So it's not relevant there.) Yes. As an overall discussion of Ryan's academic abilities, I think it's relevant. It does a good job in summing it up. It's great at the beginning of the year in September, pulling out the OSR (Ontario School Record) and see what was going on last year but as far as pulling it out daily I'm looking at Ryan in class and ... can he do this? No. So I've got to try something different.

Tim's approach is by no means universal. For students who are in Special Education classes, the Ontario Curriculum is not necessarily used. Lisa explained that she uses the IEP as the curriculum in her special education class:

(Interviewer: Now when it comes to actually implementing the IEP, how do you use what you've written in this document to help you in the classroom?) In the class? I do use it in my planning, so what I'll try and do is, just let me think. This would be the first term reading goals. It's hard because it's so broad. They're at such at such an early level. It's not specific, like it is more so in the math. I'll actually use that as my planning for the term. So I'll go through and say, "Okay, these are the goals that I had set for Jae-Lynne. All right, well let's start here, and this month we'll do money, and this month we'll do time, and see where she's at". And with the reading and the writing it's more of an overview. Although sometimes one term I might pick to do character study and one term I might pick to focus on setting, just to break it up for them. (Interviewer: So you use the IEP as a guide? To keep you on track?) As their curriculum, yes, more so than the curriculum, yes.

One of the difficulties with the IEP, as described by many of the people I interviewed including principals and resource teachers, is that the IEP is used as an assessment of student needs in order to allocate funding (the ISA claim) in addition to its purpose as an explanation of instructional practice. The different purposes of the IEP create a conflict between instruction and policy. In Lisa's school, it is common for teachers to write up two separate IEPs, one for instruction and one for submission to get funding:

(Interviewer: Oh, so there are two IEPs for her?) Yes. This would be the one that I wrote that was totally from me that I would use for planning during the year. But the one that they would see would have a lot more of those life skills things on the behavioural (Interviewer: And is it painting her in a more negative light?) Definitely, yes. Which is the one thing you have a problem with. Because you think you see the progress that they've made, and then you get to this meeting at the end of the year where they bring them back to where they were at the beginning, and you're thinking, "Oh..." (Interviewer: Yes, they're penalized for their progress. Now how was that conveyed to the parents? Did they know that there are two IEPs?) Oh, no. They wouldn't even see that other one. They would have no idea. (Interviewer: So they just know that this one exists.) Yes, and that's the one that goes home and gets updated and that's the one they see. (Interviewer: And do they know about the link between the IEP and the ISA claim?) I don't think it's very well laid out, because they come to the IPRC and they get the label, MID. I send this one home throughout the year as I update it. But they might find out if they got ISA funding with an Ed Assistant the following year when it happens. But I wouldn't even say most of them know (Interviewer: And how many kids with ISA claims have you got in those twelve?) Well, as of September, I had none because eight out of twelve of my class weren't formally identified. But two of them they looked at. And ironically it was the two kids, her and her brother (referring to Jae-Lynne and her brother who was not a participant in the study).

Similarly, Dennis says it is difficult to be honest in the IEP because of the link between assessment of achievement and allocation of funding:

Maybe you need something in writing to make sure that this child is being worked with. Yes, accountable ... which isn't even accountable, but I mean, that word "accountable" is kind of tricky. I'm *afraid* of where that's going is what accountable means. (Interviewer: Yes. That's been the big buzzword with the IEPs to some extent, and in other education initiatives accountability is a concern.) But obviously then teachers are just going to make them as *vague* as possible. Because if you're talking about how this child is, well, this child could go up a reading level, you're not going to put something like that. You're going to put something so vague that if the kid slips, which might happen ... *that's always the problem, too, is kids are always progressing in the school system* [emphasis added].

Jason explains that if the IEP were not negative the effect would be the loss of resources to support the Education Assistant (EA):

We write the document (the IEP) because it's necessary to get support ... through the ISA. (Interviewer: Right, and even that's a bit of a fudge.) And

127

that's a fudge, because probably if we were *completely* honest, we might not get EA support with him.

Barry explains how the link between assessment and resources can lead to an inaccurate assessment of student achievement:

Because of the difficulty getting the funding and the stringent requirements in order to get that, which I think are too stringent, you have to keep justifying. Maintaining that service doesn't lend itself to truth, quite frankly, because you'll be penalized as a result of showing an improvement, and even though in Rory's case with medication being adjusted, you could lose the SNA (Special Needs Assistant), have something altered that could affect it, and then have to go through the process again to re-enact it. It doesn't lend itself to truth. (Interviewer: So this is a pretty useless document (the IEP). I think so. (Interviewer: So when you go around to assess Rory in his accomplishments, especially in terms of behaviour, do you feel then that you can have an accurate voice?) Not entirely, no. And all the parties involved, we're all in this conspiracy together.

Aside from the relationship between assessment and funding for resources, there is confusion about the relationship between IEPs and report cards. Much of this confusion comes from a lack of consensus about how to report grades for student achievement on material that has been modified for the student. Leslie explains why she thinks parents are more likely to read the report card than the IEP:

I haven't spoken to the parents about these (the IEPs) but I've never had a parent come to me and say, "Can you explain this to me", like they do with the report cards. So I'm thinking that parents aren't putting a lot of weight on this, most of them. They're just looking at it and saying, "Okay, that's nice". And you have all these things here, assessments … I mean it's saying sixteenth percentile, forty-second percentile … well if I was a parent looking at this and my child came home I might think they're getting 5% and 16%. It might be very confusing for them I would say.

Several teachers disliked the current reporting process, or simply found the relationship between the IEP and the report card confusing. Barry finds the report card unclear:

(Interviewer: How have you found the [computer] program, [for the report card]?) Very complex and difficult to work through. I also … understand the whole accountability thing, and this applies to the report card as well, the whole impersonality to it; the whole lack of voice to it. My voice or even the child's voice in the new report system I find very annoying and cumbersome. And I don't find it as meaningful to parents as the more personal way was. They generalize … Click on phrases I find very impersonal and annoying.

Jason explains that there can be two types of report cards and that even the report card can be used to determine funding levels:

Well I know when I did write the first term report card it wasn't clear whether or not, first of all, he was to be receiving an anecdotal report card, or whether or not he was to receive a Ministry Report Card. It was decided that he was to receive a Ministry Report Card. Then when I wrote the Ministry Report Card I was cautioned that I should be, more or less, negative in everything I said. Not to talk about what he can do, but to talk about what he can't do. And very much stress that everything is with assistance, and to give him, 40s and 50s for everything. Otherwise the Ministry might read the report card and think, "Wow, look, with some assistance. Well if he only needs some assistance then I guess we don't need an EA"; that kind of thing. So it was very much from a deficit model, when I was writing the report card.

According to the communication from the Ministry of Education, the report card should not be linked to funding. However, there is consistent confusion about the relationship between assessing students' classroom achievements and the funding that will be allocated to support students. Marlene was also told to be sure to make the report card and the IEP appropriate for a funding claim:

Rather than on a report card, we did *this* (put comments on the IEP), besides the report card. When (the program support teacher) went to the meeting, the person at the meeting said, "No, you don't need to put the comment for that term on the report card itself or on the IEP. You just put it on the report card". However, our principal is saying, "If we want *this* to draw up the ISA claim, we *should* have the comment in the evaluation box". However, the board, or whoever, at the meeting, was saying to (the program support teacher), "No, they're not looking at assessment evaluation. They're looking to see observation quizzes, how you assess ... but not what the actual evaluation is". They want to see what the expectations and teaching strategies are, on the IEP. So ... when (the program support teacher) called the head of program support for her board, *they* couldn't even give a definitive answer at the end of the first term.

Since the time of the interviews, provincial education funding for special education has been changed as a reaction to the problems described above. However, it is my belief that the problems have not been solved because there is still a link between assessment and funding. The system in place at the time of the interviews was often described by critics as "diagnosing for dollars", but it was much more than that. Diagnosis of a disability was not enough for a student to get funding; teachers also had to document the ongoing deficits of students and lack of progress. The result was "grading for dollars". Every grade or assessment of achievement was linked to the resources needed to provide appropriate accommodations for students.

Both the Ontario Report Card and the IEP are described by teachers and parents as inadequate to present the achievements of individual students. The inadequacy stems in part from the use of drop-down computer menus to select comments. The most common complaint about classroom assessment, however, was the systemic issue of tying funding to individual student achievement. The funding policy was clearly driving the reporting of achievement, despite the fact that the policy was not intended to work in this way. I think it is possible to trace some of the difficulty back to the early identification, early intervention practices described in Chapters 3 and 4. While the practice of "intervening" does help many students to overcome learning difficulties, an inappropriate message is delivered from this policy. The message is first, that a formal process of identification is necessary in order to "intervene". And second, that "intervention" is a specialist practice rather than just good teaching. Identification is always about finding those students who do not fit the norm, either who are on the low end or the high end of the learning spectrum. The result is that "kids progressing in the school system" who have been identified become a problem.

ACHIEVEMENT, ACOUNTABILITY AND INDIVIDUAL, SITUATIONAL AND SOCIO-POLITICAL BARRIERS

There are several purposes for evaluating student achievement. One of these purposes is to rank students or to assess their abilities based on the standards established for their grade. This purpose is supported by the Ontario curriculum, which establishes the norms, and is reinforced by the standardized EQAO testing that is conducted across the province to assess the effectiveness of the school system. Teachers and parents also reinforce evaluation of student achievement based on norms of the curriculum when they judge student achievement in comparison with student peers, rather than in relation to the relative gains a student makes as compared to their own earlier level of knowledge and skill. This approach is associated with Individual beliefs about barriers to learning. In addition, teachers and parents with Individual beliefs will sometimes view accommodations or modifications as an invalid evaluation of student ability. One of the problems with this approach is that the criteria for evaluation and the mechanism for evaluating student achievement lack flexibility and therefore do not allow for individual achievement levels.

Another purpose of grading and assessing achievement is instructional. This purpose allows teachers to assess what students know and what they do not know, what they are able to do and what they are not able to do, in order to align instruction with the individual needs of each student. This instructional practice can be supported by information from parents about how they understand their children's abilities based on their own observations at home. Assessment practices that support instructional goals are associated with Situational beliefs.

Finally, there is an administrative purpose for evaluating student achievement. This is evident in the use of individual student assessments to determine funding levels and allocate resources. Teachers and parents who described the administrative purposes of student evaluation held socio-Political beliefs. The result in Ontario is that the problem becomes "kids progressing in the school system".

Dennis's interview profile was scored as follows: 1.05 (Individual), 1.11 (Situational), and 3.83 (socio-Political). This was the highest socio-Political score for all teachers in the sample.

Dennis has been teaching for twenty-six years, thirteen of which he taught special education. Some of his special education teaching experience was in a self-contained class. He has taught all grades between kindergarten and grade six. At the time of the interview Dennis was team-teaching a grade five class with thirty-two students, three of whom had IEPs as well as being formally identified through IPRCs. The other teacher in the class was a special education teacher and all of the students who had IPRCs in the class were designated as having a behavioural exceptionality. The special education teacher in the class had primary responsibility for Catherine's IEP. The class was known as the behavioural-integrated class. Dennis referred to this as an inclusive placement in contrast to the self-contained classes he taught in the past. Catherine, who has been recently diagnosed with Asperger's syndrome, was new to the program in the school year in which the interview was conducted.

Dennis's dominant socio-Political belief score comes from his focus on the public policy issues which he sees as the biggest barrier to students like Catherine. Dennis gives an example of inclusive education policy breaking down barriers for a student:

> One of the reasons I stopped teaching behavioural is one of the worst children I had, my last year in self-contained, went upstairs to a *regular* classroom ... and every afternoon would be great upstairs, it would be terrible with me in the morning. And that blew my mind as to why is this kid ... terrible with just eight of them and two adults, and great when he's alone with thirty kids and a teacher. So ... it's the programs.

He has seen this same problem with Catherine, who came from a special education class the previous year. Dennis describes Catherine:

> I'm the regular teacher in the class. Catherine came to this school at the beginning of grade four, and she was described at the time as a difficult child. One of the most difficult children that ... and she was in a self-contained special ed classroom for behavioural students. So we were expecting a child that needed an enormous amount of room, space, guidance, discipline. *"We've had a lot of difficulty", "quite possibly might attack other children"; "bites other children".* That's what we were prepared for. As a matter of fact, we found this out in June, even though, as a behavioural teacher you can't believe what you hear. So over the summer I was wondering who this child was going to be. None of that stuff presented itself. And, yes, we were really on guard. We walked with her everywhere. We were prepared to ... hold her hand a lot. And I think what happened was she had been in a Special Ed program for so long that, she had somewhat been institutionalized in the

sense that she wasn't given freedom. Her strengths weren't nurtured as much as her difficulties were kind of squelched.

Although he is very focused on policy issues, Dennis does hold some Individual and Situational beliefs. His Individual beliefs are not presented when describing Catherine, but Dennis does say that some students will not progress regardless of the program:

> Let's face it, some kids don't progress. They stay the same forever (…). That makes it look like we take this piece of mud or coal, at the end they could be a diamond, but sometimes they aren't.

Dennis's Situational beliefs are apparent when he describes his own role in understanding Catherine as an individual:

> You know, I don't know how I deal with her. We play it by ear. Sometimes we're kind of curt. Sometimes we try and talk with her. A lot of times we just talk to get a sense of who she is. It's good to know how she sees the world. So we talk with her as much as we can, just to understand her mind better to help her help us.

Dennis's socio-Political beliefs are most apparent in his discussion of the IEP. Although Dennis is not responsible for writing Catherine's IEP, he is clearly involved in her program and gives input on Catherine's IEP. The formal responsibility for Catherine's program lies with the Behaviour teacher with whom Dennis team-teaches. In discussing IEPs in general, Dennis articulates the problems with Individual beliefs:

> This is not a scientific process. And the problem with the IEP, I think, is it supposes that this is a kind of western science. You know, that here's the problem: we're going to fix it. We're going to lay out all the things and then we're going to work on those things and then, three months later we'll check 'em off. It'll be okay. And it's just … much more … rich. Children's personalities are much more rich than that. They cannot be compartmentalized in that way.

Unlike Tim, the teacher with a dominant Situational profile, Dennis does not view the IEP as a means of understanding the student's individual needs:

> Once you know it (the student's needs) too, well, I don't want to say what's the point in writing it up, but I mean in some ways what's the point of writing it up? It's never really used, I don't think. I think it becomes, kind of, stored.

Finally, still talking about IEPs, Dennis articulates his view of the main socio-Political barrier created in IEP policy:

> You would often tailor what you had to write. That's the way it finally goes. I guess that's one of the things about it … in order to get funding, children need labels. That's just the way it is. So … you want to label, because that's the way the system works. So if the kid doesn't have a label, you make up a

label so that kid can get money. Because you know the kid needs help. So, I guess that's good but it's so sad. I don't know if that'll ever change.

Dennis's Individual beliefs are evident in his description of students who he believes will never succeed in school. However, in describing Catherine, Dennis is able to articulate significant socio-Political barriers that come from labelling students for funding, and segregating students in special education classes.

CHAPTER 7

"I Just Want Him to be Happy"

The Social Climate of the Classroom

The issues presented in the preceding chapters evoked strong opinions from teachers and parents, but none more than the issue of social relationships in the classroom. The social dimensions of school and classrooms are often described as the most important for parents who just want to see their children happy. The social dimension of the classroom is also a barometer for the inclusivity of the classroom. When children are identified as having a disability and are in regular classrooms, they are not necessarily being included, unless they also feel welcome and part of the group (Hutchinson, 2007). This subjective feeling is also affected by the many other social undercurrents in the classroom and in society including class division, racialization, issues of sexual orientation and gender, and the many complex experiences that make up the social identity of human beings. Certainly the many social divisions of society are reinforced in the identification of disabilities in schools. Students from economic, ethnic and cultural minority groups have been found to be over-represented in special education programs (Harry & Klingner, 2006; Hosp & Reschly, 2004; Losen & Orfield, 2002). Researchers have also found that students from ethnic minority families are more likely to be placed in special education programs rather than inclusive programs (Losen & Orfield, 2002).

Several reasons for focusing on social relationships in the classroom are cited in the literature. First, healthy social relationships in the early years are predictive of good social relationships later on (Buysse, Goldman, & Skinner, 2002). That is social relationships are developmental in the same way that literacy skills are developmental. For this reason, some teachers and parents understand social relationships as a component of the curriculum and social development as an important goal in the classroom. Social development and skill are also impacted by academic performance in the classroom. Students' self-esteem is closely linked to their identity in social situations, and teachers and parents repeatedly described how students who were performing academic tasks at a lower level than their peers felt "stupid" and had low self-esteem. Many parents were concerned about the stigma attached to identification of disabilities and to getting extra help. There was inconsistency in how disability status was incorporated into the identity of students as described by their teachers and parents. Some parents described their children as having a disability and others took offence to the term disability. This was an interesting distinction in light of the growing acceptance of disability culture amongst disability groups and in disability studies courses at universities, particularly in the humanities. While the parents in this study who denied the term disability were doing so in order to avoid stigma, it can be argued that this denies the children access to the culture of people with shared experience. This view is particularly prevalent in the deaf community, a unique group because of their distinct language which is a critical component of culture. Furthermore the disability movement in North America is now actively promoting literature, film, and other arts with a disability focus. Embracing disability as an identity can therefore mean inclusion in the disability community. However, some argue that the promotion of disability culture can be undermined by inclusive education if congregation of students with disabilities is discouraged at all costs (Hall, 2002).

Several students were identified as having behaviour problems. For all of these students, their behaviour was affecting their academic achievement. There were concerns about how these students affected other students in their class. In many cases, students identified as having behaviour problems were blamed for bad behaviour of other students. Research suggests that regular classroom teachers find students with behaviour difficulties in their classrooms to be the most challenging students and the most likely to be segregated (Hedeen, Ayres, Meyer, & Waite, 1996; Visser, 2002). This is counter-intuitive if we consider that students with behaviour difficulties are exhibiting difficulty with a social skill. In special education classrooms students have fewer opportunities to interact with other students, and in one study they were found to form fewer friendships in school, but not fewer friendships outside of school (Panacek & Dunlap, 2003). In my study there were eleven students, eight boys and three girls, identified as having behaviour problems. These students were Dwayne, Rory, Cooper, Sherman, Maria, Dylan, Isabel, Dalia, Jawad, Elias and Greg. In addition Owen and Abigail, both identified as having developmental disability were described by their teachers as having serious problem behaviours. Two of these students are black and one is aboriginal, which is consistent with a report by the Ontario Human Rights Commission that some ethnic groups are part of racialized minority groups whose members are more likely to be labelled as having behaviour problems and who are unfairly targeted through zero-tolerance disciplinary policies in Ontario (Bhattacharjee, 2003). In addition, students with disabilities are at greater risk of being punished with suspension or expulsion through zero-tolerance policies. (James & Freeze, 2006)

METHODS OF SUPPORTING SOCIAL DEVELOPMENT

The social climate of the classroom has two important components. The first is the overall classroom climate, and the second is the individual development of positive behaviour in the classroom. The overall classroom climate can be affected by the expectations of the class as a whole. In schools where classes are grouped by ability there can be low expectations for the lowest ability groups, but it can equally affect high ability groups who are left to work independently and without enough guidance (Boaler, William, & Brown, 2005). In order to ensure positive overall classroom climate Doveston and Keenaghan (2006) suggest building a collaborative environment in which all students have some common goals to work toward, ensuring that all students are consulted and given credit for their contributions and ensuring the projects with common goals are inclusive, which they suggest involves projects without writing. Doveston and Keenaghan also suggest that activities with common goals should be active and have a brisk pace, and include time for reflection and positive feedback. These are consistent with effective teaching practices in other areas of the curriculum (McGhie-Richmond, Underwood, & Jordan, 2007). None of the teachers I spoke with talked explicitly about the need to build a positive climate for social inclusion in their classes.

The literature on social skill development indicates that teachers are particularly concerned with social skills that are related to academic skill development and a professional atmosphere in the classroom. One large scale study found that the two social skills rated most important for teachers from elementary through to high school and across special education and regular education classes were self-control and assertion. Self-control was considered important across the grades; however, high school special education teachers viewed it as significantly more important than high school regular education teachers. Assertion skills were considered to be relatively more important to elementary and middle school teachers than for high school teachers (Lane, Wehby, & Cristy, 2006). Teacher expectations for behaviour are extremely important because failure to meet these expectations can lead to disciplinary action, referral for special education, and poor peer and adult relationships in the school (Lane, Wehby, & Cristy, 2006). Teachers, however, can play an important role in helping students to develop positive behaviours. In recent research on behaviour management in inclusive classes, the focus is on supporting positive behaviours and viewing negative behaviours as a way for students to communicate distress (Hedeen & Ayres, 1998; Hedeen, Ayres, Meyer, & Waite, 1996; Hutchinson, 2007). Negative behaviours may result from changes in routine, feelings of isolation or frustration in the classroom. Male (2007) reports that lower social acceptance leads to more aggressive and inappropriate behaviours. From this perspective all negative behaviours are the result of the interaction between an individual student and their environment, a Situational belief. Interestingly, in the Safe Schools Act (the zero tolerance policy in Ontario) there is a clause that exempts students from disciplinary action if there are "mitigating" circumstances. This clause is sometimes used to exempt students with disabilities from disciplinary action if the behaviour is directly related to a disabling condition. However, if we assume that negative or disruptive behaviours are communication signals from students that there is a problem for them in their environment, then all negative behaviours are products of mitigating circumstances. James and Freeze (2006) note that zero tolerance policies are designed to ignore mitigating circumstances instead using punishment as a deterrent in the tradition of behaviourism. They go on to argue that zero tolerance policies are in fundamental opposition to inclusive practice.

Beverly describes how changes she made on the IEP reflect current legislation (although she does not say it by name, Beverly is referring to the Safe Schools amendment to the Education Act, which is similar to zero-tolerance policies elsewhere). In this case Beverly is using the IEP to protect her daughter from being suspended or expelled for her behaviour:

> When I looked at her IEP originally I said, "Well, this is really, really vague". It's going to be put on a shelf somewhere because it meets the requirements for paperwork, but you know, I can't see how it's going to be used. So I wrote out what I considered to be an IEP – I made it overly specific because I thought what's the point of having an IEP that's vague. I also added a behaviour plan, because she didn't have one. And I know that if you do have a behaviour plan, (...) an amendment to the Education Act or whatever it is, that the zero tolerance, (or) automatic consequences don't need to be applied to exceptional students who have a behaviour plan, because they're superseded by the behaviour plan. I thought it would be important for her to have a behaviour plan that explains what consequences are meaningful and work for her, because the point of consequences isn't to make kids feel bad. The point is that hopefully that behaviour won't happen again. If the behaviour *is* happening again then it's not working. If you're not getting the desired behaviour, then whatever it is isn't working. So she needs to have a behaviour plan that says what works for *her*. And it may be very different, and it tends to be with kids who have Asperger's because they have, you know, almost the opposite problems that most other kids have.

Teachers were much more likely to talk about how they deal with individual behaviours. This may be because I was talking to teachers about particular students. For the most part teachers described dealing with students who had behaviour issues. These teachers overwhelmingly described needing to separate students with difficult behaviours from other students. Lisa, a Special Education teacher teaching a self-contained class, describes how she approaches social skills development with Jae-Lynne:

> (Interviewer: In terms of social skills, how is Jae-Lynne?) She has a lot of difficulty. A lot of difficulty with getting along with others, making friends. A lot of issues around bullying. She's quite a petite little girl, and it took me a long time to figure out that she was actually doing a lot of bullying outside. A lot of threatening, you know, "Give me-", and she's got some issues around food and candy. "Give me your candy or my brother's gonna come after you", and other kids would say, "Okay". Because they themselves have social problems as well. I've got one kid that has a behavioural page, who's definitely a handful. You know, he's got a behavioural page [in his IEP], whereas I find the other ones, the life skills, the social skills, they don't show up nearly as much, I think, as they should. Because they focus so much on, "Well, where are they in reading and writing?", and I think ... when the special ed people come in to talk to us about what they expect and what they want, unless it's a behavioural issue, they're very big on making sure that it's a two year gap and that they're as noted as being as low as they can be to get funding.

Lisa acknowledges that in Jae-Lynne's class there are a few students who are good role models for social skills, but she feels that she cannot focus on developing social skills because they are not part of the curriculum. Mark believes that in the intermediate grades the stigma for students is especially difficult. As a grade seven teacher he sees this in his class. His solution is to separate these students; he does not describe any plan for developing a positive social atmosphere in his class. Interestingly Mark says that Jeremy, the student he thinks should be separated from his class, has shown no inappropriate behaviours other than low self-esteem:

> (Interviewer: Were you also saying if you could put him in groups in your room or is that something else?) Not so much in the intermediate. If you put them in groups in the room kids are quite aware of that and they can put typical intermediate peer pressure which is stronger than maybe any other age group except maybe grade eight. That can be a bit tricky so it's better to get the children, if they're in an IEP program, to get them out of the classroom because they do get pressure from the other kids and it becomes a negative thing. But if they do it in an enclosed environment with another teacher what the other kids don't see doesn't have an effect on them and can be a really positive thing for them. They can achieve success and they can be around other children that are at the same ability level.

Barry teaches grade three and his student Rory has some quite serious inappropriate behaviours. In fact, Rory is back in school this year after being in a residential program for children with severe behaviour issues. A psychologist at Rory's school advocated for him to return to live with his father. Barry describes his first interactions with Rory:

> Originally it was constant inappropriate behaviour with children, sometimes of a sexual nature and sometimes in a hope to make a friend and not knowing how to go about that so he'd end up bothering a child instead of befriending. And not so much physical aggression but sometimes it took place as physical over-affection that became an aggressive harassing kind of thing. So he's had to learn how to interact with peers. What I'm finding now is he isn't interacting very much with peers and I don't know how much of that is because there's so much one-to-one adult interaction, that's what he gets himself caught up with. He does go down to recesses in the Outreach Program and goes outside. He doesn't seem as interested in peers in some ways and I don't know what to put that down to exactly, but at least the inappropriateness is not as prevalent as it used to be ... It's still there sometimes.

So, Rory's behaviours have been quelled by separating him from his peers. However, it is difficult to imagine that Rory will learn to develop appropriate behaviours unless he does get to interact with other students. Dwayne, a grade six student, had a similar program to Rory when he first went to school. Dwayne came to Canada from Jamaica at age seven and entered grade one with no previous school experience. He was immediately put in a special education placement. His mother Clare describes the program in grade one:

> Basically he had a one-to-one system. He was being monitored the whole day. So they basically watched his behaviour because they thought that was a big part of it, why he wasn't getting his work done and why he wasn't up there to his level. So they had him monitored right throughout the day on the playground, in the classroom.

For Dwayne this meant the he had very little interaction with children his own age, the primary opportunity for him to gain access to Canadian society. Not all students are aggressive. Some students are withdrawn, which can also cause difficulties in the classroom setting. Teachers seem to be less threatened by these students and more interested in helping them to gain independence. I wondered if this was because it helps the teachers if their students are more independent. Vanessa describes how Paul's passive nature has affected his place within the classroom dynamic:

> Paul gets along with all children in the class. He rarely has conflict. The problem is that many of the girls tend to coddle him. He is much shorter than most of the boys … to his credit at the beginning of the year, always the girls would come to me, "Paul doesn't understand. Paul needs help with this, Paul doesn't know where his lunch is", always, and so right from the beginning this is a skill that we've been working on – is him building his confidence to be able come to me himself. Sometimes he'll fall back on it, having someone else, even one of the boys coming and tell about something, but usually he will come to me now, and whether that's confidence that has all of a sudden come, or whether he's more comfortable with me, but all of a sudden he's started to become more of an advocate for himself. That's good growth. No, I wouldn't say bright in the sense of alert but he makes the connections that surprise you, and show that he really is thinking. But he tends to come to school very tired a lot, and he finds it a struggle to persevere because even though the tasks are at his level, for the most part and modified and accommodated for, he still finds to maintain focus for a long period of time is difficult in a large group situation and that's what I need to point out to you. I think what's very important is that small group settings, quiet small group settings and partners, seemed to be the more preferred choice and work to his benefit.

Vanessa has clearly made Paul's social interactions a priority in her class in order for Paul to advocate for himself. Although Vanessa does not say this, I imagine this gives Vanessa more time to work with other students. She has appropriately worked with Paul to develop these skills and it has benefited her as well. Tim also feels that social skills are an important area of development for his student Ryan:

> (Interviewer: It sounds like you've provided a lot of social supports to help him.) Yes. That seems to be the real focus. (Interviewer: Is that something that's been written in his goals?) It is. It's more of an informal goal. I mean it

is in here in different ways but when we're thinking about programming we're much less concerned about Ryan being at a grade seven level in math as we are with him communicating and just having those kinds of skills.

Tim and Vanessa describe supporting social development, but this was not a common practice amongst the teachers I spoke with particularly in relation to students with aggression or inappropriate behaviours. This may be partly because social development is seen by both teachers and parents as the responsibility of families, or as an internal characteristic of students, rather than as a school responsibility. Many parents were very concerned about their children's social development and were actively engaged in supporting this development. Jawad is described by his teachers as aggressive and difficult. Jawad's teachers also explained to me that his mother was difficult because she didn't show up for meetings and would be unco-operative with their plan for discipline. However, Jawad's mother explains that she didn't agree with the schools approach to Jawad's behaviour:

(Interviewer: Well it sounds like you've implemented a lot of strategies around their behaviour.) Yes, well, he's having problems at school, but he wasn't having at home at the time. The other thing is, when I know that he's not having a good day at school, I don't give him a severe punishment at home, but I take something small away. And I tell him why. I tell him, "Well, you didn't have such a good day at school, so this is what we're going to do today". Well, I take an hour of TV away. Something not huge, because I believe that whatever he does at home, if I call the school, the school is going to say, "Excuse me, Mrs. Brown, this is your problem, your responsibility, your business, not ours". They're not going to punish him at school for something he does at home. So why should I give him – he's already getting a punishment at school.

In addition to dealing with disciplinary issues, several parents expressed concerns about their children balancing their academic and their social lives. Most of the students in this study struggle with the amount of work they have to do because they are often slower than their peers in completing school tasks. Parents for the most part seem supportive of their children completing homework, but they are also concerned with their children balancing their school life and other interests. Harvey describes how his son, Stephen feels about the extra time he has to work on his reading:

He feels if we tell him to go and read, it's like a punishment ... "Oh no, I have to read? I don't want to read". I get after him everyday and I'll say, "Stephen, I'd like you to read a chapter of this book", and just for kicks I'll say, "and write me a couple lines of what you just read, or whatever". But he feels that ... "I just got home from school! I could be watching TV". So still he doesn't understand reading is really important and that he has to ...

Clare has a similar approach with her son Dwayne:

> And we would do stuff at home in the summertime. I know my mother would say to me all the time, "Don't just leave him there. Don't just put him in the books all the time". I said, "Yes, I have to". And she'd say, "Yeah, but you gotta give him a little break too". I said, "Yes, I do that too". I don't let him hit the books, you know, 24/7. He does get break time. But I'm hard on him with the books, yes.

Lana explains that there is also a large time commitment on the part of parents. For parents of children with IEPs there are tremendous expectations with regard to them attending meetings, reviewing IEPs and report cards, on top of the support they give to their children who are struggling with their homework:

> I would like to say [I am] not very involved but at the same time I'm trying to encourage all these things that are here [in the IEP]. And you do what you have to or you do the homework and all the rest. But I mean at the end of the day there's not much time left for anything else.

Overall, while parents described social development as a big concern, particularly with regard to developing friendships and good self-esteem, teachers most often described behaviour problems as the responsibility of specialists or parents. This was coded as an Individual belief. Some teachers, however, described social development as part of the daily goals in the classroom. This was most often described in relation to passive or quiet students. These teachers supported the social development of students and were coded as having Situational beliefs. There were also socio-Political barriers to supporting social development as described by Lisa who said that she was discouraged from documenting social development goals because they were not part of the curriculum.

SOCIAL SKILLS AND ACADEMIC LEARNING

One of the predominant themes that emerged from talking to teachers and parents was the relationship between students' social standing and skills and their academic standing in the class. Repeatedly both teachers and parents described the effect of low academic achievement on students' self-esteem, with students feeling "dumb" or "stupid". Academic achievement was also enhanced or hindered by the social dynamics in the classroom as described by parents. Peer rejection based on academic achievement as well as disruptive behaviour has been documented in other studies (Male, 2007). Most teachers describe self-esteem as an internal characteristic of a child rather than as reflective of expectations set for them in the class. Leslie describes how Corinne's self-esteem affects her self efficacy:

> I would say it (her self-esteem) is sensitive. It's not very high but it's not extremely low either for the most part. I think it doesn't take much to upset her and I'm not sure if it's self-esteem … she doesn't put herself down but when we write goals she doesn't set her goals very high either.

Parents also see the connection between school success and student self-esteem. However parents were more likely to describe environmental factors as the source for self-esteem. Ellen describes how her daughter Dalia felt after her success in a science project:

> She had to do a speech on her favourite thing and it was worth a lot of her mark. It was a science project. And she wrote on desert animals, nine or ten desert animals. And what we did was we got this pamphlet with all these animals on it and each one had a name to it and she talked about each animal. The only thing I had to help her with was her appearance and standing and not moving about and turning around. (Interviewer: Presentation skills.) Yes. She got like an A and she got chosen to speak publicly for the school region area of her class and a few other schools, but unfortunately it fell through because the person who was organizing it got extremely sick and it had to be cancelled. It was on a weekend.

Parents' non-academic concerns are often about student self-esteem. It is in this discussion that parents' hopes and love for their children standout. For many it is painful to talk about the difficulties that their children face and to imagine the future. Dana expresses concern that all the work her son has been doing will be unrewarded in high school because education policy will bar him from getting a high school diploma:

> And my oldest is doing fine, but he's struggling through high school and ... he's not even complaining doing grade nine work, (but) he's not getting a diploma when he graduates. Well that *bothers* me! I want (my son) to get one!

Parents are very aware of the connection between academic identity and self-esteem. Self-esteem is a central issue for parents and was described as a primary concern in almost every parent interview I conducted, but parents are also very concerned about academic achievement. Sheila was hopeful that identification and intervention would help her daughter to do better academically with the expectation that her daughter's self-esteem would improve:

> I was hoping to find that yes, she did have a learning disability and she would get help to get her through school and not feeling at the bottom of the barrel all the time and that she wasn't accomplishing anything, because she was. (Interviewer: It sounds like self-esteem was becoming an issue at this point as well.) Yes. (Interviewer: What kinds of things were you finding with Fatima?) She just had no confidence within herself. It's taken a long time to build that up.

Celia has similar concerns for her daughter Isabel:

> And I know that the more you struggle and the poorer your self-esteem is because you're dumb ... and that's what she thinks she is because she just doesn't get it. I just want to keep her in school and that's becoming ... with the exception of now that she's involved in this program, I have quite a lot of confidence that she may complete her high school education.

Katie also sees the relationship between her son David's self-esteem and his academic success. She believes that his academic performance is having an impact on self-esteem and she feels that more intervention will help the problem:

> I think if he had more one-to-one, that would help him. I would *love* to see him ... get up to grade level ... and then *do* a little bit more, understand a little bit more of what he's doing. I'd like to see that; I'm hoping that'll happen. And, I know they're always maybe a year or two behind in that, but (...) so that he doesn't figure ... he is that *stupid*.

The relationship between self-esteem and academic success can also be used in negative ways. Lana uses the threat of social stigma as a motivator for Corinne:

> Yes. I say to her, "Do you want to be the kid who's behind all the time, who has the lowest mark, and everyone looks at you and makes fun of you?" And she says "no". So I say, "Well you have to work harder and you have to pull that mark up". And she has that understanding. It goes like this though because she goes through periods where she wants to study and then it just sort of ... I don't know what it is, if it's the time in her life or ... I don't know.

Academic success can also effect broader social position than just relationships in school. This is evident in the relationship between education and employment, health status and social participation (Raphael, 2004). Some parents are aware of this broad relationship between academic success and future social status. Tracy describes her concerns about her daughter Maria's future:

> How much can she do and what's going to happen when high school is finished? Because her older sister is in high school and I've seen the stuff that she has to do. I just don't know how ... well I know that she'll be modified. She won't have the same program but it's still going to be a lot. I don't know if she'll cope with going to high school because she has refused to come to school here.

The social dynamics of the classroom can affect academic performance just as academic performance can affect social dynamics. Fiona's concerns about her son Caleb are that the social setting in the classroom make him anxious and unable to perform well academically:

> But I worry as he gets older because he really isn't identified with any specific disorder; this psychometrist saw him recently and she gave me this rather lengthy report but basically he still has some word processing difficulties, word retrieval difficulties. So that in the classroom, even though he's participating more and more active in putting up his hand and answering questions now, he will stutter or get very excited and he wants to share, but then with all the attention with all the people looking and waiting and anticipating, he starts to get flushed. He starts to stutter, and he can't always share the information that he knows.

For most parents and teachers the relationship between academic standing and social standing is self-evident, whether it is in the relationships they have in school or in their future social standing. For most teachers and parents the first solution is to get students working at grade level. The problem with this solution is that in a competitive environment there will always be some students who are not at the top of the class. If the comparative aspect of academic achievement, which is reinforced in standardized assessments, is removed from the classroom dynamic there is still the issue of valuing individuals based on external criteria rather than encouraging an atmosphere in which each individual is a valued member of the classroom community.

SOCIAL DEVELOPMENT AND PEER RELATIONSHIPS

In addition to the impact of social skills on academic achievement, social development impacts friendships and relationships with peers. Friendships are exceedingly important relationships for students and they become increasingly important as students advance in age. This is equally true of students with and without disabilities (Male, 2007). Several factors are believed to support friendship development: proximity, similarity in attitude, demographics and personality (Male, 2007). Proximity is determined through placement in regular or special education classes and similarities are found through interaction. Bunch and Valeo (2004) in a study of Ontario students in elementary through high school classes found that students in inclusive school systems were more likely to form friendships and advocate on behalf of peers with disabilities and reported less abusive behaviour and acceptance of inclusive practice than their counterparts in a school system that used a special education model. Similarly, Jordan and Stanovich (2001) found that in classrooms where teachers had inclusive instructional practices students with and without disabilities reported closer social relationships.

In my study there were widely varying perceptions of the capacity for friendship and the relationship between students with IEPs and their peers. Some teachers viewed the presence of students with problem behaviours as a negative. Catriona was clear in her assessment of the negative impact that Owen, a kindergarten student, had on his peers:

> I had one very quiet little boy who was attending a daycare in our school, and father switched him over to the school where Owen's attending, and since then this little guy has just really deteriorated. He's sort of right in Owen's back pocket imitating everything Owen does, and so I've seen a very negative influence in some of his classmates.

Students with disabilities may also be negatively influenced by their classmates and peers. Parents are concerned about their children developing positive relationships as well as not getting bullied. Amanda sees negative attitudes toward her son Alexander's behaviour as the cause of some of his difficulties:

> But there are still a couple of kids, too, who are a little bit on the … rough side, I guess. The school takes it as if its Alexander's way (and) why he

145

doesn't have so many friends. But I look at too where each teacher hasn't seen Alexander since he started with everybody in the same class. So I see certain kids who, you know, flip up their desk and throw it across the room. And I'm thinking, "That's why. Not because of Alexander". But there are some children that just ... violently why ... is why he's not playing with them. But a lot of the times they assume it's because of him. You know, that he's not social.

Sometimes even when students do find friendships they are judged to be inappropriate or not at grade level for development. Melinda, a grade six teacher, describes Stephen's social skills. Of interest is the fact that Melinda says that social development is not part of the curriculum yet she is assessing social skills.

I guess different weaknesses, some social skills, difficulties in that area, how to behave with other peers. He's at a lower level. Socially, he's maybe a grade one (or) a kindergarten student. The way he interacts; he has one friend in the class who's also got difficulty socially. So they'll run around on the playground, hooting and hollering and running, and just the way they're behaving with one another would be, like, maybe a five or six-year-old way.

Conversely, some teachers actively engage their class in social participation. These teachers understand self-esteem to be a product of external factors such as proximity and shared experience or similarities. Marlene describes how she includes a student in her class:

I just include her in everything. She's really well accepted by the other children, but I've made *sure* that, you know, those things *happen* at the same time that when it's a group, I make sure I choose who she's in with, that I know that there's someone who will ... help bring the good parts out in her.

Stigma was an issue not only for children within school but for families as well. Sheila explains how important it was for her to talk to a neighbour whose son also had an IEP because her usual support network of family who stigmatized her daughter Fatima:

I was aware of all of this because my neighbour has a son who's on an IEP as well and she had explained it all to me and actually she was the one telling me what to do. (Interviewer: So she helped you negotiate the school system and sort of figure out – well very often people do reach out to various resources and sometimes its neighbours and family or friends.) But when you tell your family they look at you like, "What does she need that for?" She's perfectly fine. Like it's a bad thing but it's not. It's going to make me cry.

Family relationships often involve siblings. In this study, many of the students had siblings who also had IEPs. In two cases the students were in the same class as their brother or sister. In Jae-Lynne's case, her younger brother was in the same class because they were in a self-contained special education class that spanned several grades. This created problems for Jae-Lynne according to her mother:

I don't want her younger brother in the same class anymore, because it's bringing problems to him and Jae-Lynne doesn't seem to want to do her work, and it's lacking, and the Special Education teacher agreed. She said, "Yes, Jae-Lynne's work is lacking, because she doesn't want to pay attention to class, because she wants to be the big sister. And then they don't know if her brother will be staying with the Special Education teacher and just going out for normal ... (that) every other class will be normal. But he'll go to her class for the two subjects.

Dylan and Isabel are also in the same class. In this case they are twins and they both have been identified as having behaviour problems. They are particularly aggressive with each other and their mother Celia described how this had affected them over the past year:

It's improving. They had a really difficult year or year and a half where there was a lot of conflict and physical abuse with each other and just downright nastiness – and you better get there soon mum or someone's going to get hurt – and they're better friends now and I think that that has a lot to do with ... Isabel was the peacemaker and the peacekeeper and for the most part she would go along to keep the peace or whatever. Now I find that that's a little bit changed and Dylan will make a little bit more effort now and she will be more ... well now I don't want to and I'm going to make you wait ten minutes. If Dylan wants Isabel to do something like in a game sense ... she might agree if she likes him that day or he's been nice to her or the dynamics of the household would be fairly smooth then she would cooperate. But if it hasn't been then she ... so they have a lot of conflicts but I'd have to say in the last six months they've been better friends, there's not so much physical....

Clare is very clear about how she thinks Dwayne should handle his social difficulties in school. Clare feels that Dwayne has some friends at school but he has some difficulty getting along with other students. In fact his teacher says he has no friends and that other students do not want to interact with him because he is "in your face" and aggressive. But Clare seems to be trying to teach Dwayne how to cope with rejection:

I mean, he is a kid, and he probably thinks, "Oh, all the other kids don't like me." And I say, "So what. You have to like yourself", you know? You can't base your whatever you have for you on whatever people think, because not everybody's going to like you. Believe it or not, not everybody's going to like you. Whatever you do, you can try to please people but you can't please them all. You've got to please yourself. You've got to do things that you know are right. (Interviewer: You're building up his self-esteem?) Yes, that is a big (thing) ... I think that has a lot to do with it, because if you try to please people all the time, for people to like you and for people to be your friend, you're going to get into a lot of trouble. Because then you're going to

want to do what they want you to do and not what you want to do, and then
who's going to say they're going to want you to do all good.

Social relationships with classmates and brothers and sisters are important for
social development as well as for self-esteem. Teachers sometimes use these
relationships to support students within their classes, intervening to ensure that
students are sitting with supportive peers. But these relationships are complicated
and students can influence each other in both positive and negative ways. In
judging peer relationships amongst students, teachers and parents can be biased,
attributing the negative behaviours to those students who have been labelled
troublemakers. In addition, stigma attached to poor academic performance can lead
to stigma in the classroom and in the larger community. Social rejection is a
painful experience for both students and for their parents. Equally, both students
and parents are deeply affected by social acceptance.

THE SOCIAL CLIMATE OF THE CLASSROOM AND INDIVIDUAL, SITUATIONAL AND SOCIO-POLITICAL BELIEFS

Several studies indicate that children who are identified as having disabilities are
more likely to be rejected or have fewer friends than their peers in both special
education and regular education classes. However, students in regular classrooms,
particularly those in which teachers are engaging students in learning, are more
likely to have closer friendships than those students in special education classes or
in regular classes without appropriate teaching (Bunch & Valeo, 2004; Jordan &
Stanovich, 2001; Panacek & Dunlap, 2003). Teachers who described working
toward social as well as academic goals had Situational beliefs. Teachers who
indicated that students had difficulty with social situations, including having overly
aggressive or overly passive relationships with peers and who described these
social characteristics as intrinsic characteristics of the student, were coded as
having Individual beliefs. These teachers were also more likely to judge the
relationships that did exist, including blaming students for being a negative
influence or for being easily influenced and describing friendships as immature.
One of the biggest differences between teachers and parents with Situational
beliefs and those with Individual beliefs was their attribution with regard to the
cause of social difficulties. Both teachers and parents with Situational beliefs were
likely to relate social difficulties to student awareness that their skills were at a
lower level than their classmates, and these parents and teachers were very
concerned with students' self-esteem. However, all teachers and parents seemed
aware of the stigma attached to getting extra help. From a socio-Political
perspective the question is do school programs reinforce the stigma or do they
promote acceptance of diversity in ability, physical appearance, skills, and
behaviours. Childhood and adolescence are a time of conformity with peers. As
students get older social acceptance becomes more and more important. The
systemic concern is whether teachers and parents are helping students to make
good decisions about social choices or whether schools are reinforcing rejection
and stratification of society.

Aside from the themes that emerge in the areas of academic achievement, parents have several concerns that relate to non-academic issues. These include concerns about social stigma, balancing students' academic lives with non-academic activities, social interactions, and self-esteem. The issue of labelling and social stigma struck a nerve for some parents. One parent became emotional when describing how her daughter has been stigmatized because of her learning difficulties. This is coded as a Situational belief.

Another issue that arises in consideration of the social dynamics of the classroom is the way in which students gain acceptance. Many teachers and parents suggested that if students were able to do the same academic work as their peers, their self-esteem would improve and then their social skills would improve. Additionally, some teachers and parents tried to hide the students' disabilities in order to avoid stigma. However, in my opinion, avoidance of stigma has two problems. First, by avoiding the problem it does not get solved. Sapon-Shevin (2001) deconstructs the notion that good inclusion is invisible, a comment that I have heard many times. She notes that in a class where you cannot see the accommodations taking place, there is no modelling for other students to interact with a child who needs to be treated differently. Differential treatment does not have to be inequitable treatment; in fact differential treatment is often fair treatment for a student who has a disability. In addition, making differential treatment visible can validate that difference is a normal and acceptable part of social engagement and part of the classroom. Accepting difference is also important for those students who cannot hide their disability. By accepting difference it becomes okay to acknowledge and accept difference rather than hiding it. The social dynamics of the classroom were perhaps the most emotionally charged topic I discussed with teachers and parents because both agreed that it was predictive of the future for these students.

The belief profile for Diane's interview yielded a score of 0.37 (Individual), 1.63 (Situational), and 4.00 (socio-Political).

Diane's son Nigel was in grade six at the time of the interview. He has cerebral palsy and learning disabilities. Diane describes his academic difficulties as "severe", compounded by seizures and other physical difficulties. Diane sees most of the problems that she and her son have faced to be the result of working within the bureaucratic system of the school board with guidelines set by the Ministry of Education. Much of her energy is directed at trying to bring about change at the level of the school system, rather than through instructional accommodations or modifications for her son. This accounts for the high socio-Political belief score for her interview.

Diane describes Nigel's difficulties along with her view on assessment. She begins with a description of Nigel's disabilities (coded as Individual), then she says that assessment will help her understand Nigel's difficulties and give him support (coded as Situational). Finally, Diane says that assessment is used for bureaucratic purposes such as funding within the school system (coded as socio-Political):

> He has a lot of physical difficulties that you don't see first hand and he has even more severe academic difficulties. We're in the process now of really learning what those are (Individual belief). I've had a feeling all along but it's hard to communicate that to a Board and a school where they have to follow protocol and guidelines, and so on. Because of it I asked for an assessment at (a local children's hospital) last year. (Interviewer: Independent.) Independent from the school. I wasn't interested in a diagnosis; I just wanted to know why he was having so many difficulties in some areas and not others (Situational belief). (Interviewer: You were looking for resources?) More so how we could help him cope with his difficulties and maybe why he was having so much difficulty in certain aspects of his learning and not in other aspects. That was very confusing for me and I just didn't figure his needs were being met adequately or that he was fully understood. So he's a diverse child. He's very hard to figure out and he's very hard to fit into the little boxes they have. But recent assessing as demanded by the ISA funding has changed his category (socio-Political belief).

The change in category from Learning Disability to Intellectual Disability will likely generate more funding to support Nigel. Diane is very concerned about the issue of labelling her son for the sole purpose of meeting the bureaucratic needs of the education system. Diane's view of assessment as a bureaucratic tool demonstrates a socio-Political belief, in contrast to Katie's Individual belief that assessment is a tool to confirm a deficit, or Dana's Situational belief that assessment is a tool to plan for her son. Diane describes here why she sees assessment as a major obstacle for Nigel:

Part of the problem is I refuse to label him developmentally disabled for the sole purpose of securing funding. I won't do it. So they have to find other resources to come up with the support that the ISA needs to find funding to fit him into one of those boxes. Now they did the intelligence test and it supports the intellectual disability. And (a local children's hospital) had done an adaptive functioning assessment which you had to get one or less on two categories along with the intelligence test to fit into that category, and he did get one on one of them and less than one on the other. So those support that diagnosis, but I will not diagnose him. Not for the sole purpose of funding. I won't do it. It's dangerous and I'm not doing it. So they're going to submit on that information alone and if that doesn't work then I'll reinvent the wheel again. If I have to diagnose him for funding, I won't have any other choice but I'll fight it every step of the way. (Interviewer: It sounds like you've had some experience with having to fight these things.) Well yes, absolutely. I've been extremely politically active with the Intensive Support Amount (ISA) funding. I don't agree with it.

Throughout the interview, Diane's focus is on systemic level problems, rather than instructional level problems. Beyond Diane's concerns about funding policy as presented above, Diane is also concerned with human resource policies in the board which directly affect her son's education:

Well his EA he's very close to. And that's another reason we came back here (Nigel went to a different school for one year) was because he's had this EA since kindergarten and he adores her and the support he got over at (the other school) was nil, pretty much as far as the EAs went. I'm not comfortable with the EA program in this Board. I think as a parent you should have a say as to who is working with our children but its unionized so there's nothing we can do about it and I don't agree with that. However, we've been fortunate so far, other than six months last year, we've done pretty well that way. (Interviewer: That's the main thing; you want to be able to choose EAs.) Not necessarily choose but I think we should have some representation into that. I think that that's not addressed through the EAs. The EAs are not included in the program as much as I'd like to see them included. They are the main person working with our children and I don't believe that their teachers even ... they may develop the program but the EAs will implement it. The teacher will assist and modify where needed but that EA, at least in our case where she works fairly closely with our child ... (Interviewer: He's with an EA almost all day?) Diane: Almost all day, off and on all day. So at least in our case where this EA is with them for the majority of the day I think that they should have more input into all aspects. I've broken a few moulds along the way. I was one of the first ones that demanded the EA be part of the team meeting. I refused to have a team meeting unless the EA is there.

When asked what she thinks could be done to improve the program, Diane again focuses on change which would address the school as a community rather than directly changing her son's program. She says, "I'd like to see more disability awareness programs within the school". She says:

> The IEPs are all geared to supporting the need of funding although ... (Interviewer: The IEP reflects that funding need, not just the program need.) Yes. However, I would not be without an IEP. And every parent I talk to, if they haven't heard about the IEP or if they haven't signed ... and that's the other thing, they've changed the IEP signature thing, usually you had to sign it here. (Interviewer: On the front.) They changed that this year. So when I first got the IEP the first time I got nothing, I didn't even get this. So I said, I don't think so. (Interviewer: You didn't get the back page.) I said, "What's going on here?" (Interviewer: You need space to make comments.) Exactly. I have to sign this and you're not getting it back 'til ...

Diane's socio-Political beliefs are again apparent when she describes her recent experience with an ISA application. The problem is perceived to be in the education system rather than with the individuals who work in the system, such as the school psychologist in the next example:

> I didn't want to do the intelligence test. I didn't want to put him through another assessment because he's been assessed to death. And basically they told me you do have a choice ... you can not do this assessment, that's fine or do the assessment. And I said, "If I don't do the assessment then he doesn't get a submission for funding because there's no qualifications there". So in other words it's not a choice, it's an ultimatum. You either do this assessment so you can put in some sort of documentation of proof of need for your ISA funding or don't do the assessment and don't get any funding. So it's not a choice, it's an ultimatum. And I wrote that right on the consent form for the intelligence test. And I got a call from the psychologist from the Board who had a problem with that because he said, "But you do have a choice". I said, "Okay, I do have a choice. We can do it or we can't, yeah, I understand that but it's not a choice". He said, "I don't understand your comment". And this is the Board psychologist. I said, "What part don't you understand?" It's not a choice; it's an ultimatum. But it's not his fault either. (Interviewer: And where do you see the problem?) The problem is ISA funding guidelines, the criteria. They should just burn it. I don't agree with it at all. It's crap. It's the Ministry's way of paving the way to segregation. They're making it so that there's only a minority amount of children that are going to fit into these categories so that the rest of the children have to be mainstreamed or are going to be put into their own little classrooms. Your MR (mental retardation) classes will come back, segregation's going to come back because nobody's going to qualify for the funding, and in order to get any sort of education done within a classroom they're going to have to segregate. It's paving the way to segregation. I said that the day it came out and it's going faster than I thought. I have a big problem with it.

CHAPTER 8

How Disability is Constructed in Our Schools

The practices associated with teacher and parent beliefs as described in the preceding chapters illustrate the link between ones "worldview" and how one operates in the world. It is the combination of beliefs and practices in schools which define "disability" in the context of education. If teachers, parents and students believe that disability is an individual condition resulting from pathological factors, then they will respond to individuals as though they had pathological conditions. This is true if teachers, parents and/or students believe that disability is a situational condition resulting from their own attitudes and the environment in the classroom or if they believe that disability is a socio-political condition resulting from systemic factors. In this way the classification of people as "disabled" is born out in schools. The practices and beliefs that I have described throughout this book are specific to the educational context which is particularly ripe for classification of students into categories of abled or disabled because schools by nature are institutions for developing abilities. However, school systems are also known to reproduce inequities already present in societies despite the goals of meritocracy. The capacity for schools to "disable" individuals is evident in the numbers of students in special education programs. National survey data indicates that in Ontario approximately 3% of children aged zero to fourteen have participation limitations (Statistics Canada, 2001) while almost 13% of students in Ontario schools are getting "special education services" (Bennett & Wynne, 2006). This indicates that pathological conditions cannot be blamed for the vast majority of learning difficulties. The question then is why are these students in need of "special education"? Why can't the regular education system meet their needs? And, if the school system were to adequately meet the needs of all students, regardless of their diverse pathologies, characteristics and abilities, would the category of special be necessary? In this chapter I will revisit the key issues addressed in Chapters 3 through 7 with regard to school practice showing how they build on one another and how they ultimately lead to the construction of disability in our schools.

Practices Associated with Individual Beliefs

Both teacher and parent Individual beliefs were evident in the coded practices across the range of practices described in both teacher and parent interviews. The individual belief about disability is based in a pathological view of the student. Learning difficulties are perceived to be a result of something being physically, emotionally or intellectually wrong with the student. The difficulties faced by the student are not considered to be a result of their social interactions or the community to which they belong and therefore the locus of control for solving the problem lies within the student. The overriding philosophy of this belief is that some students have characteristics that make it hard for them to learn. Both parents and teachers holding individual beliefs were likely to attribute the causes of academic failure to internal factors in the student and thus take less responsibility for instructional interventions.

Practices associated with Individual beliefs were those that focused on the inherent and pathological characteristic of the child. These practices included psycho-educational assessments that were used to confirm the nature of ability and/or disability, monitoring for the stability of the condition in order to assess if the student should continue to get support, and assessing students' capacity to learn rather than their gains relative to their own previous learning. In addition, self-esteem, attitude and social behaviour (including friendships) of the student are also considered to be stable, inherent characteristics of the student (rather than the result of environmental factors), and are blamed for learning problems, such as incomplete homework. These students are expected to work more independently because their limited abilities and attitudes, it is reasoned, preclude their participation with the rest of the class. Both the classroom teacher and parent are considered to lack the necessary knowledge to "help" students with limited abilities which impacts the collaborative process between school staff, parents and other professionals (such as itinerant support, administrators, etc.). Thus Individual beliefs affected the ways that teachers interacted with each other, with parents and with students. The family characteristics may also be thought of as a fixed part of the character of a student. Ferguson's (2002) review of the parent literature found that parents of children with disabilities are often held responsible for the disability resulting in teachers' believing that parent defiance or denial of disabilities is the cause of student learning difficulties. Individual beliefs about barriers, thus, are aligned with the notion that student ability is fixed and that barriers to learning are a result of factors internal to the student and/or their family.

The explanations of education practice coded as Individual beliefs both corroborate and conflict with other research. Consistent with the Individual belief, Pivik, McComas, and LaFlamme (2002) found that one of four types of barriers that parents reported for their children with physical disabilities was their physical limitations. Also consistent with the Individual belief, Vincent (2000) describes one type of collaborative relationship between parents and teachers as "parents as consumers", in which parents see the school as a service provider for their children. This practice is informed by the belief that education professionals know more about the learning characteristics of students (including pathological conditions) than anyone else. Vincent judges this to be the least desirable relationship for teachers and parents. It is generally accepted that parent involvement impacts student outcomes, but Corter and Pelletier (2004) say that the evidence of this impact is inconclusive in the research. Epstein (2001), on the other hand, has found a link between family characteristics and the characteristics of students (as an internal characteristic of the student), and says that teachers, parents and students themselves believe that parent participation in education is important. Minke and Vickers (1999) also found positive attitudinal effects for teachers when parents are involved. Thus, from the Individual belief perspective parents may be described as shaping the characteristics of their children (supported by Epstein 2001; also Goodnow, 1997; Lightfoot & Valisner, 1992), but they might be excluded from educational planning and decision making. This excluding relationship with the school is described by Vincent (2000) as a "parent as consumer" model, because the parents are viewed (both by teachers and by themselves) as lacking professional knowledge and thus unable to support student needs. Professional knowledge is treated in most research as superior to lay knowledge. Professional knowledge of students' pathological identification is important in delivering the type of programs that are proclaimed to be the most effective by traditional special educators such as Kauffman (1999), Sasso (2001) and Barrow (2001).

Teachers reported that early on in their interactions with students they would assess their abilities through observation, assignments and school records. For teachers who had Individual beliefs, these assessments were used to confirm that the student had limitations, and were thus "special" or not normal. Similarly, parents who held Individual beliefs also viewed assessment as a means of confirming their child's deficits. For children with disabilities, regular classroom teachers would defer to specialist teachers for all formal assessments of disability characteristics under the assumption that regular teachers could not teach these students. In some cases Individual beliefs were associated with class assessments used to inform specialist teachers rather than as part of the regular classroom teachers' need to understand the student. In other cases informal assessment, such as quizzes, anecdotal notes, teacher-student dialogue, were not done at all because student abilities were thought to be too limited for any information to be collected in such assessments (e.g., poor writing skills, poor analytical skills). Several teacher statements coded as Individual were associated with descriptions of not accessing information about students. For example, these teachers would say they did not read the student records or they did not ask anyone else about the student because they felt this type of information was not useful for their teaching. Ultimately, Individual beliefs resulted in teachers doing far less teaching for these students because assessments had confirmed that they were different, and therefore it was believed that regular classroom program could not be effective for these students.

Teaching practices associated with Individual beliefs were limited by student ability or disability. One teacher said, "The parents don't understand that there is nothing I can do for their child. The problem is him. He has to change or he will fail". Teachers describe not knowing what to do with these students and therefore the students are expected to work independently from the rest of the class doing what they refer to as "busy work". Teachers, who do not differentiate instruction, still expect independent work from students who are getting far less instruction. So, a student who does not understand a class assignment is asked to work alone on something they already know how to do, such as colouring or looking at a picture book, rather than the teacher working with the student until they understand the material. In some cases, the Education Assistant is given full responsibility for the student's program because the teacher says she does not have time to provide a separate program for one student. The students' deficits are thought to preclude an academic program. Lack of student progress makes monitoring redundant. One teacher suggested that funding should be based on the likelihood that a student will succeed, taking into account how much support is offered by the family and if the student is motivated. There was an underlying emphasis on making the program and monitoring practices someone else's responsibility. Teachers who subscribe to Individual beliefs often do not familiarize themselves with student needs because primary responsibility for student program is with a specialist teacher or EA. This creates a compounding problem with teachers saying they do not know students well enough to provide a good program, but they do not get the opportunity to get to know the students because the students are out of the class with specialist teachers. In this pattern, reporting to parents often becomes the responsibility of someone other than the classroom teacher because they are the least familiar with the student.

Parent statements coded as Individual were also associated with the assumption that someone other than the parents should be responsible for their child's learning. Some professional parents expressed a lack of understanding for their child who was viewed as very different from themselves. Parents viewed teachers as experts and said they could not understand their own children's needs as well as the teachers. Parent statements associated with Individual beliefs stressed that primary responsibility for student learning should belong to specialist teachers. One parent said, "I don't put as much time into helping with his homework anymore. He doesn't have a clue to what he is reading anyway". In some cases, teachers attribute learning difficulties to characteristics of the parents. Teachers also discourage some parents from giving input into the individual program for students because they don't agree with the parents' perspectives. This practice is in fact contrary to education policy as consultation with parents is mandated in provincial standards. Parents saw report cards and teacher meetings as a means of confirming student deficits. One of the deficits commonly described by parents was a lack of motivation on the part of students to complete homework, and parents said they could not force students to do their homework.

Self-esteem and social difficulties were described by parents and teachers under the Individual beliefs as internal characteristics to the student that were amongst their deficits. This included descriptions of students not getting along with their classmates (including their own brothers and sisters), which precluded using peer support or peer modelling as instructional strategies. The student deficits described included low self-esteem and low motivation. The social relationships were also described as being influenced by the inability of the student to catch up to classmates. Evidence for these deficits included students' poor homework habits and low grades on tests. Thus monitoring was done to verify the deficits rather than identify strategies to support the student.

People with Individual beliefs behaved in ways that made their belief systems come true. The learning problem for individual students was a function of their internal characteristics because teachers and parents held the individual students responsible for their learning difficulties. When the problem was defined as being an intrinsic problem of the child, parents and teachers could then deny their own responsibility in the learning process. This model of disability fits well with a positivist view of the purpose of schooling. If we understand schools to be meritocratic institutions with clearly defined curricular goals, then it makes sense that individuals either have merit or do not, which can be defined by their ability to meet the curricular goals. The underlying belief that informs this thinking is an ableist attitude that people who do not learn in the way that is defined as "normal" do not merit the attention of classroom teachers. In addition, this model does not account for the unquestionable reproduction of social inequities in schools that uncover the flaws in the meritocracy. Further, the so-called hidden curriculum, the skills that are not listed on the Ministry documents but which are learned in schools, such as networking and social patterning, mean that traditional testing of school achievement does not accurately capture many of the achievement gains that occur in classrooms. Teachers and parents who act on their Individual beliefs create an atmosphere in which students alone are responsible for their achievement. These teachers and parents make a distinction between expectations for independent learning that are consistent with the skills and demonstrated abilities of students and inappropriate expectations that blame students when they do not learn as quickly as their peers or when they react to systemic discrimination.

Practices Associated with Situational Beliefs

Situational beliefs were the most prevalent across both the teacher and parent interviews. Participants with Situational beliefs viewed educational difficulties as their responsibility and sought information and support in order to teach students to the best of their abilities. The Situational belief about disability is based on the idea that the student's difficulties are a function of interactions with individuals and physical spaces in their immediate environment. These interactions are affected by the attitudes of the people with whom the student interacts, or physical barriers to full participation for students with physical or sensory disabilities. The student's difficulties are not attributed to policy issues, nor are they perceived to be due to the impairment itself. The responsibility for breaking down barriers lies with all of the group members such as teachers and classmates, parents and siblings. The overriding philosophy of this belief system is that individuals are responsible for removing barriers.

Within the framework of the Situational beliefs, the child's learning characteristics are considered to be a product of their environment. For example, if a student cannot understand a concept, the teacher or parent believes this is due to his or her own level of responsibility in supporting the student (either academic, social or emotional). This is consistent with Brophy's (2002) description of learning taking place within the dialogical interactions between teacher (or parent) and student. Brophy, however, cautions that the interaction between teacher and student is affected by contextual factors such as grade level and instructional goals. Social behaviours are also viewed in the context of the student's learning environment. Therefore, if a student is not motivated, this is thought to be an effect of learning difficulty such as frustration, not the cause of the learning difficulty. Stigma about the student is also considered a cause of learning difficulty under the Situational belief code.

Situational beliefs about barriers are associated with practices in which teachers contribute to student learning through dialogue and scaffolded instruction, so that barriers to learning are circumvented through adjustments in instruction. In addition, teachers and parents support students' organizational and social needs. In order to provide this highly individual instruction, teachers must have a wide repertoire of teaching strategies as well as knowledge of individual students. This echoes the assertions of Borko and Putnam (Borko & Putnam, 1996) and Shulman (1987) that teachers need both general pedagogical knowledge and knowledge of individual students to be effective. Parents too are implicated in this learning process through their attitudes and support for students' learning environment and culture. They are expected to help with homework, attend meetings, provide support for discipline strategies and volunteer in the school. The research of Hanson, Horn, Sandall, Morgan, and colleagues (2001) supports the notion that a family's willingness to advocate for the student and find information is integral to students staying in inclusive placements. Situational belief statements from both teachers and parents are linked to practices which describe them taking responsibility for their own role in the child's education. Consistent with Situational beliefs, Pivik, McComas and LaFlamme (2002) found that attitudinal barriers (both intentional and unintentional) were described by parents of children with physical disabilities as comprising at least half of the major barriers for their children with physical disabilities.

Teachers coded as having Situational beliefs described doing informal, early assessments to inform their practices. Teachers used assessment to understand the students' skill level and learning patterns, and they took time to get to know the student as a person rather than only understanding their deficits. One teacher said, "Even though we lay out expectations in the IEP, we know Ryan as an individual, not just as expectations". Formal assessment reports were also used by these teachers to understand students' individual needs rather than as a reason to defer to specialist teachers. Assessment, monitoring and collaboration practices are implicated by the Situational belief that these activities are meant to better understand the individual child and his or her learning characteristics. The results of both formal psycho-educational assessment and informal assessment by the teacher in the classroom are used by teachers and parents to better understand the individual characteristics of students and to make instructional decisions based on knowledge of these students. Monitoring students' progress allows parents and teachers to reassess students' needs as they progress through the school year. The class lessons are designed for all of the students in the class based on an understanding of the needs of each student. Teachers and parents also describe the importance of collaboration with each other and with other staff in order to meet their responsibilities in the child's education. Teachers and parents assert that collaboration is important for informing all team members (school staff and parents) about the individual needs of students. Collaboration as a means to provide more effective educational opportunity is consistent with Minke and Vickers's (1999) finding that parent participation leads to more effective schools. Further, the notion that teacher collaboration with other staff leads to improved performance for students with disabilities is supported by Graham and Harris (Graham & Harris, 1999).

Parents coded as having Situational beliefs selected schools with philosophies and policies that best met the needs of their children. Some of the parents felt that their opinions were not taken seriously by school staff. This was thought to be harmful because parents felt that it was very important for teachers to know their child as a person in order to understand their child's learning needs. One parent said, "I made a book about him to show the teacher. Like a get-to-know you, so that they could understand him".

Teachers who held Situational beliefs designed their instructional programs to meet the learning objectives of all students in the classroom. The instruction was then adjusted based on individual needs and designed for success. Continual monitoring of all students in the class ensured that teachers understood individual student needs. Teachers said that knowledge of student needs leads to reassessment of goals based on achievement. In some cases, teachers described the IEP as important in outlining the individual goals for students. In most cases, teachers with Situational beliefs individualized programming independent of the IEP. Teachers described student success in their program as their responsibility.

Parents who hold Situational beliefs describe working to help students overcome barriers by helping with homework, targeting specific goals such as reading or math. Some parents say that teachers undermine this support by not giving clear enough instructions for parents to understand homework. Parents also introduced accommodations such as reducing the number of questions assigned in homework when they felt that their child needed these kinds of adjustments. Some parents said they struggled in school themselves and that they could not provide sufficient support to their child. In this case, the parents would help to identify the difficulties a child faces but they said they needed the school and teachers to take responsibility for their child's learning. Parents also reported that they saw different behaviours at home than those reported from the school. This means that parents have a different perspective of their children from school staff. Parents have specialized knowledge that helps them to understand their children's needs in ways that are not necessarily understood by teachers. Several parents suggested that teachers did not treat parent consultation as a collaborative process but simply informed them of what was happening at school. These parents wanted reporting to reflect the individual goals of students rather than standards based assessments.

Aside from the collaborative relationship with parents, teachers are also expected to collaborate with colleagues such as special education and resource teachers. Teachers with Situational beliefs describe a team approach to collaboration with the classroom teacher maintaining primary responsibility as ideal. Specialists thus provide support rather than controlling the programming needs of students. IEPs and reporting provide opportunities for all members of the team to monitor the child's needs, and more importantly, his or her progress.

Both teachers and parents described self-esteem and social difficulty as products of the environment in which students were learning. Some parents suggested that teachers and other students stigmatized their children leading to low self-esteem or causing students to react with behavioural outbursts. The social needs of students were treated by both teachers and parents with Situational beliefs as important to the learning outcomes of students and were addressed like other individual needs. Low self-esteem was also thought to be a result of poor academic achievement which spurred additional support for high achievement based on individual ability.

Situational beliefs about disability, like Individual beliefs, are grounded in the notion of responsibility. While Individual beliefs situate responsibility for learning with the child, Situational beliefs situate the responsibility with the teacher. For teachers and parents with this belief system, there is a focus on breaking down barriers for each student. One of the recommendations here is that teachers get pre-service and in-service training that acknowledges the teaching approaches that benefit all students. These include direct instruction, differentiated approaches, universal access and time management for the classroom (Hutchinson, 2007; McGhie-Richmond, Underwood, & Jordan, 2007; Snider, 2006).

Practices Associated with Socio-Political Beliefs

While socio-Political beliefs were the least likely to be dominant in the teacher and parent interviews, they were prevalent throughout the interviews as secondary beliefs. Participants who held socio-Political beliefs viewed students' educational attainment as linked to policy definitions of success, funding criteria, and curriculum constraints. These participants situated learning difficulties within a political context. Within this belief systemic pressures such as the economy and the status quo are thought to influence decision making and whether or not the needs of all students are supported. Learning difficulties are thus a function not of individual attitudes but the underlying values of society, the educational system and education policy. The overriding philosophy of this belief system is the system is not equitable.

Socio-Political beliefs about barriers are associated with educational policy constraints and systemic problems in schools which hinder both teachers and students from full participation in learning goals. Several systemic barriers are described by teachers and parents: long wait-times for assessments leading to delay in providing services or to parents paying for private assessments when they can afford to do so; lack of individual support leading to ineffective programs or to parents paying for private tutoring when they can afford to do so; and documentation such as the IEP and Ontario Report Card designed with computer-generated comments that do not reflect individual students. In particular, the Report Card is thought to be inappropriate for students with disabilities since it is designed for students who fit a normative mould of ability. In addition, the Ontario Curriculum is described as a systemic barrier, again because it is designed for a norm, not to meet the needs of individual students. As described in Chapter 1, Pearson (2000) found that school culture directly affected the content and effectiveness of IEPs, over and above the needs of individual students. These findings are also consistent with the findings of the Ontario Human Rights Commission which outlined several areas of discrimination toward students with disabilities inherent in the Ontario special education system (OHRC, 2003)

People who hold socio-Political beliefs view collaboration between teachers, parents and other support staff as dictated by school policy rather than by individuals involved in the collaboration. This leads to decisions based on school policy rather than a true understanding of the individual student and the context of the classroom. Stanovich (1994) found that school environment operationalized by principal's beliefs was a stronger predictor of classroom teaching practice than teachers' own beliefs. This is consistent with teacher and parent socio-Political beliefs that school level policy governs practices such as collaboration.

Documents such as the IEP and the Ontario Report Card are described as confusing rather than supportive of the teacher, parent and student. These documents are considered to be especially problematic when considered in relation to Special Education Funding. Despite the fact that schools are told that Intensive Support Amount (ISA) funding should not be linked to the IEP and Ontario Report Card, teachers and parents who expressed socio-Political beliefs consistently said that in practice they are linked. Teachers and parents described being told that negative comments on the IEP and the Ontario Report Card were more likely to result in funding application approval. Further, parents described pressure to ensure that medical documentation of disability is filed in the Ontario School Record (OSR) by the funding deadlines to ensure that students received support. Although there is no policy to this effect, and it is in fact illegal to falsify these documents, there was ample anecdotal evidence that teachers and parents felt obliged to "stretch" the deficits of students maximizing the negative descriptions in order to secure funding. This need for documentation was described in accounts of assessment, monitoring and collaboration practices.

In addition, people who held socio-Political beliefs stated that individual learning characteristics of students are thought to be irrelevant because the curriculum, documents (such as the IEP or Report Card) and bureaucratic processes do not meet the needs of individual students. These perspectives are an addition to the understanding of teacher and parent beliefs that I did not find in previous research on teacher or parent beliefs. This perspective, however, is evident in the disability studies literature. Oliver (1990) claims that people with disabilities have been separated from the mainstream across historical periods, across cultures and across institutions including education. The Ontario education system, by providing curriculum, IEPs, Report Cards, and supports that do not meet the needs of students with disabilities, in fact excludes these students from accessing jobs, from social integration, and from full participation in our society.

Teachers and parents described many policies which affected their practice. A few of the most often cited socio-Political barriers included limited resources such as lack of computer programs, class sizes that were too large, lack of appropriate materials for the skill level of students, and limited time for planning. Time for planning was also impeded by the amount of paperwork required for students who had IEPs. A lack of trained staff to interpret psycho-educational testing was described as a barrier to the tests being useful to teachers. Long wait-times for assessment were cited by parents who often had assessments done privately because they had been told their children could not get individualized support without a psycho-educational assessment. Collaboration between school staff was controlled by the administrators who could support or undermine collaboration. Similarly, the level of involvement of Education Assistants and other school support staff was dictated by unions and the number of itinerant support staff hired by school districts with tight budgets. For many parents, scarce resources were made available only after they had advocated for their child at the school and school district levels.

The funding policy was probably the most often cited problem with the school system. At the time of the study, there was a funding mechanism in place called the Intensive Support Amount (ISA). ISA funding used the level of need determined in psycho-educational testing to determine the level of funding. This funding mechanism had been nicknamed "diagnosing for dollars" and it was considered by many to be regressive because if a student showed improvement the funding would be clawed back. In fact some school personnel disclosed that they kept two sets of records, the positive ones to show parents and the negative ones to show Ministry of Education officers. In many cases, school staff described documenting students with the most negative language they could in order to secure funding.

IEPs were also reported by both teachers and parents to contain inappropriate information. The IEP designed at the school district level is a standardized form, sometimes with a computer drop-down menu from which to select teaching strategies and descriptions of student characteristics. Parents and teachers said that this form provided little personal information about the student. Some parents insisted on adding personal details about their child and viewed the IEP as a contractual agreement between them and the teacher. The teachers, on the other hand, saw the IEP as a guideline only. The teachers who described spending the most time differentiating instruction usually had another system in place to monitor their instruction and found the IEP to be just a lot of paperwork. Some teachers also described the IEPs as a tool to monitor their teaching, which intimidated them. Teachers who saw value in the IEP described it as important for reporting to other people about the student, but did not view it as a working document guiding their daily program, the intended purpose of the IEP according to provincial policy. The IEP, like other special education policies, was described by teachers and parents as being implemented for the sake of bureaucratic simplicity not based on individual student needs. One parent described the systemic resistance to individualized approaches. She said, "It's hard to communicate his needs to a Board and a school where they have to follow protocol and guidelines". Written documentation required for students with disabilities created fear amongst some teachers who were concerned that they might be legally liable for their comments.

Other systemic concerns included the issue of homework. Parents described students having a large amount of homework but in some cases parents were not available to help students complete the work. These students fell further and further behind. Similarly, the stringent curriculum, which was relatively new at the time of the study, was considered to be too rigid, leaving little room for the individual goals and achievements of students identified as having disabilities. Once students fell behind they were at risk of being streamed into a non-credit program which could result in an alternate diploma with little value in the workforce. This policy exposes the underlying assumption in the school system that some students could not or should not be in the workforce.

Finally the Ontario Report Card was described as a problem for students with disabilities. There was confusion from both teachers and parents about how to report accommodations and modifications in the program. Parents did not understand how marks were determined for students with IEPs. The format of both the IEP and the Ontario Report Card were described as too formulaic leaving little room to describe the individual achievements of students.

The socio-Political concerns described in this section might best be understood if we consider that for the most part they are the result of existing policies that do not meet the needs of individual students. It is also helpful to consider how school policy might be failing other students in the same areas. For example, if students identified as having a disability are not getting enough individual support, are the other students in their class getting individualized support? If students identified as having disabilities are getting assessments that do not actually inform teaching processes, are other students in the system getting assessments that accurately determine their pre-instruction skills? And if students identified as having a disability are getting grades and report cards that are difficult to understand and are invalidated by getting support (or appropriate instruction), do the other parents and students understand their grades and report cards? My point here is that these basic school mechanisms are not designed to meet the needs of all students, and the problems with them may point to general problems in the school policy.

Interaction Between The Individual, Situational
And Socio-Political Beliefs In Practice

There is a relationship between the Individual, Situational and socio-Political beliefs. The commonality between these beliefs as they are defined in this project is in the positioning of responsibility. Each of these belief systems has a differing perspective on the locus of responsibility for learning and lack of learning. And the difference between locating responsibility for learning within the student, the teacher or parent, or in the system naturally affects the practices of teachers and parents. Individual understanding of the locus of responsibility leads to targeted advocacy toward the mechanism each individual believes to be most effective. In identifying these various loci of responsibility I hope this relationship amongst the belief systems and between beliefs and practices becomes more transparent. Additionally, it becomes evident that there may be more than one level of responsibility for learning. If the school system is to become truly inclusive it may be vital to address all levels of responsibility. I will talk more about this in the next chapter.

A summary of the characteristics of educational practice, as informed by the teacher and parent data are presented in Table 8.1 in order to contrast the three positions. These contrasting positions are a composite of practices aggregated from the analysis of teacher and parent practice.

Table 8.1. Summary of contrasting practices by ISP belief category.

	Practices associated with Individual beliefs	Practices associated with Situational beliefs	Practices associated with socio-Political beliefs
Purpose of practice	Confirmation of disability is sought in assessment, monitoring and collaboration.	Understanding of the individual is sought in assessment, monitoring and collaboration.	Documentation of disability is sought in assessment, monitoring and collaboration.
Attributions	Student attitudes or abilities are locus of control for outcomes	Locus of control for outcomes is shared with teachers, parents and the student	Outcomes are attributed to public policy, e.g. Curriculum
Explanations	Responsibility for outcomes is transferred to others	Responsibility for outcomes is owned by individuals	Responsibility for outcomes is systemic.
Judgements	Learning characteristics are internal to the student	Learning characteristics are a product of social interactions	Learning characteristics of the student are irrelevant because the system is based on a norm

Conclusions

The research I have presented in this study primarily examines the teaching and parenting practices associated with the Individual, Situational, and socio-Political (ISP) beliefs about the nature of disability. I think, however, there are some additional comments to be made about the research itself and how this type of research contributes to overall knowledge in the fields of education and disability studies. In this chapter I will discuss the ISP theory and the research methods employed in the study and make some final comments on the application of the theory presented in this book.

THE ISP THEORY AS A COMPREHENSIVE EXPLANATION OF TEACHER AND PARENT BELIEFS

In publishing a study of this kind there are always concerns about the validity of the data: in this case whether the ISP belief construct, as developed from the critical disability studies literature, is a valid measure of teacher and parent beliefs about the nature of barriers to learning. The evidence of the validity of the construct comes from several different analyses. First, the ISP construct is an expansion of existing theory about disability, building on both the Social Model and the Pathognomonic-Interventionist (PI) construct (Stanovich & Jordan, 1998). Previous theory has supported the notion of a bi-polar theoretical construct but the ISP theory posits that there are in fact three belief categories. This new theory presents an explanation of beliefs about barriers to learning that is more congruent with the full spectrum of theory presented in the literature as described in Chapter 1.

The addition of the third dimension of beliefs – the socio-Political – is also validated by the spontaneous statements of the participants in the study, and detailed in the belief profiles presented throughout the book. The ISP coding is further analysed in relation to the contextual descriptions of practice which were coded separately from the beliefs. These practices provide additional validation of the ISP construct since they appear to cluster around the belief categories. Finally, descriptive statistics for the ISP beliefs show the variance of beliefs across the teacher and parent sample, providing a picture of the nature of teacher and parent beliefs.

Expansion of Current Theories of Disability into the Tripartite ISP Theory

As described in Chapter 1, the notion of disability theory as divided between a medical model understanding and the Social Model is ubiquitous in the literature (Barnes, Mercer & Shakespeare, 1999; Tregaskis, 2002). Medical intervention and social supports dominated discourse on disability throughout the twentieth century. However, emerging disability theory has challenged the central discourse on the "most appropriate" ways of teaching students with disabilities, particularly in light of human rights challenges to the notion that people with disabilities do not benefit from educational experience. In Chapter 1, I argued that systemic barriers and attitudinal barriers are distinct aspects of the Social Model, giving rise to the Situational and socio-Political belief theories. The socio-Political belief category also presents an addition to the PI continuum described by Jordan and Stanovich (2004). In studies of the PI beliefs Jordan and Stanovich found that 43% of teachers held what they term mid-point beliefs, those that were neither pathognomonic nor interventionist, which they say "at times were indicative of the policies and procedures in place that favored one or the other end of the P-I continuum" (2004, p. 31). Evidence of each of the ISP categories of belief is found in the belief statements in the interview data. The comprehensiveness of the tripartite ISP theory is evident in the cases described in Chapter 3.

The expansion of a theory of disability is important, but in my view, is irrelevant until it is connected to lived experience. Thus, the theory is used in this study to explore the experiences of teachers and parents. The link between theory and practice allows teachers and parents to apply current theory to their own experience and for all of us to understand our own role in constructing disability. To sum up the complex findings of the book, the underlying issue is one of responsibility.

The Belief Profiles presented throughout the book illustrate each belief category and provide face validity for the ISP construct. The teacher interview of Brenda and the parent interview of Katie are both coded as having predominant Individual belief profiles. Both Brenda's and Katie's interviews are characterized by descriptions of the students' deficits and neither Brenda nor Katie considers the responsibility for education of these students to be theirs. Throughout Brenda's interview it is clear that Brenda believes that Karen, who has multiple disabilities as a result of a rare brain disorder, requires support from specialized staff such as itinerant support workers, Education Assistants, special education teachers and Karen's parents. For Brenda this precludes her own responsibility for Karen's program. Similarly, Katie describes her son's disabilities as resulting from the actions of his birth mother (alcohol and drug consumption resulting in Foetal Alcohol Syndrome) and attributes David's learning difficulties to David's own attitude. Both Brenda's description of the barriers for Karen and Katie's description of barriers for David are evocative of Barnes, Mercer, and Shakespeare's (1999) assertion that some people view disability as a functional limitation of the individual and that this view does not take into account the socio-Political environment of people with disabilities.

The teacher interview of Tim and the parent interview of Dana are both coded as having a predominant Situational belief profile. In both of the interviews the predominant belief is coded as Situational because both Tim and Dana emphasize their own responsibility in supporting the educational needs of the students. Both Tim and Dana describe social interactions, such as the method of communicating instructions or the capacity for others to communicate with these students, as the basis for educational success. These underlying beliefs are consistent with Kalyanpur and Harry's (1999) assertion that the individuals who interact with a person with a disability on a daily basis are the ones who create the impetus for including them in classroom and family routines just as other students in the class or family are included.

The teacher interviews of Dennis and Diane are coded with predominant socio-Political belief profiles. Dennis, as a teacher with experience in both Special Education settings and regular classroom settings, and Diane, with experience as a parent advocate, have in-depth knowledge of the services available to students with IEPs in the Ontario education system. Further, both Dennis and Diane describe the education system as the most significant barrier to learning for these students. Dennis's interview is dominated by the underlying belief that the nature of the placement (inclusive versus Special Education classroom) is the most important factor in whether or not Catherine will be successful. Diane describes her son Nigel's biggest barrier as being the bureaucracy of the education system which fails to provide individualized support for her son. Leicester and Lovell's (Leicester & Lovell, 1997) description of a world designed for non-disabled people captures the barriers described by Dennis and Diane including systemic discrimination and public policy that are designed for non-disabled students.

It might be easy to place blame for the failure of students who have been labelled in our schools, but I think it is more productive to identify the responsibilities of school systems, of people with decision making power and of the students themselves.

Measurement of the ISP Constructs

In addition to expanding the existing theory on disability to include a third theoretical dimension of belief, the ISP coding is more comprehensive than in previous research. Participant statements of explanation, judgement and attribution about their experiences are used as the unit of analysis in this study rather than the a priori statements of behaviour used in the PI coding system. The PI method combines the coding of beliefs and practices based on the assertion that an aggregate measure of behaviours across situations is a good predictor of behaviour in other situations (Ajzen, 1991). However, as noted in Chapter 1, Ross and Nisbett (1991) warn against overestimating the relationship between behaviours and dispositional characteristics (such as beliefs) without understanding the contextual factors that may be influential. The literature on teacher beliefs makes it clear that beliefs are a messy construct and are thus difficult to measure (Fenstermacher, 1994; Kagan, 1992a; Muijs & Reynolds, 2002; Pajares, 1992). The ISP method of interviewing and coding beliefs examines the beliefs construct more directly than those methodologies that use behaviours to approximate beliefs. As Ross and Nisbett (1991) note "everyday human behaviour, especially social behaviour, becomes explainable and predictable only when we know, or can accurately guess, the subjective interpretations and beliefs of the people involved" (p. 60). The ISP scores the subjective interpretations of participants themselves.

The reliability of the ISP coding is established in the inter-rater scoring. Two raters scored each of the first six parent and six teacher interviews establishing good inter-rater reliability scores for the ISP construct. Concurrent validity of the ISP construct is provided by the PSB and the PI as well as national data on attitudes toward people with disabilities. Analysis of the ISP coding correlated with the PI coding for the teacher interviews. This analysis indicated a significant positive relationship between the PI scale and the Situational belief category of the ISP and a significant negative relationship between the PI scale and the Individual belief category of the ISP. This shows that as hypothesized, the Individual belief is similar to the pathognomonic construct of the PI and that Situational belief is similar to the Interventionist category of the PI. However, the correlations indicated that about 25% of the variance between these variables is accounted for. This is to be expected because the ISP measures a different construct, which includes the socio-Political category, as described above. However the correlation does indicate that Individual and the Social categories and the PI scale share a common construct.

Concurrent validation of the parent interviews was conducted with the PSB, a new questionnaire developed for parent self-rating on ISP coding. Although the correlation between the PSB and the ISP coding for the parent interviews was not significant, this could be explained by the small sample of participants who completed the PSB (n = 4). Due to the small sample, this should be considered a pilot test of the PSB and further testing will be conducted. Concurrent validation of the parent ISP coding should also be studied further.

Analysis of the ISP scores showed no correlation with questionnaire data including with the demographic data. The volunteer sample in this study is one limitation of the findings, since a volunteer sample is not representative of a population. However, since the participant sample included teachers and parents from four different school boards and eleven different schools, there was variance in the school level context that might affect the systemic context of the participants (particularly in relation to the socio-Political beliefs). The demographic data (see Tables 2.1 and 2.2) also show variance in the student and parent participants by gender, disability identification, placement location, family socio-economic status, education levels, and involvement in parenting organizations. The student sample includes a ratio of almost 2:1, boys to girls. This is reflective of the Canadian population in which a disproportionate number of boys are known to have cognitive/emotional disabilities (Statistics Canada, 2001). In the parent sample, although there are participants in each of the four income quartiles, there is over-representation of families in the top quartile. Assuming that there are more resources available in households with a higher income, one would expect students in the sample to have more resources. However, in national survey data there is evidence that although higher socio-economic status (SES) is correlated with higher achievement scores on reading tests for all students, the differential between students with and without disabilities is constant for differences in SES (Statistics Canada, Program for International Student Assessment/Youth in Transition Survey (PISA/YITS, 2000). Both male and female teachers are represented, and they have varied experience (number of years teaching and Additional Qualifications in Special Education), and classroom features (class size and characteristics of students). None of the demographic variables listed were significantly correlated with measures of teacher or parent ISP beliefs.

There was also no correlation found between ISP scores and the nature of students' disability labels (such as intellectual, behavioural or physical disability). This is somewhat surprising since in National survey data on Canadian attitudes toward disability, attitudes are differentiated by disability category (Environics Research Group Ltd., 2004). Teachers' attitudes toward students with disabilities have also been linked to disability category, particular to more negative attitudes toward students with perceived behaviour problems (Cook, Tankersley, Cook, & Landrum, 2000). As an example, Mark, a teacher, says that a student's behaviour and the character of his/her family should be used to determine whether or not they qualify for support. This is an extreme view within the data used in this study. The socio-economic status of the students (as measured by parent income levels) also showed no correlation with parent ISP beliefs. However, as described in Chapter 1, Gross (1996) found that parents from high socio-economic backgrounds with strong literacy skills were able to secure more resources for their children, an implication for the practices associated with beliefs. The lack of correlation between beliefs and individual student characteristics might illustrate the disconnect between teaching practice and student characteristics. The assessment procedures described in this book illustrate the over-emphasis on pathological characteristics of students in the school system, de-emphasising the instructional characteristics of teachers, such as the ability to engage students, that are fundamental to the learning process. Finally, teaching experience (measured by number of years teaching overall and number of years teaching special education) did not correlate with teacher ISP beliefs.

Perhaps a stronger concurrent validation of the ISP findings comes from a recent national public opinion survey of attitudes toward people with disabilities (N = 1,843, using a representative sample by geographic region). The *Canadian Attitudes Toward Disability: 2004 Benchmark Survey* by the Office for Disability Issues (ODI) (Environics Research Group Ltd., 2004) shows similar proportional findings to the ISP results in this study. The Situational belief was the most predominant amongst the ISP profiles of participants in this study (62%), and the survey indicates that prejudice (from both individuals and society-at-large) is believed to be the most significant barrier for persons with disabilities (cited by 49% of Canadians). In the ISP coding, Individual beliefs were the second most predominant amongst the ISP profiles scored (24%). The Individual belief corresponds with the survey categories of limited capability of persons with disabilities (17%), lack of confidence of persons with disabilities (15%) as barriers (32% of Canadians cited these as the predominant barrier). Finally, 14% of the dominant ISP scores in this study were found to be socio-Political beliefs. In the national population, lack of government or institutional support are the least likely to be described as the primary barriers for persons with disabilities (13% of Canadians cited these as the predominant barrier) (Environics Research Group Ltd., 2004).

Although concurrent validation of the ISP construct is limited, the descriptive statistical data for the belief categories is supportive of the ISP constructs. Measures of central tendency indicate a relatively good approximation of a normal distribution for each of the I, S and P belief categories in both teacher and parent ISP scoring. Despite the small sample size, the coding indicates good variance across the three ISP categories. Three outliers are evident in the Individual belief category for the teacher interview sample (Brenda, Mark, and Melinda). In the parent interview sample, one outlier is evident in the socio-Political belief scores (Diane). For the teacher interview data and especially the parent interview data, there were fewer statements coded for socio-Political beliefs. The combination of outliers in the individual and socio-Political belief categories and the smaller number of coded statements in the socio-Political belief category might be explained by the fact that the sample of teachers and parents is unlikely to be as politically knowledgeable as would be a sample that included administrators or school board officials. This theory is supported by the fact that the one parent outlier, due to a very high socio-Political Belief score (Diane) indicated that she had in fact been very involved in her school board's Special Education Advisory Committee (SEAC), and other political activities. Further, the pervasive nature of the belief systems in the descriptive data of the six case example interviews is also evident. Less than 1% of statements across the sample were coded with the "don't know" category that indicated they did not fit with the ISP constructs.

There are some philosophical issues that are pertinent to a discussion of method, particularly in study that examines systemic oppression. In consideration of the experiences of students who have been labelled as having disabilities, I think it is important to address the place of this research within the frameworks of emancipatory and traditional research. First, emancipatory research does not shy away from the subjective experience of oppression and seeks to facilitate empowerment of the oppressed (Oliver, 1997). Emancipatory research also seeks to include the research participants in the research practice itself. One clear limitation in the scope of the ISP beliefs described in this study is that the students' own beliefs are not presented. The students discussed in the study ranged in age from grade one to grade eight. Their ages thus exclude them from having legal responsibility for decision making with regard to their programs or placements (students age sixteen or older have the legal right to participate in the design of their IEPs). The theoretical framework employed in this study comes from a tradition of research on teachers and is extended to parents; it is therefore beyond the scope of the study to examine students' beliefs. Further, the students in the study were too young to communicate at the level required for the interview technique employed in the study. However, the missing perspective of the students may in itself be a barrier for these students. Without the voice of the students, this type of research risks putting the researcher, teachers, and parents in the role of experts and subverting the independent thinking of students with disabilities. This is an area of development that will be explored in the future, perhaps with older students. Leicester and Lovell (1997) provide a good example of a study conducted with adults about their experiences in special education and their beliefs about the need for educational change.

Traditional research methods, some of which are employed in this study, take a positivist approach, and for many researchers in special education this is a moral approach to providing education for students with disabilities (Barrow, 2001; Kauffman & Sasso, 2006; Sasso, 2001). The tensions between positivist and post-modern research methods and between traditional and emancipatory theoretical positions, have created a chasm in educational research and practice that I believe is harmful for all students. Education is one of the largest social policy initiatives in our society. It is the mechanism by which we teach children and youth the skills to participate in our society. Good social policy cannot be carried out without data about the population. My research employs methods that could potentially be used in population research. However, population data alone are inadequate without the perspectives of the teachers and parents who will implement public policy. The work presented here is intended to better understand the perspectives of teachers and parents who are integral to education practice but who can potentially do harm to students. I believe that mixed methods approaches provide a much broader picture than one method alone. The framework of the ISP theory provides a foundation for the study of inclusive practice which might counter Kauffman's (1999) claim that there is no scientific evidence to support inclusion.

Limitations of the ISP Theory

The ISP model of disability appears to be a valid measure of the teacher and parent beliefs evident in the fact that all three belief constructs were found through coding of the teacher and parent interview sample. However, the only predictive variable to support the validity of the ISP construct found in this study is the correlation with the PI scale. This could be a consequence of not examining the right predictive variables. Some variables that might be used as concurrent validation in the future could be an efficacy questionnaire, or a self-rating questionnaire such as the PSB. The limited predictive scope of the ISP in this study may also be a result of the small sample size. In order for the ISP theory to be validated statistically, as the PI scale has been in a number of studies (Jordan-Wilson & Silverman, 1991; Jordan & Stanovich, 2004; Stanovich & Jordan, 1998) further research should focus on the I, S and P categories as criterion variables. In addition, there are some disadvantages to the ISP measure. First, the nature of the ISP coding is that it produces three scores for each interview. These scores are inter-dependent as an inherent part of the coding system, since the belief scores for each of the three categories sums to six for each coded statement. The belief profile is comprised of the mean scores for all statements in the interview. Since the profile is comprised of three inter-dependent scores, the application of the profile in comparative analyses with other data is limited.

Finally, the dominant belief in the profiles (or the highest scoring belief) is limiting in that it does not indicate the complexity of participants' experiences. The dominant belief alone risks labelling the participants in much the same way that people with disabilities are labelled and stereotyped based on disability labels. The frequencies of beliefs presented in Figure 2.4 summarize the dominant beliefs for the sample of teachers and parents. In order to avoid the risks associated with labelling individual participants by the coded beliefs, and to show the multi-dimensionality of participants' beliefs, a profile of beliefs is presented for each participant. The limitation of using a single belief label to describe individuals is further overcome in the analysis of practice by using statements as the unit of analysis rather than analysing the interviews as a whole.

APPLICATION OF THE ISP MODEL AND INTERPRETATION OF TEACHER AND PARENT PRACTICE

The strength of the analysis of practice is in the aggregation of data across interviews to identify practices associated with the belief categories. These practices were coded independent of the belief coding. Had the practices of each interview participant been coded at the same time as the ISP beliefs the complexity of individual experience would have been lost. The dominant belief profile tells us the prevailing belief coded in each interview, which provides important inform-ation about the total sample as described in the section above, but that does not mean that the experiences of the participants with matching dominant ISP scores were the same. Each interview belief profile contains three scores (one for each category, with the highest scoring category identified as the "dominant belief") allowing for the fact that each participant has a complex set of beliefs, encom-passing all three categories. The analysis draws on statements from many different interviews, in order to illustrate the practices associated with belief statements rather than dominant belief categories.

The explanations of practice, from teacher and parent interviews, were selected for analysis if they included explanations of practice (including justifications, attributions and judgments) and thus previously coded for ISP beliefs. These explanations of practice from both teacher and parent perspectives substantiate the claim that education practice is informed by a pervasive set of underlying beliefs. The coded practices, grouped by the five interview topics, show theoretical consistency throughout each of the three coded belief categories. These theoretical consistencies are described here starting with the Individual belief category.

The ISP model of beliefs provides a relevant and reliable framework for understanding teacher and parent beliefs about barriers in education. In future research it would be helpful to conduct further tests on the ISP theory as a criterion variable for doing further research on the parent self rating (PSB) and examining predictive variables for the teacher beliefs other than the PI scale. However, the

ISP model has the potential to provide a framework for examining the beliefs of other school staff such as Principals, Vice-principals and Resource Teachers. In addition, this framework would be useful for examining the beliefs of students themselves, as they are a significant omission from this study. The biggest contribution of the ISP theory may be in its unique interpretation of Social Model Theory (Tregaskis, 2002) and the fresh view of teachers' beliefs in combination with the beliefs of parents. The ISP theory illustrates how the characteristics of students, the attitudes of teachers and parents, and the political context of the school system interact to affect the experience of students in our schools.

The teaching and parenting practices elicited from the interviews are also potentially useful in application. The practices of individuals are only limited by the number of people asked to describe their practice. However, in an analysis like the one conducted in this study, patterns emerge that provide a picture of practice associated with the three belief categories. This picture of practice is useful for evaluation of current education policy, understanding teaching and school level practices and assessment of learning goals of students within the framework of the ISP theory. This theory provides a framework for evaluating policies and practices in relation to inclusive education, with a foundation in the rights of children to have an equitable educational experience. The Ontario Human Rights Commission has outlined barriers to education that include both practices which are Situational in nature (attitudes) and barriers that are socio-Political in nature (physical access, access to accommodations, timeliness in accessing service and funding, and discrimination in the Safe Schools Act).

Finally, the ISP construct of beliefs may be an appropriate theoretical framework for understanding beliefs about social identities other than disability, such as race and ethnicity, sexual orientation, and class, where the relationship of biological variation, socially imposed identities and systemic discrimination have been debated. In fact, the critical disability studies literature has both been informed by and contributed to theory in these other fields.

Limitations of Interpreting Practice

One limitation of the analysis of teacher and parent practices is in concluding that the practices are caused by the beliefs or that the beliefs are caused by the practices. The manner in which the data are coded starts with the beliefs and then moves to the practices. The beliefs were coded first from statements that indicated judgments, attributions and explanations of behaviours, and then the practices associated with a belief statement were aggregated from across a sample of interviews. This is not necessarily how beliefs and practices are linked, despite the assumption that teacher beliefs *inform* teaching practice in many studies of teacher beliefs (Kagan, 1992b; Muijs & Reynolds, 2002; Stipek, Givvin, Salmon, & MacGyvers, 2001). The method used in this study cannot determine cause and effect of beliefs and practices, nor can any other study, but my impression from the interviews is that the relationship is one that goes both ways. That is beliefs inform practice and practice in turn informs beliefs.

One further complication in the analysis of practices and beliefs was that occasionally the practices did not appear to be consistent with the coded beliefs. For example, Tim says that the IEP for his student Ryan was prepared by the Resource Teacher. This sounds like a practice associated with an Individual belief since the Resource Teacher appears to be the expert and the classroom teacher is not taking responsibility for the IEP. However, when the teacher is asked what he thinks of this practice he says that it is good because it is less time-consuming for him, but that he does not use the IEP in his everyday teaching because it does not match his understanding of Ryan's needs. One of the strengths of coding in this study is that this distinction between practice and beliefs is evident. The limitation is that the practices are not always predictive of the beliefs.

FURTHER CONSIDERATIONS

As a final point of discussion, the Individual, Situational and socio-Political beliefs about the nature of barriers in education might be interpreted as being either positive or negative. It seems that in their application to practice the three belief categories do indeed align themselves with "good" or "bad" practices depending on interpretation: the Individual with a traditional special education approach and a medical model approach; the Situational with individualized instruction and a participatory role for parents; and the socio-Political with a human rights approach. But in reflecting on the literature review from Chapter 1 it is clear that each of these theoretical positions has both "good" and "bad" elements. This highly subjective evaluation is grounded in my review of the literature and my experience in conducting this study. Thus, the Individual belief that education problems are pathological, a view that I consider negative, is balanced by the positive aspect of the Individual belief that feminist theorists propose. People with disabilities have variations in their physical or mental functioning that are part of who they are. This positive Individual belief might be better explored in interviews with the students themselves, but it is also evident in some of the statements in the study. For example, one parent says, "Believe it or not, not everybody's going to like you. Whatever you do, you can try to please people but you can't please them all. You've got to please yourself". This is coded as an Individual belief because the responsibility for social interaction lies with the student, but it could be argued that the mother is supporting her child's independence and self-esteem.

The positive aspect of the Situational belief is strongly supported by the research on teaching, which puts teachers at the centre of effective education. The negative aspect of the Situational belief is that it emphasizes the role of teachers and parents too strongly and risks denying the self-determination of the students. Again, interviews with the students themselves would help to flesh out this negative component of Situational beliefs avoiding the privileging of professional knowledge over personal knowledge.

The socio-Political theory has both positive and negative potential since it is concerned with systemic change which could be either negative or positive. For the most part, the participants in the sample had a socio-Political position that promoted inclusive practice, a view that I consider to be positive. But, there were examples of participants wanting what I consider to be negative systemic changes, such as wanting more segregated education, wanting the curriculum to include more "life skills" for students with disabilities, and a parent wanting more students held back when they don't meet the grade standard.

In addition to the positive and negative aspects of the ISP theory, the three constructs have an additional feature that was not explored in the study. That is, each of the categories has a different perspective on the locus of responsibility for educational attainment which could affect teachers' or parents' self-efficacy. The Individual belief and the socio-Political belief both have loci of responsibility external to the teachers and parents: within the student for the Individual belief, and within the system for the socio-Political belief. The Situational belief, on the other hand, promotes the teacher or parent as the locus of responsibility. Further investigation of this idea might provide a more thorough understanding of how beliefs implicate practice. This might also provide a predictive variable that could establish the I, S and P categories as criterion variables.

CONCLUSION

This study provides preliminary evidence of the validity of the Individual, Situational, and socio-Political theory of beliefs about the nature of barriers in education and the application of this model in an analysis of educational practices reported by teachers and parents. It is clear from the literature in education that teacher beliefs are accepted as an important component of teaching. This study examines teacher and parent beliefs about barriers by analysing explanations of practice while independently coding for these practices. Although some of the validation measures for the ISP coding were more successful than others, neither teacher beliefs nor parent beliefs have been examined within this framework before. Thus, the ISP model of beliefs provides a new framework for understanding teacher and parent beliefs with more depth and accuracy than in previous studies.

The analysis of teacher and parent descriptions of practice, in light of the ISP coding, provides evidence of the practices related to these beliefs. Although we cannot know whether beliefs inform practice or practice informs beliefs, this study illuminates the relationship between teacher and parent beliefs and the educational practices that both inform and are informed by those beliefs. The beliefs of teachers and parents span three constructs of understanding about the nature of barriers in education, and the practices associated with each of the belief categories are widely divergent. It is my opinion that all three belief systems are legitimate explanations of barriers but that there has been an over-emphasis on the individual barriers for students with disabilities in our school system. This imbalance, which I believe has been swinging toward a greater understanding of situational barriers in education with the limited implementation of inclusive practices, is one of the biggest challenges to fully inclusive education for all students. Until we truly understand the impact of public policies that are inequitable, as well as the nature of attitudinal barriers in the education system, the goal of fully inclusive education as called for in the Salamanca Statement (World Conference on Special Educational Needs: Access and Equality, 1994) will not be realized. This study is a step in understanding these barriers from the perspective of some of the stakeholders – teachers and parents – who are closest to the students affected by these barriers.

ISP Scores

Table A1. *ISP belief profile scores for teacher interviews.*

Name	Dominant belief	Belief profile		
		Individual belief score	Situational belief score	socio-Political belief score
Erica	Individual	2.27	2.07	1.67
Jillian	Individual	2.28	1.88	1.84
Julianne	Individual	2.29	1.52	2.19
Nancy	Individual	2.58	1.77	1.65
Donald	Individual	3.19	2.50	.31
Vanessa	Individual	3.42	2.47	.11
Jennifer	Individual	3.64	1.64	0.36
Melinda	Individual	3.92	2.08	0.00
Mark	Individual	4.25	1.62	0.13
Brenda	Individual	4.62	1.14	0.05
Sharon	Situational	2.00	2.23	1.77
Marilyn	Situational	1.63	2.23	2.13
Joslyn	Situational	1.44	2.31	2.25
Donna	Situational	2.00	2.33	1.67
Nathan	Situational	1.61	2.57	1.82
Barbara	Situational	1.41	2.74	1.85
Sherry	Situational	1.36	2.78	1.86
Sarah	Situational	1.73	3.09	1.18
Anne	Situational	.24	3.09	2.67
Shane	Situational	1.25	3.15	1.60
Caroline	Situational	2.00	3.57	.43
Evan	Situational	1.30	3.75	0.95
Catriona	Situational	1.41	3.77	.82
Carla	Situational	1.33	3.87	0.80
Leslie	Situational	1.14	4.09	0.77
Tim	Situational	0.38	4.24	1.24
Melissa	Situational/socio-Political	.22	2.89	2.89
Jason	socio-Political	1.59	1.86	2.50
Lisa	socio-Political	1.07	2.27	2.67
Marlene	socio-Political	0.80	2.17	2.83
Alexandra	socio-Political	.29	2.71	3.00
Barry	socio-Political	0.77	2.23	3.00
Dennis	socio-Political	1.05	1.11	3.83

Table A2. ISP belief profile scores for Parent interviews.

Name	Dominant belief	Belief profile		
		Individual belief score	Situational belief score	Socio-Political belief score
Laura	Individual	3.20	2.26	.54
Jasmine	Individual	3.27	1.50	1.23
Patricia	Individual	3.39	2.57	0.04
Fiona	Individual	3.75	1.90	0.35
Susan	Individual	3.78	1.57	0.65
Ellen	Individual	3.80	1.27	0.93
Ellen	Individual	3.80	1.27	.93
Tracy	Individual	4.00	1.79	0.21
Katie	Individual	4.23	1.76	0.00
Todd	Situational	1.67	2.48	1.85
Carrie	Situational	.87	2.87	2.26
Marianna	Situational	1.58	2.96	1.46
Lynn	Situational	.79	2.96	2.25
Angela	Situational	2.46	3.04	.50
Jean	Situational	2.85	3.05	.10
Connie	Situational	2.71	3.12	.17
Doreen	Situational	1.06	3.12	1.82
William	Situational	2.61	3.22	.17
Janet	Situational	.75	3.25	2.00
Sheryl	Situational	2.47	3.35	.00
Paula	Situational	2.29	3.37	.34
Judith	Situational	1.18	3.45	1.36
Moira	Situational	1.50	3.62	.88
James and Sally	Situational	1.83	3.72	.45
Genevieve and Matthieu	Situational	.75	3.75	1.50
Maria	Situational	1.33	3.86	.81
Ted and Michael	Situational	.09	3.86	2.05
Margaret	Situational	.58	3.88	1.54
Tia and John	Situational	.79	3.96	1.25
Hellen	Situational	1.06	3.97	.97
Clare	Situational	1.83	4.10	.07
Sheila	Situational	0.87	4.13	1.00
Celia	Situational	1.57	4.19	0.24
Harvey and Marg	Situational	0.46	4.29	1.25
Lana	Situational	0.86	4.59	0.55
Dorothy	Situational	1.25	4.75	0.00
Dana	Situational	0.42	5.01	0.54
Sophia and Harold	Socio-Political	1.37	2.00	2.63
Amanda	Socio-Political	0.37	2.47	3.17
Pramila	Socio-Political	1.04	1.74	3.22
Beverly	Socio-Political	0.07	2.37	3.56
Diane	Socio-Political	0.37	1.63	4.00

Table A3. *Names of subjects and table of relationship.*

Teacher	Parents	Students
Erica	Agnes	Vincent
	James/Sally	Sherman
	Ellen	Dalia
Jillian	Tracy	Maria
Julianne	Sophia/Harold	Dustin
Nancy	Paula	Charlotte
Donald	Janet	Cooper
	William	Greg
Vanessa	Patricia	Paul
Jennifer	Tia/John	Neil
Melinda	Dana	Robert
Mark	Doreen	Jeremy
Brenda	Angela	Karen
Sharon	Harvey/Marg	Stephen
	Clare	Dwayne
Marilyn	Diane	Nigel
	Genevieve/Matthieu	Isaac
	Celia	Dylan and Isabel (twins)
	Connie	Charles
Joslyn	Jasmine	Alistair
Donna	Judith	Christopher
	Katie	David
Nathan	Sheila	Fatima
Barbara	Dorothy	Aaron
Sherry	Nicole	Jawad
Sarah	Fiona	Caleb
Anne	Carrie	Jordan
Shane	Pramila	Rita
Caroline	Lynn	Jahneil
Evan	Sheryl	Abigail
Catriona	Ted/Michael	Owen
Carla	Laura	Naima
		Noah
Leslie	Lana	Corinne
Tim	Margaret	Ryan
		Aiden, Gavin, Liam
Melissa	Marianna	Bruce
Jason	Hellen	Marcus
Lisa	Susan	Jae-Lynne
Marlene	Amanda	Alexander
		Jacqueline
Alexandra	Moira	Tiffany
Barry	Jean	Joyce
	Todd	Rory
Dennis	Beverly	Catherine

Note: Several teachers have more than one student in his or her class who participated in the study. In addition, some teachers refer to students who were not participants. For clarity, these students are also listed here in order to provide the reader with a guide to the students in each teacher's class.

Glossary of Acronyms

ADD – Attention Deficit Disorder
ADHD – Attention Deficit Hyperactivity Disorder
CYC – Child and Youth Counsellor
EA – Education Assistant
IEP – Individual Education Plan
ISA – Individual Support Amount
ISP – Individual, Situational, and socio-Political
IPRC – Individual Placement and Review Committee
ODD – Oppositional Defiance Disorder
OHRC – Ontario Human Rights Commission
OSR – Ontario School Record
PI – Pathognomonic-Interventionist
PSB – Parent Self-rating questionnaire on the nature of Barriers in education.
SEAC – Special Education Advisory Committee
SES – Socio-economic status
SNA – Special needs assistant

References

Ajzen, I. (1991). The theory of planned behavior. *Organizational Behavior and Human Decision Processes, 50*, 179–211.

Antonak, R. F., & Larrivee, B. (1995). Psychometric analysis and revision of the opinions relative to mainstreaming scale. *Exceptional Children, 62*(2), 139–149.

Antonak, R. F., & Livneh, H. (1988). *The measurement of attitudes towards people with disabilities.* Springfield, IL: Charles C. Thomas.

Apple, M. (2001). Creating profits by creating failures: Standards, markets and inequality in education. *International Journal of Inclusive Education, 5*(2/3), 103–118.

Barnes, C., Mercer, G., & Shakespeare, T. (1999). *Exploring disability: A sociological introduction.* Cambridge, UK: Polity Press.

Barrow, R. (2001). Inclusion vs. fairness. *Journal of Moral Education, 30*(3), 235–242.

Bennett, S., & Wynne, K. (2006). *Special education transformation: The report of the co-chairs with recommendations of the working table on special education.* Toronto, Canada: Ministry of Education (Ontario).

Berliner, D. C. (1994). Expertise: The wonder of exemplary performance. In J. N. Mangieri & C. C. Block (Eds.), *Creating powerful thinking in teachers and students.* Fortworth, TX: Harcourt Brace.

Bhattacharjee, K. (2003). *The Ontario safe schools act: School discipline and discrimination:* Ontario Human Rights Commission.

Boaler, J., William, D., & Brown, M. (2005). Students experiences of ability grouping: Disaffection, polarisation and the construction of failure. In M. Nind, J. Rix, K. Sheehy, & K. Simmons (Eds.), *Curriculum and pedagogy in inclusive education: Values and practices* (pp. 41–55). London, UK: Routledge Falmer.

Borko, H., & Putnam, R. T. (1996). Learning to teach. In D. C. Berliner & R. C. Calfee (Eds.), *Handbook of Educational Psychology.* New York: MacMillan.

Brophy, J. (2002). Introduction. In J. Brophy (Ed.), *Social constructivist teaching: Affordances and constraints* (Vol. 9). Boston: JAI.

Browder, D. M., Wakeman, S. Y., & Flowers, C. (2006). Assessment of progress in the general curriculum for students with disabilities. *Theory into Practice, 45*(3), 249–259.

Bunch, G., & Valeo, A. (2004). Student attitudes toward peers with disabilities in inclusive and special education schools. *Disability and Society, 19*(1), 61–76.

Buysse, V., Goldman, B. D., & Skinner, M. L. (2002). Setting effects on friendship formation among young children with and without disabilities. *Exceptional Children, 68*(4), 503–517.

Cole, C. M., Waldron, N., & Majd, M. (2004). Academic progress of students across inclusive and traditional settings. *Mental Retardation, 42*(2), 136–144.

Cook, B. G., Tankersley, M., Cook, L., & Landrum, T. (2000). Teachers' attitudes toward their included students with disabilities. *Exceptional Children, 67*(1), 115–135.

Corbett, J. (1996). *Bad-mouthing: The language of special needs.* London, UK: Falmer Press.

Corter, C., & Pelletier, J. (2004). The rise and stall of parent and community involvement in schools. *Orbit, 34*(3), 7–12.

Danforth, S., & Rhodes, W. C. (1997). Deconstructing disability: A philosophy for inclusion. *Remedial and Special Education, 18*(6), 357–366.

Doveston, M., & Keenaghan, M. (2006). Improving classroom dynamics to support students' learning and social inclusion: A collaborative approach. *Support for learning, 21*(1), 5–11.

Earl, L., & LaFleur, C. (2000). Editorial. *Orbit, 30*(4), 2.

Education Act. (1998). *Identification and placement of exceptional pupils* (O. Reg. 181/98 Cong. Rec). Ontario.

Engel, D. M. (1993). Origin myths: Narratives of authority, resistance, disability, and law. *Law & Society, 27*(4), 785–826.

Environics Research Group Ltd. (2004). *Canadian attitudes towards disability issues: 2004 benchmark survey* (No. PN 5431). Ottawa, ON: Office for Disability Issues.

REFERENCES

Epstein, J. L. (2001). *School, family and community partnerships: Preparing educators and improving schools.* Boulder, CO: Westview Press.

Evans, J., Lunt, I., Wedell, K., & Dyson, A. (2000). *Collaborating for effectiveness: Empowering schools to be inclusive.* Philadelphia: Open University Press.

Fenstermacher, G. (1994). The knower and the known: the nature of knowledge in research on teaching. *Review of Research in Education, 20,* 3–56.

Ferguson, P. M. (2002). A place in the family: An historical interpretation of the research on parental reactions to having a child with a disability. *The Journal of Special Education, 36*(3), 124–130.

Finkelstein, V. (1980). *Attitudes and disabled people.* New York: World Rehabilitation Fund.

Fuchs, L. S., Fuchs, D., Hamlett, C. L., Phillips, N. B., & Karns, K. (1995). General educators' specialized adaptation for students with learning disabilities. *Exceptional Children, 61*(5), 440–459.

Fuchs, L. S., Fuchs, D., Prentice, K., Burch, M., & Paulsen, K. (2002). Hot math: Promoting mathematical problem solving among third-grade students with disabilities. *Teaching Exceptional Children, 35*(1), 70–73.

Fulcher, G. (1998). *Disabling policies? A comparative approach to education, policy, and disability.* London, UK: Falmer Press.

Giangreco, M. F. (2003). Working with paraprofessionals. *Educational Leadership, 61*(2), 50–53.

Giangreco, M. F., Edelman, S., Cloninger, C., & Dennis, R. (1993). My child has a classmate with severe disabilities: What parents of nondisabled children think about full inclusion. *Developmental Disabilities Bulletin, 21*(1), 77–91.

Glaser, B. G., & Strauss, A. L. (1967). *The discovery of grounded theory: Strategies for qualitative research.* Chicago: Aldine Publishing Company.

Goodnow, J. J. (1997). Parenting and the transmission and internalization of values: From socio-cultural perspectives to within-family analysis. In J. E. Grusec & L. Kuczynski (Eds.), *Parenting and children's internalization of values: A handbook of contemporary theory.* New York: John Wiley & Sons.

Gould, S. J. (1996). *The mismeasure of man* (Revised and expanded ed.). New York: W.W. Norton & Company.

Graham, S., & Harris, K. R. (1999). *Teachers working together: Enhancing the performance of students with special needs.* Cambridge, MA: Brookline.

Gross, J. (1996). The weight of the evidence: Parental advocacy and resource allocation to children with statements of special educational need. *Support for learning, 11*(1), 3–5.

Hall, J. P. (2002). Narrowing the breach: Can disability culture and full educational inclusion be reconciled? *Journal of Disability Policy, 13*(3), 144–153.

Hall, K., Collins, J., Benjamin, S., Nind, M., & Sheehy, K. (2004). Saturated models of pupildom: Assessment and inclusion/exclusion. *British Educational Research Journal, 30*(6), 801–817.

Hamrich, P. L., Price, L., & Nourse, S. (2002). *Daughters with disabilities: Reframing science, math and technology for girls with disabilities.* Arlington, VA: National Science Institute.

Hanson, M. J., Horn, E., Sandall, S., Beckman, P., Morgan, M., Marqhuart, J., et al. (2001). After pre-school inclusion: Children's educational pathways over the early school years. *Exceptional Children, 68*(1), 65–83.

Harris, K. R., & Graham, S. (1996). *Making the writing process work: Strategies for composition and self-regulation.* Cambridge, MA: Broadline Books.

Harry, B., & Klingner, J. (2006). *Why are so many minority students in special education?* New York: Teachers College Press.

Hauser-Cram, P., Warfield, M. E., Shonkoff, J. P., & Krauss, M. W. (2001). Children with disabilities: A longitudinal study of child development and parent well-being. *Monographs of the Society for Research in Child Development, 66.*

Hedeen, D. L., & Ayres, B. J. (1998). Creating positive behavior support plans for students with significant behavioral challenges. *Rural Special Education Quarterly, 17*(3–4), 27–35.

Hedeen, D. L., Ayres, B. J., Meyer, L. H., & Waite, J. (1996). Quality inclusive schooling for students with severe behavior challenges. In D. H. Lehr & F. Brown (Eds.), *People with disabilities who challenge the system.* Baltimore: Paul H. Brookes.

Hofer, B. K., & Pintrich, P. R. (1997). The development of epistemological theories: Beliefs about knowledge and knowing and their relation to learning. *Review of Educational Research, 67*(1), 88–104.

Hosp, J. L., & Reschly, D. J. (2004). Disproportionate representation of minority students in special education: Academic, demographic, and economic predictors. *Exceptional Children, 70*(2), 185–199.

Hutchinson, N. (2007). *Inclusion of exceptional learners in Canadian schools: A practical handbook for teachers* (2nd ed.). Toronto, Canada: Pearson Prentice Hall.

James, S., & Freeze, R. (2006). One step forward, two steps back: Immanent critique of the practice of zero tolerance in inclusive schools. *International Journal of Inclusive Education, 10*(6), 581–594.

Jordan-Wilson, A., & Silverman, H. (1991). Teachers' assumptions and beliefs about the delivery of services to exceptional children. *Teacher Education and Special Education, 14*(3), 198–206.

Jordan, A., Kircaali-Iftar, G., & Diamond, C. T. P. (1993). Who has the problem, the student or the teacher? Differences in teachers' beliefs about their work with at-risk and integrated exceptional students. *International Journal of Disability, Development and Education, 40*(1), 45–62.

Jordan, A., Lindsay, L., & Stanovich, P. J. (1997). Classroom teachers interactions with students who are normally achieving, at-risk, and exceptional. *Remedial and Special Education, 18*(2), 82–93.

Jordan, A., & Stanovich, P. (2001). Patterns of teacher-student interaction in inclusive elementary classrooms and correlates with student self-concept. *International Journal of Disability, Development and Education, 48*(1), 43–62.

Jordan, A., & Stanovich, P. (2004). The beliefs and practices of Canadian teachers about including students with special needs in their regular elementary classrooms. *Exceptionality Education Canada, 14*(2 & 3), 25–46.

Kagan, D. M. (1992a). Implications of research on teacher belief. *Educational Psychologist, 27*(1), 65–90.

Kagan, D. M. (1992b). Professional growth among preservice and beginning teachers. *Review of Educational Research, 62*(2), 129–169.

Kalinowski, T. (2003a, February 18). Boards cry foul. *The Toronto Star.*

Kalinowski, T. (2003b, November 10). Disabled teen sets precedent: School board forced to comply. *The Toronto Star.*

Kalinowski, T. (2004, March 12). Family fights for gifted son's education. *The Toronto Star*, p. B2.

Kalyanpur, M., & Harry, B. (1999). *Culture in special education.* Baltimore, MA: Paul H. Brookes.

Kaplan, L. S., & Owings, W. A. (2001). Teacher quality and student achievement: Recommendations for principals. *National Association of Secondary School Principals Bulletin, 85*(628), 64–73.

Karkee, T., Lewis, D. M., Barton, K., & Haug, C. (2003, April 22–24). *The effect of including or excluding students with testing accommodations on IRT calibrations.* Paper presented at the annual meeting of the National Council on Measurement in Education, Chicago, IL.

Katz, S., & Earl, L. (2000). The paradox of classroom assessment. *Orbit, 30*(4), 8–10.

Kauffman, J. M. (1999). Commentary: Today's special education and its messages for tomorrow. *The Journal of Special Education, 32*(4), 244–254.

Kauffman, J. M., & Sasso, G. M. (2006). Towards ending cultural and cognitive relativism in special education. *Exceptionality, 14*(2), 65–90.

Kenworthy, J., & Whittaker, K. (2000). Anything to declare? The struggle for inclusive education and children's rights. *Disability and Society, 15*(2), 219–231.

Kierstead, A. G., & Hanvey, L. (2001). Special education in Canada. *Perspectives, 25*(2).

Lane, K. L., Wehby, J. H., & Cristy, C. (2006). Teacher expectations of students' classroom behavior across the grade span: Which social skills are necessary for success? *Exceptional Children, 72*(2), 153–167.

Larrivee, B. (1986). Effective teaching for mainstreamed students is effective teaching for all students. *Teacher Education and Special Education, 9*(4), 173–179.

Leicester, M., & Lovell, T. (1997). Disability voice: Educational experience and disability. *Disability and Society, 12*(1), 111–118.

Leithwood, K., & Janitzi, D. (1999). Transformational school leadership effects: A replication. *School Effectiveness and School Improvement, 10*(4), 451–479.

Lightfoot, C., & Valisner, J. (1992). Parental belief systems under the influence: Social guidance of the construction of personal cultures. In I. E. Sigel, A. V. McGillicuddy-DeLisi, & J. J. Goodnow (Eds.), *Parental belief systems: The psychological consequences for children* (2nd ed., pp. 393–413). Hillsdale: Lawrence Erlbaum Associates.

Lipsky, D. K., & Gartner, A. (1996). Equity requires inclusion: The future for all students with disabilities. In C. Christensen & F. Rivzi (Eds.), *Disability and the dilemma of education and justice* (pp. 144–155). Philadelphia: Open University Press.

Livingstone, D. W., Hart, D., & Davie, L. E. (2002). *Public attitudes towards education in Ontario 2002*. Toronto, Canada: Ontario Institute for Studies in Education, University of Toronto.

Lock, C. L., & Wilson, R. J. (2000). Two solitudes: Classroom teachers and psychometric researchers. *Orbit, 30*(4), 11–13.

Losen, D. J., & Orfield, G. (Eds.). (2002). *Racial inequality in special education*. Cambridge, MA: Harvard Education Press.

MacArthur, J. (2004). Tensions and conflicts: Experiences in parent and professional worlds. In L. Ware (Ed.), *Ideology and the politics of (in)exclusion* (pp. 166–182). New York: Peter Lang.

Male, D. B. (2007). The friendship and peer relationships of children and young people who experience difficulties in learning. In L. Florian (Ed.), *The sage handbook of special education* (pp. 460–471). Thousand Oaks, CA: Sage.

Mattingly, D. J., Prislin, R., McKenzie, T. L., Rodriguez, J. L. & Kayzar, B. (2002). Evaluating evaluations: The case of parent involvement programs. *Review of Educational Research, 72*(4), 549–576.

McGhie-Richmond, D., Underwood, K., & Jordan, A. (2007). Developing effective instructional strategies for teaching in inclusive classrooms. *Exceptionality Education Canada, 17*(1), 27–52.

McGlaughlin, M., & Jordan, A. (2005). Push or pull: The forces that shape inclusion in the USA and Canada. In D. Mitchell (Ed.), *Contextualizing inclusive education: Evaluating old and new international perspectives*. London: Routledge Falmer.

Ministry of Education. (2000a). *Individual education plans: Standards for development, program planning and implementation*. Toronto, Canada: Government of Ontario.

Ministry of Education. (2000b). *Standards for school boards special education plans*. Toronto, Canada: Ministry of Education (Ontario).

Ministry of Education. (2001). *Student-focused funding: Intensive Support Amount (ISA)*. Toronto, Canada: Ministry of Education (Ontario).

Minke, K. M., & Vickers, H. S. (1999). Family-school collaboration. In S. Graham & K. R. Harris (Eds.), *Teachers working together: Enhancing the performance of students with special needs*. Cambridge, MA: Brookline.

Morris, J. (1992). Personal and political: A feminist perspective on researching physical disability. *Disability, Handicap and Society, 7*(2), 157–166.

Muijs, D., & Reynolds, D. (2002). Teachers' beliefs and behaviours: What really matters? *Journal of Classroom Interaction, 37*(2), 3–15.

Nespor, J. (1987). The role of beliefs in the practice of teaching. *Journal of Curriculum Studies, 19*(4), 317–328.

Nilholm, C. (2006). Special education, inclusion and democracy. *European Journal of Special Needs Education, 21*(4), 431–445.

OHRC. (2003). *The opportunity to succeed: Achieving barrier free education for all students with disabilities*. Toronto, Canada: Ontario Human Rights Commission.

Oliver, M. (1990). *The politics of disablement*. Basingstoke, UK: MacMillan.

Oliver, M. (1996). *Understanding disability: From theory to practice*. New York: St. Martin's Press.

Oliver, M. (1997). Emancipatory research: realistic goal or impossible dream? In C. Barnes & G. Mercer (Eds.), *Doing disability research* (pp. 15–31). Leeds, UK: The Disability Press.

Ouellete-Kuntz, H. (2005). Understanding health disparities faced by people with intellectual disabilities. *Journal of Applied Research in Intellectual Disabilities, 18*, 113–121.

Pajares, M. F. (1992). Teachers' beliefs and educational research: Cleaning up a messy construct. *Review of Educational Research, 62*(3), 307–332.

Panacek, L. J., & Dunlap, G. (2003). The social lives of children with emotional and behavioral disorders in self-contained classrooms: A descriptive analysis. *Exceptional Children, 69*(3), 333–348.

Pearson, S. (2000). The relationship between school culture and IEPs. *British Journal of Special Education, 27*(3), 145–149.

Pivik, J., McComas, J., & LaFlamme, M. (2002). Barriers and facilitators to inclusive education. *Exceptional Children, 69*(1), 97–101.

Polkinghorne, D. E. (1988). *Narrative knowing and the human sciences*. Albany, NY: SUNY Press.

Raphael, D. (Ed.). (2004). *Social determinants of health: Canadian perspectives.* Toronto, Canada: Canadian Scholars Press.

Rea, P., McLaughlin, V., & Walther-Thomas, C. (2002). Outcomes for students with learning disabilities in inclusive and pullout programs. *Exceptional Children, 68*(2), 203–222.

Rieck, W. A., & Wadsworth, D. E. D. (2005). Assessment accommodations: Helping students with exceptional learning needs. *Intervention in School and Clinic, 41*(2), 105–109.

Rodger, S. (1995). Individual Education Plans revisited: A review of the literature. *International Journal of Disability, Development and Education, 42*(3), 221–239.

Ross, L., & Nisbett, R. E. (1991). *The person and the situation: Perspectives of social psychology.* Philadelphia: Temple University Press.

Rozanski, M. (2002). *Investing in public education: Advancing the goals of continuous improvement in student learning and achievement.* Toronto, Canada: Ministry of Education (Ontario).

Sapon-Shevin, M. (2001). Making inclusion visible: Honouring the process and the struggle. *Democracy and Education, 14*(1), 24–27.

Sasso, G. M. (2001). The retreat from inquiry and knowledge in special education. *The Journal of Special Education, 34*(4), 178–193.

Schraw, G., & Olafson, L. (2002). Teachers' epistemological world views and educational practices. *Issues in Education, 8*(2).

Sen, A. (1999). *Development as freedom.* New York: Knopf.

Shulman, L. S. (1987). Knowledge and teaching: Foundations of the new reform. *Harvard Educational Review, 57,* 1–22.

Skrtic, T. M., Sailor, W., & Gee, K. (1999). Voice, collaboration and inclusion: Democratic themes in educational and social reform initiatives. *Remedial and Special Education, 17,* 143–157.

Slee, R. (1997). Imported or important theory? Sociological interrogations of disablement and special education. *British Journal of Sociology of Education, 18*(3), 407–419.

Slee, R. (2006). Limits to and possibilities for educational reform. *International Journal of Inclusive Education, 10*(2–3), 109–119.

Snider, V. E. (2006). *Myths and misconceptions about teaching: What really happens in the classroom.* Lanham, MD: Rowan & Littlefield.

Stanovich, P. J. (1994). *Teachers' sense of efficacy, beliefs about practice, and teaching behaviours as predictors of effective inclusion of exceptional and at-risk pupils.* Unpublished PhD dissertation, University of Toronto, Toronto.

Stanovich, P. J. (1996). Collaboration – The key to successful inclusion in today's schools. *Intervention in School and Clinic, 32*(1), 39–42.

Stanovich, P. J., & Jordan, A. (1998). Canadian teachers' and principals' beliefs about inclusive education as predictors of effective teaching in hetergeneous classrooms. *The Elementary School Journal, 98*(3), 221–238.

Stanovich, P. J., & Jordan, A. (2004). Inclusion as professional development. *Exceptionality Education Canada, 14*(2 & 3), 169–188.

Statistics Canada. (2001). *Participation and Activity Limitation Survey (PALS).* Ottawa, Canada: Government of Canada.

Statistics Canada. (2004, March 1). *Children with special needs in Canada.* Paper presented at the Canadian Education Statistics Council.

Statistics Canada. (2001). *Program for international student assessment/youth in transition survey.* Ottawa, ON: Statistics Canada.

Stipek, D. J., Givvin, K. B., Salmon, J. M., & MacGyvers, V. L. (2001). Teachers' beliefs and practices related to mathematics instruction. *Teaching and Teacher Education, 17*(2), 213–226.

Strauss, A. L. (1998). *Basics of qualitative research: Techniques and procedures for developing grounded theory.* Thousand Oaks, CA: Sage Publications.

Swanson, H. L., & Hoskyn, M. (1998). Experimental intervention research on students with learning disabilities: A meta-analysis of treatment outcomes. *Review of Educational Research, 68*(3), 277–321.

The Report of the Expert Panel on Early Reading in Ontario. (2003). *Early reading strategy - Help for children with reading difficulties.* Toronto, Canada: Ministry of Education.

Thousand, J. S., Villa, R. A., & Nevin, A. I. (2006). The many faces of collaborative planning and teaching. *Theory into Practice, 45*(3), 239–248.

Tregaskis, C. (2002). Social model theory: The story so far... *Disability and Society, 17*(4), 457–470.

REFERENCES

Trent, S., Artiles, A. J., & Englert, C. (1998). From deficit thinking to social constructivism: A review of theory, research, and practice in special education. *Review of Educational Research, 23*, 277–307.

Uberti Zrebiec, H., Mastropieri, M. A., & Scruggs, T. E. (2004). Check it off: Individualizing a math algorithm for students with disabilities via self-monitoring checklists. *Intervention in School and Clinic, 39*(5), 269–274.

Underwood, K. (2002). *Parents' understanding of disability: An exploration of the culture of special education in Ontario.* Unpublished M.A. thesis, University of Toronto, Toronto.

Underwood, K. (2006). *Inclusive education v. special education: Risks for migrant students in Ontario, Canada.* Paper presented at the Education for Migrant Integration – Integrating Migration into Education: European and North American Comparisons, Toronto, Canada.

Underwood, K. (2007). The case for inclusive education as a social determinant of health. *Munk International Centre Briefings, Comparative Program on Health and Society Working Paper Series 2005–2006.*

UPIAS. (1976). *Fundamental principles of disability.* London, UK: Union of the Physically Impaired Against Segregation.

Vincent, C. (2000). *Including parents? Education, citizenship and parental agency.* Buckingham, UK: Open University.

Visser, J. (2002). Inclusion for students with emotional and behaviour difficulties. *The Journal of International Special Needs Education, 5*, 5–9.

Vygotsky, L. S. (1978). *Mind in society.* Cambridge, MA: Harvard University Press.

Walther-Thomas, C., Korinek, L., McLaughlin, V., L., & Williams, B. T. (2000). *Collaboration for inclusive education: Developing successful programs.* Boston: Allyn & Bacon.

World Conference on Special Educational Needs: Access and Equality. (1994). *The Salamanca statement and framework for action.* Salamanca, Spain: UNESCO.

Index

Lightning Source UK Ltd.
Milton Keynes UK
18 September 2009

143886UK00001B/36/P